C000217265

Alison Morgan is a star! Combinii experience as a Christian teacher an think afresh about what it means tc for churches to be communities wl develop their relationship with Him. A wise and prophetic book which challenges us to consider the question 'How do I make my faith in Christ real today?'

The Archbishop of York, Dr John Sentamu

God has already used Alison Morgan's inspired writing to touch very many lives. This wonderful new book addresses the question of discipleship, a crucial one for today's church. She insightfully and engagingly elucidates what it means to be a disciple of Jesus and rightly insists that only as disciples together, as church, shall we be a truly effective part of God's great mission to transform not just individuals but the whole creation in Christ.

John Inge, Bishop of Worcester

Discipleship is an absolutely central part of our theology and of our Christian practice. And Alison Morgan is one of our finest Christian writers. In this excellent book she brings to discipleship her scriptural and doctrinal skill together with her commitment to a Church that makes a real difference to the world God loves. She draws on her rich knowledge of Dante, of Shakespeare, of the great writers of Christian spirituality. But her real inspiration is the work of God in the Church she has seen – in Africa, in the UK, all around the world. Her poetic and creative talent invests her writing with delight and joy. I commend this book to anyone who wants to grow in Christ and to see their community grow too, spiritually, numerically and as Christ's mature followers.

Paul Bayes, Bishop of Liverpool

Alison has once again put her finger on the pulse of issues at the heart of mission in contemporary life. As we seek to develop disciples in our nation this will add significantly to the response to that challenge.

David Picken, Archdeacon of Newark and Chair of the On Fire Mission network

Alison Morgan has done a great service by bringing together many strands of the emerging chorus that being a disciple of Jesus is what being a Christian is all about. Yet she frees the word from limiting links to informational and individualistic meanings. She tracks how this change is occurring, and puts the case for disciple meaning 'apprentices of Jesus, in community.' She beautifully balances the passionate individual following of Jesus in order to become more like him, with the well-argued emphasis and practical application that the plural of disciple is Church. The title should surprise some but become normal thinking. To ground both emphases there are stories of changed lives and tasks for groups to engage with. It should become standard reading, thinking and living.

George Lings, Church Army Research Unit

Alison Morgan writes with a rare blend of wisdom and inspiration. This beautiful book is peppered with story, challenge and hope. I cannot recommend Alison's work highly enough.

Mark Russell, Chief Executive, Church Army

Here is an ever-expanding vision of what it means to be disciples of Jesus. It is simply written but exciting and profoundly challenging – calling us to a deeper experience of God's life and a more engaged participation in God's mission. It is a call to rediscover discipleship in community. Such discipleship is sacrificial, world-changing and wonderfully fulfilling. Full of real life stories, it beckons us to abandon ourselves to God's great story and thereby discover life in abundance.

Martin Breytenbach, Bishop of the Diocese of St Mark the Evangelist, South Africa, and Chair of Growing the Church

Brilliantly written on a key issue. Creative, fresh, and inspiring from one of our leading practitioners.

Canon Roger Simpson, Archbishop's Evangelist to the North

More and more I hear it said that creating disciples is the greatest challenge facing the church today. *Following Jesus: the Plural of Disciple is Church* is timely, filling the great need for an accessible, inspiring, easily understood and practical book on this vital subject. Alison Morgan addresses the issues surrounding discipleship chapter by chapter, including some very useful group studies. I was particularly challenged by the chapter which carries the book's title, as it helped me see more clearly that discipleship is not about what the church DOES, it's about what the church IS – a community of disciples. Highly recommended.

Charles Whitehead, International Catholic author and speaker and Chairman of the Ecumenical International Consultation on World Evangelisation

What a helpful book! Alison clearly identifies the central calling of every Christian – to be a disciple of Christ – and explores what that means for us in the realities of modern life. She inspires with great testimonies, instructs with clear teaching, shapes with a coherent framework of discipleship, encourages with gritty realism, and through broad experience beautifully portrayed, she invites us afresh into the grace and freedom of lives fully given to Christ. I shall be recommending this book to my students.

Revd Mark Tanner, Warden, Cranmer Hall, Durham University

Alison Morgan has written a fine book on the Church's greatest challenge of our time – discipleship. I strongly recommend that church leaders, and Christian wanting to take their faith seriously, do not read it. ... unless they intend to practice what it says! Live this book and discover how God can change your life, your church and your community.

Bishop Graham Cray, former leader of Fresh Expressions

Alison writes with great clarity and conviction in reminding us that, 'Discipleship is a form of apprenticeship undertaken in community'. This is our calling and our privilege. Through engaging with the text of Scripture and with poignant, practical illustrations and group study sections – and never shrinking from the inherent cost of following Jesus – Alison enjoins us and gives us the tools – whatever our 'tradition' – to become intentional, welcoming, attractive and Christlike communities of faith. Essential reading for all God's people.

Stuart Robinson, Bishop of Canberra & Goulburn, Australia, and author of 'Starting Mission-Shaped Churches'

Recent years have seen a growing consensus that making disciples of Christ who live out their faith in daily life should be a priority for every church. Alison Morgan writes with passion about the urgent need to rediscover a practical and transformational discipleship, taking us back to the New Testament to study how Jesus coached his followers and how the early churches provided 'apprenticeship in community.' Alison draws on her own experience as director of the *Rooted in Jesus* discipleship programme in Africa and illustrates her argument with encouraging stories and examples from a wide variety of contexts. For ministers, leaders and others involved in planning church courses and programmes, this is a timely, challenging and practical exploration of how to make disciples today.

Paul Moore, Archdeacon of Mission Development, Diocese of Winchester, and author of 'Making Disciples in Messy Church'

When Jesus calls you to 'follow', he also call you to 'go'. The disciple who learns from Jesus is also the apostle sent out by Jesus. The church is the company of men and women who follow and go, learning from him and being sent out by him. This timely book will help it all make sense.

Stephen Cottrell, Bishop of Chelmsford

Following Jesus is a timely resource for the whole church: rich in stories, resourcing deep reflection, full of practical wisdom.

Steven Croft, Bishop of Sheffield

Drawing on her deep love and knowledge of the scriptures, Alison Morgan explores the exciting business of being a disciple of Jesus Christ and living as part of his church - illustrated with some excellent true life stories. I hope many people will read this book and benefit from its wisdom.

Alan Smith, Bishop of St Albans

A fresh and refreshing account of what discipleship looks like, with many helpful nuggets of teaching, reflection and living testimony.

Phil Potter, Archbishops' Missioner and Team Leader of Fresh Expressions

Alison Morgan combines a fine intellect with a profound spirituality, and practical grasp of the Christian life. She offers a rich vision of a life in God, seen as a joyful dance, the true answer to the spiritual homelessness of the modern world.

Peter Forster, Bishop of Chester

Following
Jesus

The Plural of Disciple is
Church

ALISON MORGAN
Foreword by Bishop James Newcome

First published in the UK by ReSource
13 Sadler Street, Wells, Somerset BA5 2RR
Email: office@resource-arm.net
www.resource-arm.net
Registered Charity no. 327035

ISBN 978-1-906363-40-6

British Library Cataloguing in Publication Data.
A catalogue record for this book is available from the British Library.

Typeset by Troubador Publishing Ltd, Leicester, UK
Printed and bound in the UK by TJ International, Padstow, Cornwall

ReSource is an independent charity based in Wells, Somerset. Our
patron is John Sentamu, Archbishop of York. ReSource's vision is
to help build a church which is diverse, local, renewed in the Spirit
and effective in mission, and we work with churches, dioceses and
regional groupings throughout the UK and beyond. Please do
contact us if you think we may be able to help you, either through
through our websites www.resource-arm.net and (for Africa)
www.rootedinjesus.net; by email on office@resource-arm.net; or
by phone at 01749 672860. Alison Morgan may be contacted via
alisonmorgan@resource-arm.net.

For Martin

Acknowledgements

Unless otherwise stated, all Bible translations are taken from the New Revised Standard Version of the Bible, Anglicized edition, copyright © 1989, 1995 by the Division of Christian Education of the National Council of the Churches of Christ in the United States of America, and are used by permission. All rights reserved.

Every effort has been made to trace copyright holders and to acknowledge them appropriately; we apologise for any errors or omissions and would be grateful to be notified of any corrections.

The following images are used by permission:

> Images on pp 12, 13, 15, 23, 36, 42, 74, 79, 185, 186, 203, 233, 265, 266, 267, 268 © Alison Morgan
> Image on p 18 © Slavujac, www.biblicalartist.net
> Image on p 91 Used by permission of Nazareth Village and photographer Reynold Mainse
> Image on p 116 © Ian Mitchell
> Image on p 132 © William Mather
> Image on p 180 © Helen Van Koevering
> Image on p 55, 264 © Rooted in Jesus

The following images are reproduced under licence:

> Images on pp 132, 158 © istockphoto.com
> Images on pp 199, 215 © 123RF.com
> Images on pp 51, 64, 70, 78, 108 © Fotolia.com

Image on p 122 © Dreamstime.com
Image on p 138 © Stockxpert.com

Additional acknowledgements:

Image on p 67 reproduced from bbc.co.uk
Image on p 82 reproduced from
    johnpridmore.yolasite.com
Image on p 106 reproduced from ReSource magazine, issue 25
Image on p 169 reproduced from religiousbuildings.net
Image on p 172 reproduced from langport-somerset.btck.co.uk
Image on p 242 reproduced from freshexpressions.org.uk
Image on p 250 reproduced from churcharmy.org.uk
The extract on pp29-30 is reprinted by permission from
    Unreachable – *One Man's Journey through Drugs, Violence,
    Armed Robbery and a Miraculous Encounter with God in
    Prison*, Darrell Tunningley, 2011, Sovereign World Ltd,
    Lancaster, England. All rights reserved.

The following images are in the public domain:

Image on p 6 by Paolo Veronese
Image on p 8 by William Shepherd
Image on p 28, 258 by David Teniers the Younger
Image on p 40 by Lucas Gassel
Image on p 98 by James Tissot
Image on p 112 by Samuel and Nathaniel Buck
Image on p 148 by Frank Newbold
Image on p 194 Brother Lawrence
Image on p 268 The Passion of the Christ, 13th century,
    Catalonia

Most of the stories in this book come directly from those who
have experienced them, and every attempt has been made
to ensure their accuracy. Some of the names have been
changed. Any errors of fact are mine alone.

Contents

Foreword   xiii

Introduction   1

Chapter 1 : Called by Jesus   7

Chapter 2 : What is a disciple?   33

Chapter 3 : Following Jesus today   62

Chapter 4 : Learning on the hoof   87

Chapter 5 : The plural of disciple is church   110

Chapter 6 : Community with a purpose   147

Chapter 7 : Take up your cross   183

Chapter 8 : Living in God's story   208

Chapter 9 : Growing together   236

Appendix 1 : A Group Study – called as disciples of Jesus 259

Appendix 2 : A meditation on the journey of discipleship   264

Endnotes   270

Bibliography   295

Foreword

There seems to be a growing consensus around 'Discipleship' as the greatest challenge facing Christians in the West – and, as usual, Alison Morgan has not only identified the key issue but also provided a lucid and practical insight into what it means. I love her writing. Somehow she manages to combine substantial scholarship with highly personal reflection and down to earth illustration, so this book – like her previous work – is easy to read as well as intellectually and spiritually stimulating.

A recurring theme is 'community': Alison has discovered from her own wide-ranging experience that discipleship is something we learn and develop together. A significant part of her own journey, which I have been privileged – in a very small way – to share, has been promoting the tremendously successful *Rooted in Jesus* course in Africa. The challenge African culture poses to complacent, bored, individualistic Christians in the West comes across forcefully in the specific examples she provides of discipleship being worked out in countries such as Kenya and Tanzania. Part of this has to do with 'signs and wonders' and the importance of seeing as well as hearing. But much of it is about people learning with and from each other. Growth in discipleship involves commitment to other disciples as well as to Jesus. So she defines discipleship as "a form of apprenticeship undertaken in community".

I also like the way in which Alison roots her theological reflection firmly in Scripture. She draws out particular emphases in the four gospels and shows how – in the Bible as well as in experience – 'making disciples involves a lot more than just leading people to faith.' This book is about living and sharing Christianity; not just being taught it. It is about becoming a practitioner rather than an observer, which means both being accountable to other Christians and engaging deeply with the Bible. That's why the helpful 'group-study' questions at the end of each chapter focus on passages from Scripture as well as the experience of group members.

What's more, in considering what is really involved in following Jesus today, Alison doesn't ignore or attempt to side-step some of the difficult issues – such as what it means to 'be lost', which she suggests has to do with heading in the wrong direction. She readily acknowledges that of the 33 million people in England who describe themselves as 'Christian', only a small percentage actually attend church or have what might be described as a living relationship with Jesus. And for those who really are trying to become more like Jesus, she is honest about the mistakes made, sacrifices endured, and pain suffered along the way.

This leads her to the inevitable conclusion that 'if the Church is not about making disciples, it is not Church.' As Alison points out, the health of the church depends on the depth of our discipleship – and for many congregations in this country that is immensely challenging. It has far-reaching implications for the way we live, and how we worship together and engage with our communities as well as each other. It also indicates that the way forward is not 'dumbing-down' the message. In the course of her travels Alison has seen quite clearly that 'turning a tough option into a soft one' doesn't lead to church growth. She has also seen that it is difficult to develop discipleship without small groups of one sort or another.

This book is full of stories and insights which, in Alison's own words, 'help us to evaluate the hidden voices of our culture and assess the validity of the assumptions on which we base our lifestyles.' It is about accepting the invitation to enter into Jesus' story – rather than simply inviting him into ours – and that is the secret of our true identity. If you are looking for something to excite people about Christian Discipleship: – this is it. That's why, in a diocese whose vision is for 'growing disciples', I will be sending a copy of *Following Jesus: The Plural of Disciple is Church* to all our clergy: with gratitude, yet again, to Alison Morgan for providing such a compelling contribution to such a crucial subject.

James Newcome
Bishop of Carlisle

The Plural of Disciple is Church

Last April I spent a few days in Venice with my daughter Katy. I'd been to Venice once before, as a student, when my brother and I explored arched bridges and glittering mosaics in the cold clear air of a deserted January. Now it was Katy's turn. She set the agenda, and I experienced Venice in a different way – for it's not just the travelling, but the travelling-with, which creeps into your soul. One day, walking along a tangle of silent canals, the only sound the gentle lapping of the turquoise waters against the ancient steps, we came out in front of the parish church of the Madonna dell'Orto. I recognised it: it was where Tom and I had stayed thirty years before, offered unexpected hospitality by Padre Giuseppe when everywhere else was shut. It had been a good base; but the church was dark, the paintings big. Missing the delicacy of the medieval mosaics, we'd passed them by.

But Katy wanted to look at them. Again our visit began with an unexpected bonus. A notice over the entrance desk said 'Venetians and clergy: no charge.' I said politely to the attendant that I am a minister in the Church of England – did that count? She was smilingly sure that it did; and we found ourselves alone, welcomed once more into this out of the way parish. Walking into its shaded interior, we discovered that it had been the local church of the sixteenth-century painter

1

Tintoretto, who had decorated it himself over a period of nearly thirty years. We began with the Presentation of the Virgin Mary in the Temple, high on the right hand wall. Mary stands silhouetted against the sky at the top of a steep flight of steps, the priest towering over her; people peer round, mothers hustle their daughters forward or sit impatiently waiting their turn; everyone is busy – except Mary and the priest, who stand motionless in the still centre of all this activity. Leaving Katy transfixed by the painting, I wandered off to inspect the two enormous canvasses which filled the side walls of the chancel: on the right, the Last Judgment; on the left, Moses receiving the tablets of stone. Here was the same energy, the same violence of movement; the Last Judgment portrayed a swirling mass of humanity, painted in all poses and conveying all possible emotions. Tintoretto, the guide book explained, was known as 'il furioso' for the sheer dynamism of his art. And it occurred to me that while all this undoubtedly lacks the stillness, the meditative clarity of the Middle Ages, it isn't really possible to keep your faith tamed and under respectable wraps with all that energy bursting out of the walls at you. It is clear that something is going on, something active and powerful, something which demands your attention. It had been the same in Santo Stefano, where Tintoretto's Last Supper dominates a whole wall and pulls you in, as if you are sitting at the next table, or carrying in the next pitcher of wine; 'vigorous', the guide book had said.

On our last day we went into San Sebastiano just over the canal from our little flat, and into the sacristy, the place where priests robe before the services. Here too it was dark, with wooden panelling framing a whole series of paintings which filled every inch of the walls. It was a majestic effort by an entire workshop of artists, a jumble of scenes from both Old and New Testaments: the baptism of Jesus, the sacrifice of Isaac, the Nativity, the passing through the Red Sea, Jacob's vision of the ladder, the Agony in the garden, the plague of serpents, the resurrection.[1] Back in the church, Tintoretto's equally energetic contemporary Veronese had painted scenes from the book of Esther on the ceiling. Except they weren't just pictures for people to crane their necks to admire; he'd painted openings, great holes in the plaster, with biblical characters leaning out and looking down at you. One, Mordecai, rode a horse, rearing up dangerously near the edge.

All these paintings seemed to ask the same question: What about you, what's your part in this grand story of life, and are you playing it properly, with all the energy which comes from the God who made you, the energy which bursts out of these walls and ceilings at you? As I ducked to avoid Mordecai and his horse, I was reminded of something I once heard Archbishop Rowan Williams say: church is not supposed to be a memorial meeting for the late lamented distinguished Jesus of Nazareth. Church is *about* something: it's about now, about you and me and God, about life and how you live it. These Venetian churches were not intended as refuges *from* reality, but as ways of injecting God into the *midst* of reality. One was built in the aftermath of a dreadful plague. Another has a ceiling shaped like a ship's keel, mirroring the trading life of the city. Another still offers life-giving kindness and hospitality to strangers today. Walk into any one of them, and you cannot help but notice their message: you are part of a world which is far bigger than you can imagine – and which has been going on for a very long time. In these churches, history leaps off the walls at you.

My first real encounter with God took place three years after my first visit to Venice. I've spent much of my life since then learning what it means to be a Christian, and in particular what it means to be a follower, or disciple, of Jesus. I've discovered it's not something you can do alone; it's as we travel with others that we move into new places – seeing through their eyes, opening ourselves up to their understandings, following their priorities. Visiting Venice with Katy was very different from visiting it without her.

I've discovered too that being a Christian is not just about what you know or even what you believe. Tintoretto and Veronese did not paint primarily to provide the congregation with information; their aim was much bigger than that, and it carried a question. This is real, they said. This happened. This is *about* something. And so now as you look at it, as you flinch to avoid being trampled by Mordecai's horse, as you stand with Mary before the high priest or serve at the Last Supper, the question is this: what about you? Are you willing to be drawn into this enormous story, or are you going to remain an observer? It was a revolutionary approach. And as Katy and I stood beneath the paintings in the churches where Tintoretto and Veronese came week by week to worship, we were reminded that for generations people have lived in the knowledge that they are part of something much bigger than themselves – part of a shared history, part of something powerful and meaningful. You can't walk into one of these churches and go out saying, oh yes, nice pictures. You have to say yes, or no: for the question is, are you part of all this, or are you just an onlooker? And if you say yes, you are acknowledging that your faith is not just something you

4

nurture quietly at home, but something that draws you into a community – a historical community, for these scenes are your past – and a contemporary community – for this is not a museum but a church in which you are standing, a living community which finds its identity in a common story. The story is still being told today. God is as present in the world now as he was when Tintoretto and Veronese were commissioned to paint history on the walls of the churches of Venice.

Our world is not always an easy place to live in. But it has a depth to it, a depth which becomes more profound as we learn to see beyond the surface events and find our own part in a story which echoes down the centuries, and yet which unfolds in the details of our own lives. What I want to do in this book is share some of the things I have learned about what this means – what it means to be a Christian, a follower or disciple of Jesus, and to find my part in his story. Some of these things I have learned by sitting alone in my study reading the scriptures, or opening myself up to God in prayer. Some I have learned by engaging with others – travelling with Katy to Venice, or to far flung parts of Britain with my friends and colleagues at ReSource, or to Africa with *Rooted in Jesus* teams. Many I have learned simply by being part of a local church community, together facing the challenges which life throws up. What *does* it mean to be a disciple of Jesus? That, I think, is the big question facing us as a church today. And the kind of answers I want to give are the kind of answers painted by Tintoretto and Veronese: big ones, energetic ones. Not answers which fill moments; answers which fill walls.

Paolo Veronese, The Triumph of
Mordecai, San Sebastiano, Venice

CHAPTER ONE

Called by Jesus

The best decision anyone can make at any time in their lives is the decision to be a disciple of Jesus Christ.

Archbishop Justin Welby

One day, probably in the year 30 (as we now know it), Jesus of Nazareth was walking by the shore of the Sea of Galilee. Jesus was just a carpenter, but his family had a history. His father Joseph could trace his genealogy right back to Abraham, and Jesus had been brought up knowing all the stories which centuries later would be painted on the walls of the churches in Venice. Just recently he had been baptised in the River Jordan by his cousin John. It had been a remarkable event, marked by an outpouring of the Holy Spirit; and John had suggested that history was now reaching its climax. This man, he had cried, is the one you have been waiting for, the one whose coming was announced by our ancient prophets. Abraham is our past; this man is our future. Take heed.

So as Jesus walked along the shore, past the fishing boats and the nets and the baskets, there must have been a bit of a frisson in the air. Who was he? What did John mean? Jesus passed two brothers, Simon and Andrew, casting their nets into the sea. He passed two more, James and John, the sons of Zebedee, sitting in their boat mending their nets. To these four

Jesus simply said, "Follow me." And the remarkable thing is that they did. The next day Jesus passed Philip, and Philip fetched Nathaniel; "Follow me," said Jesus again. Now there were six.

A little while later Jesus was walking along the street when he saw a tax collector, Matthew, sitting at his stall. Most people must have avoided Matthew, for tax collectors then were even less popular than Inland Revenue Inspectors today; but Jesus stopped. "Follow me," he said. And so it went on. Thomas, a twin; James, the son of Alphaeus; Thaddaeus; Simon, a political activist known as 'the Zealot'; and lastly Judas Iscariot. All these men except possibly Judas were, like Jesus, from Galilee, one of three administrative regions in northern Israel. Twelve of them.

Galilee in about AD 50,
by William Shepherd

But Jesus did not stop there. As he travelled around Galilee in these early days he invited many others to follow him. Some did; some chose not to. Others followed without being invited. Soon people were flocking from all over the region to be with him. All these people are described by both Luke and John as Jesus's disciples. At this point Jesus decided to narrow things down a bit. He spent the night in prayer, and of all those said to be his disciples, Jesus chose just twelve to be his inner circle, to learn from him, to help him carry out his mission and, as it turned out, to take it forward after his death. Later he would extend this group to include another seventy. By the time he died, his close followers numbered a hundred and twenty, and they included members of his own family, various women who had travelled with him and supported him, and members of the religious establishment. We know the names of twenty-eight of them.[1] Many more, people who had remained in the towns and villages where he had ministered, had also regarded themselves as his disciples; and in the days and weeks following Jesus's resurrection thousands more were added to their number.[2]

Jesus spent three years teaching and training his disciples, not just in Galilee but also in neighbouring Samaria and Judea. At the end of this period he travelled to Jerusalem, where he was arrested, condemned to death and crucified. His disciples, men and women, had accompanied him; Peter was recognised by his accent. Two of them, Joseph of Arimathea and Nicodemus, buried Jesus's body in a rock tomb, and a couple of days later Mary Magdalene, Mary the mother of James and wife of Alphaeus, and Salome the mother of James and John went to the tomb to anoint the body. Horrified to find it empty, they were addressed by a young man in white clothing. 'Don't be alarmed,' he said. 'Go back to Galilee. Jesus will meet you there.'[3] Moments later they encountered Jesus himself. He said the same. 'Go and find the others, and tell them to go back to Galilee; there they will see me.'

This raises a question. Why did Jesus, who had been

9

crucified and resurrected in Jerusalem, and whose closest followers were still cowering a short walk away in that same city of Jerusalem, suddenly tell them to go all the way back to Galilee? Why did he want to meet them there, over a hundred miles away, when they were only a stone's throw from where he was? It seems a very odd thing to ask.

As I have thought about it, I've come to the conclusion that this is not a geographical imperative but a spiritual one.[4] 'Go back,' Jesus seemed to be saying, 'to the place of our first meeting, to the place where you first heard my call. A lot has happened since then. Some of it has astonished and delighted you, some of it has terrified and disheartened you. So let's take it gently. Let's go back to where we first began our journey together, and start again from there.' It seems that Jesus is inviting them to pause at this key moment, and look back over the last three years. He wants to take them away from the hubbub of the city and the trauma of his death, back to the villages of their home territory. 'Go back,' he says; 'and then (and only then) I will tell you how I want you to go forwards.' If you want to know where you are going, you need first to remember where you have come from.

If we are to understand what it means for us, personally, to follow Jesus, to find our own part in the great sweep of history, the sweep in which Jesus claims his place as the pivotal point – what it means in practice to be his disciples – I think we too need to be willing to go back to Galilee: our own Galilee. Life can be confusing, discouraging, or just tiring. It's good to go back, to remember how it started, how it felt. For each one of us Galilee will be different. But then, for each of those first disciples it was different, too – or at least, their story is told in different ways by the four gospel writers.

Named disciples of Jesus in the gospels and Acts

1. Simon Peter
2. Andrew
3. James son of Zebedee
4. John son of Zebedee
5. Philip
6. Nathaniel, also called Bartholomew
7. Thomas
8. Matthew, also called Levi
9. James, the son of Alphaeus
10. Thaddaeus, also called Judas son of James
11. Simon the Zealot
12. Judas Iscariot
13. Mary Magdalene (Lk 8)
14. Joanna, wife of Herod's steward Chuza (Lk 8)
15. Susanna (Lk 8)
16. Jairus (Lk 8)
17. Zacchaeus (Lk 19)
18. Joses (Mk 15)
19. Mary the mother of James the Younger and Joses (Mk 15)
20. Salome (Mk 15) – perhaps the wife of Zebedee; 'who used to follow him and provided for him when he was in Galilee'
21. Lazarus of Bethany (Jn 11)
22. Mary of Bethany (Jn 11)
23. Martha of Bethany (Jn 11)
24. Nicodemus (Jn 19)
25. Joseph of Arimathea (Jn 19)
26. Cleopas + 1 (Lk 18)
27. Joseph Barsabbas known as Justus (Acts 1)
28. Matthias (Acts 1)

Many others whose names we don't know also became disciples of Jesus. Some of these stayed at home; others travelled with him: at the end of his gospel Mark tells us that 'there were many women who had come up with him to Jerusalem,' and Luke tells us that Matthias was chosen to replace Judas from among many men 'who have accompanied us during all the time that the Lord Jesus went in and out among us.'

'The disciples of Jesus were all those who responded to Jesus' call to follow him. It was a call to salvation, a call to the kingdom of God, a call to believe on Jesus for eternal life. The term disciple designated a believer in Jesus'

– Michael J Wilkins, *Following the Master: A Biblical Theology of Discipleship*

Follow me – the simple call

The earliest of the four gospels is that written by Mark, usually identified with the Mark who worked closely with Simon Peter.[5] Writing in an ordinary, unpolished Greek, Mark tells the simple story of how Jesus called his first disciples:

As Jesus passed along the Sea of Galilee, he saw Simon and his brother Andrew casting a net into the sea – for they were fishermen. And Jesus said to them, "Follow me and I will make you fish for people." And immediately they left their nets and followed him. As he went a little farther, he saw James son of Zebedee and his brother John, who were in their boat mending the nets. Immediately he called them; and they left their father Zebedee in the boat with the hired men, and followed him. (Mark 1.16-20)

Fishermen by Lake Malawi

Jesus went out again beside the sea; the whole crowd gathered around him, and he taught them. As he was walking along, he saw [Matthew] Levi son of Alphaeus sitting at the tax booth, and he said to him, "Follow me." And he got up and followed him. (Mark 2.13-14)

Mark reports no proof of identity, no explanation, no trial period. "Follow me," Jesus had said; and they did. And as we read on into the history of the early church we find others responding to Jesus in this same certain, compelled way. Saul was blinded by a light from heaven and given a simple, audible instruction to go into the city of Damascus, where he would be told what to do. The moment he heard the voice and took the decision to obey it, his life changed course: abandoning his programme of persecution, he became Paul, founder and leader of churches all over the empire. Cornelius, a Roman military commander, saw an angel telling him to send for Peter; Peter told him about Jesus, and he too committed himself instantly. Lydia, a cloth dealer in the city of Philippi, became the host of a fledgling church after a single conversation with Paul and Silas on the riverbank; 'the Lord opened her heart,' Luke explains.[6]

Many people respond to Jesus in just this simple, same-day way today. Some have their hearts opened, like Lydia. Clare, whom I met on an ordination retreat, had first responded to Jesus when she found herself suddenly filled with the unexpected knowledge that God loved her. Tony, resisting God for years, had been overwhelmed by the presence of God as he reluctantly walked into a church porch in Norfolk. Kevin, separated and homeless, had dreamt vividly of a love he had never known, and found himself the next week in church.[7]

Still others have an experience more like that of Paul, an experience marked not simply by inner certainty but by outward events. A Muslim imam was standing one day in his mosque when an audible voice thundered, "I am the Lord – Christ Jesus – I want you to be saved." The walls shook, the

14

windows shattered. The imam ran out of the mosque and down the street into the nearest church, asking "How can I be saved in the name of Jesus?" He gave his life that day to Jesus, emerging to cries of "the great Sheikh has become a Christian!" He went on to complete a theological degree course at All Nations Christian College in Hertfordshire. Having survived several assassination attempts, he is now working as a Christian minister in this country.[8]

Over the years I have met many people who have found themselves catapulted, much to their own surprise, into a relationship with Jesus. I am the director of a discipleship programme for Africa called *Rooted in Jesus,* and in 2009 we took a team to SW Kenya at the invitation of David ole Kereto, businessman and leader of a network of churches in Kenyan Masailand. There, in a dusty landscape punctuated by flat topped acacia trees, emblazoned by the flowing red and orange wraps of the Masai women and grazed by herds of zebu cattle under the whistling care of small boys, David told us how it was that he had first met Jesus.

David's father was the village witchdoctor, a man of substance in the community, a man with five wives. David, or Tiway as he was then named, was his first-born and therefore the one appointed to succeed him. Tiway had been from an early age apprenticed to his father, learning

the incantations, divinations and curses necessary to his future role. One day his best friend from primary school, Daniel, became a Christian. Tiway could see the difference in Daniel, and yet resisted Daniel's repeated invitations to accompany him to a Christian meeting; "Christianity and witchcraft can't mix," he said. Eventually he agreed to go – but only on condition that his father was not told, and that he could stand unseen at the back. It was the first time Tiway had been inside a church or seen Christian worship; and as soon as the speaker invited a response, he found himself almost forcibly propelled by the Holy Spirit to the front, where he knelt and gave his life to Christ. In that moment an immense battle was unleashed. As they walked home through the darkened landscape, Tiway found himself under devastating spiritual attack, which he is convinced he was able to resist only through the constant prayers of Daniel beside him. It was a foretaste of what was to come. When he got home, Tiway told his father he was now a Christian, and could not become a witchdoctor. His father, knowing that while his first-born son was alive no one else could be appointed to succeed him, gave him three months to think about it. Tiway stuck to his decision, and so his father decided that he had no option but to poison him. When this failed, the village elders decided that Tiway should be killed so that one of his brothers could take his place. Tiway fled for his life, was sheltered by Christians, trained at Bible College under his new name David, and eight years later returned to his village proclaiming the good news of Jesus Christ. He started his first church, and saw many come to faith. Three hundred churches later, David's Covenant Church International was said in 2008 to be the fastest growing denomination in Kenya. David had neither expected nor intended to become a Christian; it just happened.

Watch this – now follow me

So it seems that for some people, Galilee is a specific moment, a moment of overwhelming emotional or intellectual certainty that Jesus is Lord; a single moment of unforeseen, life-changing commitment. For others, it's more complicated. Even after three years on the road with Jesus, Thomas remained unconvinced when his fellow disciples told him that Jesus had appeared to them alive three days after he had been put to death. Thomas wanted visible, tangible proof: "Unless I see the mark of the nails in his hands, and put my finger in the mark of the nails and my hand in his side," he said, "I will not believe."[10] Thomas was not alone in wanting to see before he believed, and of the four gospel writers it is Luke who is most sympathetic to this response. Luke, like Mark, tells the story of how the first disciples responded to Jesus that day in Galilee; but Luke starts a bit further back. This is how he begins:

After leaving the synagogue [Jesus] entered Simon's house. Now Simon's mother-in-law was suffering from a high fever, and they asked him about her. Then he stood over her and rebuked the fever, and it left her. Immediately she got up and began to serve them. As the sun was setting, all those who had any who were sick with various kinds of diseases brought them to him; and he laid his hands on each of them and cured them. Demons also came out of many, shouting, "You are the Son of God!" But he rebuked them and would not allow them to speak, because they knew that he was the Messiah. (Luke 4.38-41).

Jesus heals Simon's mother-in-law, by Slavujac

So before Simon hears the simple "Follow me" described by Mark, he has not only already seen Jesus at work, he has on that very day seen Jesus do something very personal and particular. But there was more.

While Jesus was standing beside the lake of Gennesaret ... he saw two boats there at the shore of the lake; the fishermen had gone out of them and were washing their nets. He got into one of the boats, the one belonging to Simon, and asked him to put out a little way from the shore. Then he sat down and taught the crowds from the boat. When he had finished speaking, he said to Simon, "Put out into the deep water and let down your nets for a catch." Simon answered, "Master, we have worked all night long but have caught nothing. Yet if you say so, I will let down the nets." When they had done this, they caught so many fish that their nets were beginning to break. So they signalled their partners in the other boat to come and help them. And they came and filled both boats, so that they began to sink. Simon Peter ... and all who were with him were amazed at the catch of fish that they had taken; and so also were James and John, sons of Zebedee, who were partners with Simon. Then Jesus said to Simon, "Do not be afraid; from now on you will be catching people." When they had brought their boats to shore, they left everything and followed him. (Luke 5.1-11)

For Luke, it was clearly important that Jesus's calling of these first disciples came after (and not before) they had seen him at work. In this account, Simon, James and John were responding to Jesus on the basis of the things they had seen him do. Later, others respond in the same way to the disciples as they continue the ministry of Jesus. In Joppa, many come to faith after seeing Tabitha restored to life through the prayers of Peter. In Lystra, a disabled man is healed through the prayers of Paul, which produces an electric reaction in the watching crowd, who proclaim themselves ready to worship (to his horror) Paul himself. In Ephesus people are healed and delivered simply by touching handkerchiefs or aprons that Paul had touched; many who, like Tiway, had been involved in occult or magic practices gave their lives to Christ and brought their books to be publicly burned. These things still happen today.[11]

My experience is that more people respond to Jesus in this empirical way than respond to a single moment of calling. We live in a visual and experiential age, an age in which people think with their eyes as much as with their minds. "I don't really care whether it's true," a young man named John said to us recently in an Alpha group; "what I want to know is whether it *works*." I don't think John meant that he doesn't mind if it's all made up; he meant that he needs to see it demonstrated. John will know that it's true when he sees that it works.

Still today, many come to faith because they see, as Simon saw, that Jesus is able to heal the sick – or, as Jesus had put it himself only the week before, able "to proclaim release to the captives and recovery of sight to the blind." Healing is, as the gospel writers repeatedly explain, 'a sign of the kingdom'; it's meant to show us that something is going on, something out of the ordinary, something of God. "If you don't believe me, believe the works that I do, so that you may know and understand that the Father is in me and I am in the Father," Jesus would say to the religious leaders who doubted his credentials.[12]

One of the things we offer at ReSource is preparation materials and processes, and then teams, for parish missions. In October 2013 my husband Roger took a team to the village of Overton in Wiltshire, at the invitation of Ian and Sue Smale, for a full week of mission events. It was a remarkable time, with thirty adults and thirty children making first time commitments to Christ – adding 1½ percent of the village to the church in a single week. But the turning point came one evening half way through the mission. Roger had invited Paul Skelton of 'Healing on the Streets' in Bath to join the team, and Paul led an evening at which a number of people experienced complete healing from longstanding conditions – including one woman who was able to get up out of her wheelchair and walk unaided. Her husband was so overwhelmed by this sight that he immediately gave his life to Christ. Her son was also healed of shoulder pain, and he responded in the same way. They were convinced by what they saw.

In my book *The Word on the Wind* I told the story of Richard Taylor, a young man whose life was radically changed when he had a vision of Jesus on the cross whilst serving a sentence in Swansea prison.[13] I had heard Richard speak some years later in Leicester, by which time he was training as a pastor with David Carr in Solihull. At the end of his training Richard went back home to Wales, back to his own Galilee. He settled in Cwmbran, an unremarkable town just north of Newport, and there, with his family and a handful of former convicts and drug addicts, he planted Victory Church. 'Making a difference, one life at a time,' their logo says. Three years later, on the perfectly ordinary evening of Wednesday 10th April 2013, Richard preached on bringing your problem into the presence of Christ the King. One person present was Paul Haynes, a man confined to a wheelchair following a road accident ten years earlier. His wife Lorraine wheeled him to the front, and as Paul was prayed for his legs began to vibrate. He found he was able to move them, and then to stand. As he realised what was happening (and filmed by someone present) he lifted his wheelchair above his head, and then walked back and forth, carrying it; he had been healed. More healings followed, on that day and on subsequent days.

Many people have entered into a first time living relationship with Jesus as a result of what they have seen and experienced in Cwmbran. Andrew Parsons, one of the surprised pastors at Victory, said: "We do get a lot of people coming with no faith. One chap like that, the power of the Spirit visibly touched him, he fell to the floor. He said it felt like electricity. It was only later on he came to us and said, 'How do I get to know this Jesus?' Another big guy said to me afterwards, 'What the eff was that? Really, what was that?'" Over the next five months, over two hundred people said that they had been healed, many with subsequent medical corroboration, and some, remarkably, through contact with 'handkerchiefs' that had been anointed and blessed by the church leaders, in just the same way as happened in Jerusalem with Paul. By the end of the following year they had seen 1600 people give their lives to Christ. 'Something is definitely going on in Wales,' David Pike, a school teacher and church leader from Cardiff and an eye-witness to these events, wrote in his blog.[14]

Healing, I cannot help observing, was never intended as an in-house perk for Christians. "What sign are you going to give us ... so that we may see it and believe you? What work are you performing?" asked the disciples. "Believe me ... but if you do not, then believe me because of the works themselves," Jesus said again.[15] For many, their faith journey begins with an experience of healing, or the witnessing of healing.

For others the journey starts, as it did for Tiway, when they see how the people they know are changed when they begin to follow Jesus. People will be won over, Peter writes, 'when they see the purity and reverence of your lives.'[16] "Nothing spectacular," said Ann, a neighbour of ours who responded to Jesus just a few weeks ago, "but I feel better, I'm happier, more at peace, I swear a lot less." Ann's journey is just beginning; but those who know her notice that something has changed. "I used to be a bad man," said Rakotonirina, an elderly catechist in a remote part of Madagascar, "but I came to the conference last year and now I am rooted in Jesus." In the eighteen months between our visits Rakotonirina had, using *Rooted in Jesus,* led 120 people from his community to faith in Christ – people who had noticed the change in him.

Catechist Rakotonirina

Listen to this – now follow me

When Mark takes us back to Galilee, he tells a simple tale of encounter and response. Caught up spiritually and emotionally as they meet Jesus, people commit themselves to him in a moment: they respond to who he *is*. For Luke it's a slower process; he shows how people see and experience the remarkable ministry of Jesus before responding to him. Luke's protagonists commit themselves to Jesus when they see the things that he *does*.

Another approach again is taken by John, himself one of the first disciples of Jesus and an eye-witness of his ministry. John presents the call of Andrew and Simon, Philip and Nathaniel by focussing not on what they felt or what they saw, but on what they *heard*.

23

The next day John [the Baptist] was standing with two of his disciples, and as he watched Jesus walk by, he exclaimed, "Look, here is the Lamb of God!" The two disciples heard him say this, and they followed Jesus. When Jesus turned and saw them following, he said to them, "What are you looking for?" They said to him, "Rabbi" (which translated means Teacher), "where are you staying?" He said to them, "Come and see." They came and saw where he was staying, and they remained with him that day. It was about four o'clock in the afternoon. One of the two who heard John speak and followed him was Andrew, Simon Peter's brother. He first found his brother Simon and said to him, "We have found the Messiah."... He brought Simon to Jesus, who looked at him and said, "You are Simon son of John. You are to be called Cephas" (which is translated Peter).

The next day Jesus decided to go to Galilee. He found Philip and said to him, "Follow me."... Philip found Nathanael and said to him, "We have found him about whom Moses in the law and also the prophets wrote, Jesus son of Joseph from Nazareth." Nathanael said to him, "Can anything good come out of Nazareth?" Philip said to him, "Come and see." When Jesus saw Nathanael coming toward him, he said of him, "Here is truly an Israelite in whom there is no deceit!" Nathanael asked him, "Where did you get to know me?" Jesus answered, "I saw you under the fig tree before Philip called you." Nathanael replied, "Rabbi, you are the Son of God! You are the King of Israel!" Jesus answered, "Do you believe because I told you that I saw you under the fig tree? You will see greater things than these." (John 1.35-50)

Here there are two different responses, but they are both based not on deeds but on words. Andrew, Simon and Philip decide to follow Jesus on the basis of the teaching they have heard from John the Baptist and the way it fits with the promises of scripture. Nathaniel decides to follow Jesus because Jesus tells him things about himself which he could not have known or seen. All of them, in John's account, are responding primarily not to what they felt or saw, but to what they *heard*.

Others would respond in the same way. One of the things

I notice from the ministry of Paul is that he presents the good news about Jesus in different ways in different places. In Lystra and in Malta Paul proclaims the gospel by praying for the sick to be healed; perhaps he knows that, like our friend John here in Somerset, some people need to see before they believe. In other places, though, Paul sets out not to heal but to teach. In Cyprus and in Antioch Pisidia he and Barnabas go through the scriptures from Exodus to Jesus, and 'the word of God spread throughout the region.' He takes the same approach in Beroea, where people pore over the scriptures together to see whether his teaching is sound and many believe, including some Greeks of high standing. In Athens too he offers reasoned argument – this time not from the Jewish scriptures but from classical philosophy; among those who respond are Dionysius the Areopagite, Damaris and their friends.[17]

I have led many church weekends and clergy retreats, and I like to invite people to 'go back to Galilee' and consider how they first experienced the call of Jesus. Are you a Mark person, a Luke person, or a John person, I ask? A small number say they are a Mark person; it happened just like that. More say they are a Luke person; they believed on the basis of something they had seen or experienced. But most identify themselves as a John person; for them Galilee was not about seeing works but about hearing or reading words.

This is how it was for me. My first question was not 'does it work?' but 'is it true?'. So I looked at the textual and historical evidence for the life, death and resurrection of Jesus; I considered whether the Christian faith worked as a philosophy; I found out about other religions; I read the gospels and most particularly the gospel of John. One of the books I found most helpful was written by a man called Frank

Morison. Frank had been so convinced that the whole story was a hoax that he set out, with all the tools of a professional lawyer, to disprove it. The investigation didn't go quite as Frank expected, and he not only gave his life to Christ, he wrote a fine book explaining why. First published in 1930, it's still in print.[18] After many books and many conversations with patient friends, I concluded that the gospel had to be true. Then, and only then, was I ready to respond to the invitation "Follow me" – and to discover that it also works.

For most people in the West today, Galilee is a listening kind of place. It takes the average person some four years to think their way into the kingdom of God; like the Athenians, we have a whole secular mental framework to deconstruct and reconstruct before we even reach the starting line. The more educated we are, the harder it seems to be. Which is why we need the kind of teaching resources provided by the various enquiry courses that are now available, why it is so helpful to read books or watch interviews with high profile Christian thinkers, scientists and business people, and above all why Christians need to be open to listening to and talking with their not-yet Christian friends. 'It takes time,' poet Robert Frost once observed, 'for the intellect to eddy about a truth.'[19]

So, Jesus calls us. He calls us just like that, as described by Mark. Or he calls us by offering visible evidence of his authority to do so, as described by Luke. Or he calls us by speaking to us through the teaching of others, or through direct words of prophecy, as described by John. So pause awhile as you read, and ask yourself this question: How was it for you, this first moment of encounter with Jesus? Are you a Mark person, a Luke person or a John person – did you respond to what you felt, to what you saw, or to what you heard? Was that a moment, or a process? How was it for you?

Making a response

We began with Mark's simple account of what happened as Jesus embarked on his public ministry. 'Jesus came to Galilee,' Mark says, 'proclaiming the good news of God, and saying, "The time is fulfilled, and the kingdom of God has come near; repent, and believe in the good news."'[20] Most of those who heard it did indeed think that this was good news. Luke describes Matthew's reaction:

After this [Jesus] went out and saw a tax collector named [Matthew] Levi, sitting at the tax booth; and he said to him, "Follow me." And he got up, left everything, and followed him. Then Levi gave a great banquet for him in his house; and there was a large crowd of tax collectors and others sitting at the table with them. The Pharisees and their scribes were complaining to his disciples, saying, "Why do you eat and drink with tax collectors and sinners?" Jesus answered, "Those who are well have no need of a physician, but those who are sick; I have come to call not the righteous but sinners to repentance." (Luke 5.27-32)

Matthew responded by inviting everyone he knew to a dinner party – and then by giving away half his wealth. I have a friend who when she became a Christian could scarcely be restrained from running down the street hugging everybody – they all looked, she said, so miserable. I know another who went straight round to ask forgiveness from someone she had wronged. Another who felt a sense of complete release from the pain of a series of broken relationships. Another who stood staring at the full shopping bags in her hands, wondering why she'd thought she needed all those things.

It's said that when things are tough, it helps to go back in your mind to an earlier time or place, a time when you knew that you were loved, or a place where life seemed to make sense. Perhaps that's why Jesus told his disciples to go back to Galilee, to that initial moment of clarity which had impelled them to leave everything and follow him. For you too it may help to go back to Galilee, and think again about what it was, exactly, that changed the course of your life. Then you will be ready to continue the journey that Jesus has planned for you.

This is how the 16th century Bible scholar William Tyndale defined the gospel in the prologue to his translation of the New Testament:

'That [which] we cal gospel is a greke word, and signyfyth good, mery, glad and joyfull tidings, that maketh mannes hert glad, and makyth hym ssynge, daunce, and leepe for joy.'

David Teniers the Younger -
"A Kermis on St George's Day" (1649) – detail

Called by Jesus : Darrell Tunningley

Darrell Tunningley was serving a sentence for armed robbery. Attracted only by the tea and biscuits, he joined an Alpha course. One thing led to another, and...

'I said the first real prayer I had ever said in my life. "All right, God. I believe. Jesus, I believe You took my sentence, that you died for me. I'm tired of feeling worthless, being an addict and being angry all the time. Take away all my anger, take my drug addiction, and take away all this mess that I've made. If You do that for me, then I'll do what You want me to do for the rest of my life." That's the clean version. I swore a couple of times, but that's how I spoke, that was real to me, it was how I was feeling, it was where I was in my life – and God met me there. You see, God isn't looking for perfection. He loves us so much that He will take us exactly as we are. But He loves us too much to leave us that way.

'I don't know what I was expecting, but nothing happened. The cell door didn't start to shake, there were no bright lights, no angel came down and no booming voice said, "Yes, My son, I can hear you." I just went to bed hoping that He had heard me. The next morning I woke up before the screws had started banging the doors to wake everyone, so it was very quiet. What happened next was a series of events that I will never forget.

I would always make a smoke before going to bed so I could just roll over and have a cigarette before getting up. I was always gagging for a smoke in the morning. This morning, I rolled over to get the cig - but the sight of it made me feel sick! I don't mean a little groggy, I mean I couldn't stand to even look at it. I grabbed it and threw it out of my window. I couldn't shake the feeling, so I grabbed all my tobacco and threw that out of the window, too. Immediately, I started feeling better.

'If I woke up early enough, I would have a spliff out of the window before the screws came. But as soon as that thought popped into my head, the horrible feeling came back worse than before. I took the little bit of weed I had and threw that out of the window as well. As soon as it had gone, I started to feel OK again.

'I was freaking out by this point, and wondering what was wrong with me. I went over to the sink to start getting washed and shaved when a new feeling started to come over me. At first it was a nice warm feeling. I was happy but had no idea why – and the feeling kept on intensifying. I had had pretty much every drug going, but what I was feeling was more powerful than any of them. It was as if someone had unscrewed the top of my head and poured freezing cold water in, I could feel it running through me, washing everything bad away – all the anger and guilt and frustration. I looked at myself in the mirror and almost didn't recognize my own reflection. I was smiling and happy. All the anger that used to feel like a cancer eating me from the inside out had gone. I couldn't fully explain how all this was happening, but I knew God had heard my prayer. I knew He had forgiven me, I knew I had been given a second chance, that I was new inside.'

from Darrell Tunningley, *Unreachable – One Man's Journey through Drugs, Violence, Armed Robbery and a Miraculous Encounter with God in Prison,* Sovereign World 2011.

Darrell gave his testimony at the HTB Leadership Conference in May 2013. He is now a minister with the Assemblies of God.

Called by Jesus – a group study

"Go back to Galilee," Jesus instructed the disciples after his resurrection. Consider your own Galilee, the time and place where your journey with Jesus first began. Take time to remember and reflect, using the gospel passages below to stimulate your thinking.

Then spend some time in prayer, remembering the journey you have come on, and committing yourself to the journey that is to come.

1. Follow me – the simple call (Mark)

Mark 1.16-20 – Simon and Andrew, James and John
Mark 2.13-14 – Levi

- Imagine the scene – you are fishing, Jesus comes up, you follow – instantly
- What were you doing when Jesus first called you – what were your life circumstances?
- How did you hear his call? Was it instant like this?
- Do you know anyone who has had this kind of experience?

2. Watch this – now follow me (Luke)

Luke 4.38-41 – healings at Simon's house
Luke 5.1-11 – Simon, James and John catch many fish

- Perhaps it isn't always as sudden as all that – in this account, the actual calling isn't the first thing that happened – those called had already seen Jesus demonstrate his power through healings and miracles beforehand.
- What about you? Did you respond to Jesus out of the blue, or had you seen him do something first, in your own life or someone else's?
- Do you know anyone who has had this kind of experience?

- Is the Jesus you have committed yourself to following someone who works in this way today?

3. Listen to this – now follow me (John)

Luke talks about the disciples seeing Jesus do things which convinced them of his identity. John talks about Jesus saying things.

John 1.35-51 – Andrew and Simon; Philip and Nathaniel

- They are responding not on the basis of miracles but on the basis of teaching/prophecy/knowledge – not to what they saw, but to what they heard, through others, or directly
- Do you have experience of that, in your own life?
- Did it play a part in your first response to Jesus? Has it played a part since?
- Do you know anyone who has had this kind of experience?

4. Making a response

Luke 5.27-32 – Levi

- Did you first encounter Jesus suddenly, in one of the ways above, or was it a more gradual experience?
- If it was a gradual process, what were the key moments?
- If you haven't yet encountered Jesus in this way, would you be open to that possibility?
- When you first encountered Jesus, how did you respond?
- In what ways have you made your response public? Do your family, friends and colleagues know that you are a Christian?

CHAPTER TWO

What is a disciple?

For the follower of Jesus, discipleship is not the first step toward a promising career. It is in itself the fulfillment of his or her destiny.

Alan Hirsch[1]

I began my professional life as a student and teacher of Dante, the Italian poet who described his visionary journey down through the abyss of Hell, up the mountain of Purgatory and finally through the heavenly spheres and into the presence of God in Paradise. I wasn't a Christian then; but I read with increasing fascination of the people Dante met as he travelled through the other world – people who in their lives had taken decisions which moved them steadily further away from God, or decisions which moved them steadily further towards God. Even the ones who moved in the right direction hadn't always got it right – but it seemed it was the direction which mattered, not the detail; and now here they were, fixed for all eternity in a landscape which mirrored the inclination of their souls. Later I would notice the same process in the gospels, where we read not only of the steadfastness of Mary, the instant commitment of Matthew and the loyalty of Mary Magdalene, but also of the mistaken ambition of James and John, the impetuous violence and the outright denials of Peter, the creeping caution of Nicodemus

33

– all people who, whilst not always getting it right, nonetheless spent their lives moving in the right direction. And as in Dante, we also meet those who chose to move the other way: the rich young ruler, the many disciples who were offended by Jesus's teaching and chose to go back home, and of course Judas – who would fare particularly badly in Dante's Hell.[2] All these people were answering, in one way or another, Jesus's basic question: are you for me, or against me? Do you wish to follow me, in all your muddled fallibility – or not?

When I made my own commitment to follow Jesus, I became part of a group which understood Christian discipleship primarily as the process of studying scripture and trying to apply it to our personal lives. It was at a time when there was a great desire to rekindle the faith of the church, and it was a solid foundation on which to build – but it left me, a 'John' person, wondering where the 'Mark' and the 'Luke' people were; somehow there didn't seem to be quite enough scope for getting things wrong, and most of what was happening was in our heads, not before our eyes or in the depths of our hearts.

Shortly after that I married Roger, just accepting his first full time post as an Anglican minister; we spent the next twenty-four years immersed in the ministry of the local church. Here it became more interesting. As members of our first congregation lurched wildly about in their faith journeys, we learned that discipleship is not just about direction or instruction but also about community. It was through our commitment to one another, through our shared life of prayer, and through our floundering willingness to be guided by the Holy Spirit that we learned more of what it meant to be disciples of Jesus: we learned to pull together. Applying the same lessons in the next place, we encouraged the majority of the church to form themselves into small cell groups where they could not just study the Bible but worship and pray together, share their struggles and dreams with one another, and engage in whatever ministry they felt they were called to, both within the group and more widely within the church and the local community. The church already had an active ministry of healing, and it soon became strong in evangelism; now we were not just understanding things, but also seeing them.

In the year 2000 I met Stanley Hotay, diocesan missioner in the Tanzanian Diocese of Mount Kilimanjaro, where I had been invited to help lead a clergy conference. A couple of years later we invited him to visit us in Leicester. Stanley is a passionate evangelist, and he shared with us that the Lord had been speaking to him from Matthew 28.19-20: "Therefore go and make disciples of all nations, baptising them in the name of the Father and of the Son and of the Holy Spirit, and teaching them to obey every thing I have commanded you." Stanley said that the Lord was telling him that he was doing a great job leading people to faith, but that the key issue was to disciple them: 'You are making converts; but I want you to make disciples.' And so as we walked one day beside Rutland Water, where trees stand deep rooted on the edge of the flooded valley, a discipleship programme for Africa called *Rooted in Jesus* was born.[3] Working together and drawing in a team of people to help us, we put together a set of notes and exercises for a small group of people to follow together over a two year period. It's not a Bible study course, although it is based on scripture; it's an interactive and practical programme designed to help ordinary people follow Jesus in all aspects of their lives – to be everything, in both word and deed, that Jesus invited his first disciples to be. We've never advertised it – it never occurred to us to do so – but word got around. Thirteen years later, *Rooted in Jesus* is now in use in over 70 dioceses or denominations in 15 African countries; I have become not just its editor but also its director.

For the last ten years I have been working with ReSource, an Anglican charity based in the UK, supporting churches and church leaders across this country and beyond; *Rooted in Jesus* is now run as a project of ReSource. Most of our energy, though, is spent here. We work locally, regionally and nationally, providing resources and encouragement for churches and networks which are seeking to become more effective in mission and evangelism, in the healing ministry and in everyday discipleship.[4] My role within the ReSource team includes writing materials of one kind or another, facilitating discussion and planning days, speaking at conferences, visiting churches and leading retreats. It's an immense privilege to have this national brief, for it gives us a unique bird's eye view of the church in this country, across traditions and denominations; perhaps as much as anyone we are able to take the temperature of the church, to try to discern the signs of the times.

Increasingly, as we travel the country, we are finding the word 'disciple' on people's lips. A few years ago we'd have said the key word was 'confidence', and the question that people were asking was something like this: 'how confident can we be, in an increasingly secular culture, that the good news of Jesus Christ is still what people need and want to hear?' But as the currents of the world sweep on, more and more it seems that within the church people are talking about what it means to be a disciple of Jesus: how to make disciples, how to grow in discipleship. Why should this be? Perhaps we have become more confident as the decline in church attendance begins to turn into growth; perhaps we have simply realised that the basis of our confidence is in fact the quality of our lives as disciples of Jesus.[5] The Diocese of Carlisle has defined its strapline and the core of its 10 year vision as 'to see our churches growing disciples of all ages'; after 30 years of decline, it has now begun to grow. The incoming bishop of Dover, Trevor Wilmott, initiated a year of discipleship after being struck 'by the desire from people across Canterbury Diocese to reconnect with what makes their faith real.' In 2012 ReSource was invited to spend six days in the Diocese of Oxford, meeting with 360 clergy and 1300 church council members to think afresh about what it means to be a disciple of Jesus; in 2013 we embarked on a similar exercise across the Diocese of Portsmouth under the title 'Renewing our vision for mission.' In the autumn of 2012 a Consultation on discipleship was held in Church House, London, with representatives from many Anglican dioceses; the question was 'how can we get discipleship into the lifeblood of the Church of England?' A further consultation, 'What helps disciples grow?' followed in November 2013. At ReSource we have facilitated discussions on discipleship with different denominational networks and in many local churches. So many people have asked if they can use *Rooted in Jesus* here that we have adapted it for the UK and released it under the title *The God Who is There*, a programme which focusses, as we often say, not simply on what we know but, more profoundly, on who we are becoming.

'Discipleship,' Bishop Graham Cray has said, 'is the most strategic issue facing the western church today.' Mark Greene of the London Institute of Contemporary Christianity agrees: 'the UK will never be reached until we begin to cultivate communities that are focussed on making whole-life disciples who live and share the gospel wherever they relate to people in their daily lives.' 'Discipleship,' insist theologians Michael Frost and Alan Hirsch, 'should be the defining quality of the Christian life.' American philosopher Dallas Willard puts it more starkly: 'Most problems in contemporary churches can be explained by the fact that members have not yet decided to follow Christ.'[6]

It seems that now is the time for the church to think again about what it means to be a disciple of Jesus.

Going back to Galilee

Now the eleven disciples went to Galilee, to the mountain to which Jesus had directed them. When they saw him, they worshipped him; but some doubted. And Jesus came and said to them, "All authority in heaven and on earth has been given to me. Go therefore and make disciples of all nations, baptizing them in the name of the Father and of the Son and of the Holy Spirit, and teaching them to

38

obey everything that I have commanded you. And remember, I am with you always, to the end of the age." (Matthew 28.16-20)

After the resurrection of Jesus, the eleven remaining apostolic disciples of Jesus make the long journey back to Galilee as he had instructed. Matthew tells the story briefly: they went, they met him, they were commissioned by him. But of course it wasn't quite as simple as that. John, who was there, tells us a bit more about the time they spent together.

It seems that, once back home, Jesus's disciples are inclined to resume their old way of life. It's a natural reaction – after all, their three year adventure appears to have come to an end. And so it is that one evening, as seven of them stand on the shore of the Sea of Galilee, Peter announces he's going fishing. James and John, also previously fishermen, and the four others climb into the boat with him. They fish all night, and catch nothing. In the morning a figure stands on the shore: "Cast the net to the right side of the boat." They do; and catch so many fish that they can scarcely haul in the net. At that moment the penny drops, and John exclaims to Peter, "It is the Lord!" – the Lord who had first met them three years earlier, there on that same shore; the Lord who had filled their nets on that first day just like this; the Lord who had then called them away from their fishing and promised to make them fishers of men.[7] And, as if this were not enough of a reminder, Jesus then cooks them a meal. 'Come and have breakfast,' he says. It's a simple meal: just bread and fish. He breaks the bread, and gives it to them. And perhaps as he did so they remembered the last momentous time he had done that, the night before his death, the night when he had spoken these words: "Take, eat; this is my body, which is given for you."[8] Jesus is taking them back.

Jesus cooks some fish - Lucas Gassel (1490-1568)

But there is more. Having helped the disciples to relive these key moments of calling and offering, Jesus goes for a walk along the shore with Peter. This time he takes him back to something more painful – Peter's terrified denial of him in Jerusalem. "Do you love me?" he asks Peter three times, matching Peter's three denials. Peter, hurt, insists that he does. "Follow me!", Jesus then says, just as he had on that first day three years before. Nothing could be clearer; Jesus is saying to them, here in the place where he first chose them, 'No, I've not lost confidence in you – the invitation still stands. Come; follow me.'

That's John's account. In Luke we find yet another dimension of going back. This time it's not a personal going back but a historical one. Jesus takes them back in the scriptures. As he had done already for Cleopas and his companion on the road to Emmaus, Jesus explains to the gathered disciples – Cleopas and his fellow walker, the eleven and the wider group that is with them – how everything that has happened in the last days and weeks had been clearly announced from the very beginning of time, by Moses, the prophets and the writers of the psalms. The whole sorry business in Jerusalem had been not a disaster, but a completion; it had been a fulfilment of the cosmic purposes of God.[9]

So Jesus is taking them back, back to the beginning. It's recorded for us most vividly by John, the youngest disciple, the only one of the gospel writers who was actually there – John who many years later would begin his gospel with precisely those words: *In the beginning*. 'Go back, back,' Jesus says; 'it's your *whole* journey I want you to think about, not just the end; and, even more than that, I want you to see how it fits into the wider context of the history of the world; for the seeds of the future always lie in the past. And now that we've done that,' he continues, 'it's time to go forwards. You are my disciples; that has not changed. And here is your task: I want you to make more disciples. Baptise them in the name of the Father and of the Son and of the Holy Spirit, and teach them to obey everything that I have commanded you.'

What is a disciple?

In every life and in every movement there are times when it's important to go back, back to the beginning, back to the key moments of the past, the moments in which the big principles were first laid down. That was true for those first disciples of Jesus; perhaps it was true too for the people for whom Tintoretto and Veronese exploded history on the church walls of Venice. And I think it's true for us. We are living in changing times; and at times of change it's good to go back.[10]

So let's start with the basic question. When Jesus said, "Go and make disciples," what did he mean? What exactly *is* a disciple of Jesus? Am I a disciple? Are you a disciple? It's an

41

unexpectedly confusing question – Michael Wilkins, author of a classic book on biblical discipleship, says that when he asks his students to raise their hands if they are a true disciple of Jesus, few do so; most are confused and hesitant. But when he asks them to raise their hands if they are a true Christian, they all confidently do so. Why the hesitation? Luke tells us that even after his death, 'disciple' remained the normal word for any person who believed in Jesus – it was not until the gospel spread to Antioch in Syria that the word 'Christian' first came into use. So what *does* it mean to be a disciple of Jesus?[11]

I'm a linguist, and I think words are a bit like clothes. Each year I travel once or twice to Africa to train and support people who want to lead *Rooted in Jesus* groups. People in Africa are very kind, and sometimes they give me a shirt made from beautiful Tanzanian or Zambian cotton. And I take it home, and I wear it, and I wash it. And often I wear it and I wash it so much that the shirt shrinks or it fades; and gradually it stops looking as good as it did. I think that happens with words too – we wear them and wash them so many times that they shrink and they fade, and lose their meaning. And because it happens gradually we don't even notice.

A shrunken understanding of discipleship?

I want to suggest that this is what's happened to the word disciple. When Jesus said "Go and make disciples," he was talking about something new and big and radical, something profound, something that had never been seen before. And yet all too often after we've worn this word disciple, washed it and passed it down from one generation to another, we find ourselves left with something shrunk and faded, something much smaller than it was originally intended to be. And people look at us, and they see this rather shrivelled garment, and they are not impressed – they no longer say, as people said in those early centuries, 'where can I get one of those?'. For us, discipleship has become less than it should be: instead of lying at the heart of our identity as people called and sent by the living God, it has become a word we aren't even sure we can define.

Perhaps this always happens with words which are no longer in common use; bit by bit they lose their meaning. And the inevitable consequence of that, of course, is they are open for redefinition. The shirt which once had been cast aside as shrunk and faded is picked up by passers by, people looking for a word to fit a concept of their own; taking hold of the shirt, they stretch it to suit their own needs. This, I suggest, has happened with the word disciple: it has become something of an umbrella term, as we discovered when we devoted one of our magazines to it – everyone has their own idea of what it means. For some it suggests a programme of Bible study, for others a rather prescriptive shepherding process. For many it's simply a word attached to centrally organised training courses of one kind or another. For yet others, shying away from this academic approach, 'disciple' is just a word for a person who takes a step of commitment to Christ – 'making new disciples' seems to be the latest user-friendly phrase for evangelism. The

43

problem with this, as Stanley Hotay discovered when God spoke to him about the difference between making converts and making disciples, is that making disciples involves a lot more than just leading people to faith.

The result of this stretching of the word disciple and its cognate discipleship is that it now means almost anything you want it to mean – which is another way of saying that it means very little at all. As Dallas Willard sighs, 'the term discipleship has currently been ruined so far as any solid psychological and biblical content is concerned.'[12]

So what is discipleship? What exactly did Jesus mean when he said "Go, and make disciples"?

Apprenticed to Jesus

It depends which translation you are reading, of course, but the English word 'disciple' is used more than 250 times in the New Testament – usually in the plural. The word 'Christian,' by contrast, is used just three times.[13] A careful analysis of all these instances draws us to the conclusion that the shrinking and fading of the word 'disciple' can be seen in the loss of two features which were key to the way it was understood by Jesus.

In 2011 the Anglican Diocese of Gloucester conducted a survey among its clergy, asking what they regarded as the most important elements of discipleship. The survey reported widespread agreement across the diocese: clergy from all contexts and traditions selected 'Bible study' as the foremost activity of a Christian disciple, followed by 'prayer'. There was no suggestion that discipleship should involve any element either of ministry or lifestyle; indeed, 'personal morality' was rated bottom of the seventeen options offered, along with 'witness' and 'faith at work'.[14]

When we think about discipleship today we tend naturally to think about some form of study. The English word 'disciple' comes from the Latin verb *disco*, which means 'to learn'. We live in a culture of study, and inevitably we bring to the biblical text our own assumptions about what learning involves. For most of us, learning means classrooms and colleges; learning is about understanding, about information, about what we know – it's an activity which takes place in our heads. So it seems natural to help people to become disciples of Jesus by inviting them on a study course – perhaps a Bible study programme to start with, then for the keen ones maybe a diocesan course or some kind of further theological qualification. Viewed in this academic way, discipleship is primarily about qualifications. It's a widespread misunderstanding: the most perfunctory internet search reveals the existence of bishops' certificates in discipleship, discipleship study days and discipleship conferences, discipleship libraries and discipleship journals.

The problem is that this approach, although it fits well with the emphasis our society places on information and qualifications, does not reflect the process by which Jesus taught his first disciples. Such courses may be very helpful in themselves, but they tend to produce not so much Christians equipped to live and share their faith in the context of their daily lives, as recruits to the offices of the church – people who in being taken out of their own context have become disciples not of Jesus but of the institution. 'Sometimes, Michael Wilkins remarks, 'our discipleship programs thwart true discipleship – we can become so involved with our programs that we isolate ourselves from real life.'[15]

What then does it mean to be a disciple of Jesus? Perhaps the clue again lies in language – for we may notice that the biblical word for disciple is not Latin but Greek, and in Greek it carries a slightly different meaning. The gospel word for disciple is *mathetes*. And *mathetes* is not a classroom kind of word: in the context in which Jesus used it, it carried a bigger meaning, something more like 'apprentice' – it referred to a process which involved not just learning *from* your master but learning to actually *become* like him. So we do not see Jesus teaching his disciples in a classroom, and we do not see him encouraging or equipping them to engage in theological discussion and debate; rather the reverse, for the Pharisees who want to tempt them into this approach are given very short shrift indeed. Jesus taught his disciples in a rather different way: he taught them, apprenticeship style, to do the things which he did – how to live and how to minister. And then, as Matthew records, he told them to teach others to do these things too. So we see Jesus not so much *teaching* his disciples as *training* them, in the same practical way that he himself had been trained to be a carpenter. Jesus was indicating, TW Manson suggests, that discipleship was not a theoretical life of scholarship but a practical task of labour in God's vineyard; 'Jesus was ... a master-craftsman whom they were to follow and imitate. Discipleship was not matriculation in a Rabbinical College, but apprenticeship to the work of the Kingdom.'[16]

This was new; so new, Wilkins observes, that it took the disciples themselves some time to get their minds round what was being required of them. Other masters had disciples, so Jesus was working within a recognised framework; but he was changing it into an expression of his own particular relationship with his followers, patiently teaching them what it meant to be his kind of disciple, his kind of follower. This kind of discipleship, a following not for study but for service as ministers of the kingdom of God, had never been seen before.[17]

Mathetes : redefining discipleship

The Greek word μαθητής comes from a verb meaning to learn. It first appears in the writings of Herodotus (C5 BC), but was in wide oral use before then. First used to denote a learner or apprentice in a particular skill or craft (eg dancing, music, writing, wrestling, hunting, medicine), its meaning gradually shifted from learner to pupil, embracing the concept not just of learning but also of commitment to a great teacher or master. By the time of Herodotus, μαθητής indicates a person who was making a significant personal life commitment to the master, learning his practices and living them out.

During the Hellenistic era (C4-C1BC) μαθητής was used to denote the nature of the relationship between master and disciple, with the emphasis moving increasingly away from learning towards imitation of conduct. By the time of the New Testament, religious adherents (especially those within the mystery religions) were called disciples. Learning is minimised in these contexts; religious commitment and imitation of the religious figure's life and character characterise the relationship.

Μαθητής is used in the gospels both to describe the followers of John the Baptist and as the primary term for the followers of Jesus (those who travelled with him and also those who did not). By the time of Acts it's the normal term for any Christian believer. A disciple of Jesus is now understood to be 'one who has come to Jesus for eternal life, has claimed Jesus as Saviour and God, and has embarked upon the life of following Jesus.'

Summary from Michael Wilkins, *Following the Master – A Biblical Theology of Discipleship*, Zondervan 1992, chapter 4.

In other words, it seems that the kind of discipleship we see unfolding in the lives of Jesus's earliest followers is not theoretical, it's practical. 'Watch me,' Jesus said as he healed the sick, freed the oppressed and offered good news to the poor. Then he said, 'You go out now in pairs, try it yourselves, and we'll go through it when you get back.' Then finally, 'I'm off now, and you are to keep on doing this, and teach others to do it too.'[18] The implications of this for the way we train people for ministry today are interesting, for we so often take the exact opposite approach, deliberately removing people from the context of normal life and placing them in an artificial environment where there is no one with whom to share the good news and no opportunity to put into practice what is being learnt – which of course in turn means that what is learnt cannot itself be the ministry skills which Jesus was so concerned to impart to his disciples. Jesus wasn't training theologians; he was training practitioners, and the primary context of the training was not the classroom but the community. You cannot get to be a disciple of Jesus by going on a study course. In fact it seems that discipleship is not about what you know at all; it's much bigger than what's in your head – it's about your whole life, everything that you are and everything that you do. As the Fresh Expressions website notes, 'the term discipleship designates the whole life response of Christians to Jesus Christ.' Discipleship is indeed not about what you know; it's about who you are becoming.[19]

So what about our theological education and Bible study programmes? Bible study is of course essential, for it's in the Bible that we discover all these things. But study is not enough. Reflecting on his own theological education, Brian

McLaren laments: 'I could see absolutely no correlation between the amount of theological complexity and the amount of spiritual vitality, Christ-likeness, or fruitfulness – in my life, or in the lives of others.' 'From my desk at college,' writes Shane Claiborne, 'it looked like some time back we had stopped living Christianity and just started studying it.'[20] If we are to make disciples, we must do more than help people acquire biblical and theological information. Our task is not simply to study the Word of God; it's to get it off the page and into our lives. The Bible itself often tells us this. 'Don't read it, eat it,' God said to the prophet Ezekiel. 'Don't speak it, live it,' he said to Hosea. 'You claim to know what it says, but you have no understanding of its power,' Jesus said to the Pharisees. 'The Word of God is living and active,' said the writer to the Hebrews; 'it is meant to change us and change the people around us.' 'There is, Dallas Willard insists, 'absolutely no suggestion in the New Testament that being a disciple consists of reading your Bible and praying regularly.' It's much, much bigger than that.[21]

In the early days of *Rooted in Jesus* a woman living in Mererani, a village near Arusha in Tanzania, had a life-changing experience. Isaiah Chambala, then the *Rooted in Jesus* deanery coordinator and now the Bishop of Kiteto, tells the story. This woman was the only Christian living in her village, and each Sunday she would walk to a nearby village to attend church. She was therefore known for her faith, and one night some members of the village, followers of traditional religion, came to her house with a sick girl. No treatment had worked, and someone had told them that Christians know how to bring healing. The woman was an Anglican, a churchgoer, baptised and confirmed – but she had absolutely no idea how to pray for healing; prayer, she thought, was the pastor's job. Desperate to help, she did the only thing she knew how to do. Closing her eyes and remembering what she had been taught through the catechism, she prayed the Lord's Prayer. Nothing happened. She recited the Ten Commandments. No result. She said the Creed. Still nothing. She reviewed the sacraments, confessed her sins, and said the grace. The girl was as sick as ever. In frustration the woman burst into tears; what use was her faith? She cried and cried, Isaiah said, and rivers of tears flowed, but this time without words; just crying. "I cried not for the sick person but for myself that I didn't know how to pray," she said. When eventually she raised her head, the girl had been healed. This experience changed her life. Determined to learn how to make her faith effective in practice, the woman joined a *Rooted in Jesus* group. Soon she had led the whole family to Christ. "Why did you delay to bring this course to us?" she demanded.

The point, Isaiah explains when he tells this story, is this: discipleship is like football – knowing the theory is all very well, but it's not enough to know the theory, you are supposed to actually get the ball into the net; you are meant to win the game. It's no use us just knowing stuff in our heads; being a disciple of Jesus was never meant to be about that. It's about whether we can put it into practice, whether we can live it and help others to live it. Discipleship is not about acquiring information; it is, as Alan Hirsch puts it, 'the irreplaceable and lifelong task of becoming like Jesus by embodying his message.'[22] I notice that the Diocese of Carlisle, now growing after thirty years of decline, is consciously moving away from what it calls 'scary academic diocesan courses' to 'pathways for people on a journey of growth.'[23]

That journey, of course, may take us to places we would rather not go – as Jesus told Peter it would, and as it did for theologian Dietrich Bonhoeffer, who returned voluntarily to wartime Germany from New York in order to oppose the Nazi regime, and lost his life as a result. Bonhoeffer summed up his understanding of discipleship like this:

Discipleship means adherence to Christ and, because Christ is the object of that adherence, it must take the form of discipleship. An abstract theology, a doctrinal system, a general religious knowledge of the subject of grace or on the forgiveness of sins, render discipleship superfluous, and in fact they positively exclude any idea of discipleship whatsoever, and are essentially inimical to the whole conception of following Christ ... Christianity without discipleship is always Christianity without Christ.[24]

Our theoretical, knowledge-based discipleship is like a beautiful shirt which has shrunk in the wash; created to turn us into giants, it has become something which fits only midgets. We have reduced discipleship from a life-changing journey marked by irruptions of the divine into something so limited and vague that we can no longer even define it.[25]

What is a Christian disciple?

"Go, therefore, and make disciples of all nations, baptising them in the name of the Father, and of the Son and of the Holy Spirit, and teaching them to obey everything I have commanded you."
Jesus of Nazareth, Matthew 28:19-20

- A disciple is an active, intentional learner.

- A disciple is an apprentice and a practitioner - not just a student of the Word but a doer of it.

- A disciple is a follower of a particular teacher.

- A disciple is accountable to someone who knows them and helps them to learn and grow and live.

- A disciple is outwardly orientated, focused on helping others learn what it means to be a disciple.

Mark Greene, *Imagine How We Can Reach the UK*, LICC 2003.

Apprenticeship in community

But there's a second thing I think we have lost too, and this is not the shrinking but the fading. We live in a 'me' world, and that means we tend to see discipleship as an individual thing – as indeed we do all forms of higher education. I think of my own family; I have a son and two daughters, all at college or university, all having chosen what to study according to their own interests and aptitudes – Edward has opted for engineering, Bethy for dance and Katy for classics. We are delighted that they have chosen subjects they are motivated by and good at, and we are hopeful that in due course this will lead to appropriately remunerative employment. It is, however, not the right model for discipleship. For Jesus, discipleship was not an individual process but a community one. His disciples didn't choose a subject or a syllabus, they chose a person (or perhaps they were themselves chosen by him); and they learned not as individuals attending classes but as part of a new, mutually accountable community. Their discipleship was embedded in relationships; it required them to travel together in community with their Master.

This dynamic educational environment meant that much of their learning was done in the context of those relationships – sometimes difficult relationships, for their group included unschooled fishermen, a tax collector, and a political activist; men with very different perspectives on life. There were personality differences too; some were by nature impulsive, some reflective, some doubtful. And there were differences in age and experience; some were old, some still young enough to be accompanied by an ambitious mother. But despite this extraordinary variety in background and perspective they learned to love one another, to recognise and accept one another as brothers and sisters, not to compete with one another or judge one another. They learned to think 'we' instead of 'me'. 'You are not to be called rabbis,' Jesus said, 'and you are not to see yourselves as teachers. What you are is brothers, and your role is not to instruct but to *serve*, as you have seen me serve.'[26] The task of these first disciples was to become so united that they would seem to be, as Jesus explained to them, like the branches of a single vine.[27] Apprenticed to Jesus himself, the key to their identity lay in their relationships, not just with him but also with one another.

And it seemed that this was not just for those few who travelled with Jesus as he moved between the villages of Galilee, Samaria and Judea; it was a principle which lay at the very heart of the Christian gospel. In time, Paul would tell the Christian believers in Rome, Corinth and Ephesus that they too were no longer individuals, jostling for their rights and pursuing their own desires as they had been accustomed to do; they were now just different parts of a single body, the body of Christ. It's a clever image; for in seeing ourselves as the body of Christ we understand both our identity and our role.

For us today the challenge of community is as great as the challenge of apprenticeship, for we live in a culture which does not prioritise community. The Chief Executive of Leicester City Council, Rodney Green, once remarked that the church of Holy Trinity Leicester was the only place in the city where the gathering was not monochrome, but reflected the many different ethnic and socio-economic communities of which the population was made up. That is how it is meant to be. Being a disciple of Jesus means being joined to other people – people whom we have not chosen and perhaps would be unlikely to choose. We cannot be disciples alone; we can only be disciples together.

In Africa, of course, they still know this. "I am, because we are. We are, because He is," we said together as we prepared to take communion in Christ Church Cathedral, Arusha. Community still comes naturally to most Africans; and where people make a wholehearted commitment, despite the difficult circumstances in which they may live, to follow Jesus together,

54

then the most remarkable things can happen – now as then. The principle is neatly summed up in a proverb quoted by Bishop Jackson ole Sapit, a Masai from SW Kenya: "If you want to travel fast, travel alone; if you want to travel far, travel together."

Robert Katandula lives in the town of Mansa, in the Luapula region of Zambia, where in addition to earning his living he leads a *Rooted in Jesus* group in his local church. The group has 33 members, and divides into 6 smaller groups for discussion and prayer. *Rooted in Jesus* is not an academically demanding course; the challenges it offers are not intellectual but practical and spiritual, and it leads to radical change in the lives of those who embrace them. Many *Rooted in Jesus* group leaders have written to tell us of the transformation which has come as people commit themselves to Christ and to one another; but Robert's reports give a particularly helpful insight into how this comes about.

In January 2012 Robert wrote: 'The *Rooted in Jesus Christ* Group is a Christian group aimed at promoting spiritual growth, sharing the word of God and proclaiming the word of God to members and non members of the Anglican Church in the community. *Rooted in Jesus Christ* hold prayer meetings from Monday to Saturday in the morning daily. In the meetings on Monday to Friday the group discusses the lessons from the book *Rooted in Jesus*. Books 1, 2, and 3 have been covered so far.'

Robert went on to describe how the group are putting into practice what they have learned: 'Each afternoon on Sundays and Mondays the group meets at 1500 hours and goes into the community for visitations. The group gives spiritual support to individuals, families and groups depending on their requests. The group gives counselling, healing prayers, casts out demons and encourages those who are spiritually weak and have stopped attending church meetings. The group has received people from far villages for healing. The group is very much encouraged by the people's response to the power of prayers. The *Rooted in Jesus Christ* group is proud of their spiritual growth and the maturity in their lives. The group is seeing miracles happening to people in the community. Many people have been healed, demons are cast out, broken marriages are brought together, lost items are being recovered. Therefore the group is encouraged by how Jesus Christ is answering our prayer requests and also by how some people are changing in their lives.'

The following September Robert wrote again to report on the expanding ministry of the group now that it had completed the final book of *Rooted in Jesus:* 'I am proud in Jesus' name to inform you that our group has started charity work in the community after learning the word of

God on 'salt and light.' During our visitation to people in the community we found a lot of problems such as lack of food, clothing, proper accommodation, and school support for orphans. The group is overwhelmed with [the] challenges people have in the community. After the lesson members of the group contributed financially and materially. The group raised 24kg of maize grain, 6 bars of soap, salt, and second-hand clothes. In August our group went for a one day outreach meeting to share the word of God with St Paul's Anglican Church, which is about 35 km from Mansa town. The theme for the meeting was 'individual relationship with God.' Lessons covered were: introduction to *Rooted in Jesus*, salt and light, how to receive blessings from God and spiritual healing. I am proud that many Christians surrendered their lives to Jesus as Lord; demons and evil spirits were cast out from many people during the altar call healing prayer time. I thank the power of God [for] releasing many people from the power of darkness to light. The group has planned to reach 8 congregations before December; we are going to start with St Andrews 45 km from Mansa town.'

Robert notes that 'the committed members of the group have been transformed physically and spiritually in their lives due to the completion of the course.' Robert's pastor, Fr Teddy Sichinga, adds: 'We at All Saints Anglican church, Mansa have benefited a lot; the church has grown numerically, spiritually and financially because of the *Rooted in Jesus* programme.'

Robert's group is an excellent illustration of the nature of discipleship. The members of the group show remarkable commitment to one another; they learn together, they learn in practical ways, and they take immediate steps to apply what they are learning. The impact on their own lives and on those of the people they come into contact with is huge.

So what is Christian discipleship? I have come to define it like this: *discipleship is a form of apprenticeship undertaken in community.* It's practical, and it's corporate. To recognise this radically changes our understanding of it. It means that the focus of our discipleship should be not on what we know but on who we are becoming. And that's where the challenge lies, because we aren't becoming engineers or dance teachers, we are becoming like Jesus, the Son of God, growing into his likeness day by day as we learn to obey him. This is why the first Christian disciples were called Followers of the Way. They were following Jesus, they were going on a journey that no one had ever been on before, and they were going on it together. They were so good at going on it together that people rushed to join them, did indeed want to buy the unshrunken, unfaded T shirt; and the church was born.

Jesus and his Disciples

Jesus did not simply fit himself into the more or less standard model of the rabbi. He had no "formal" education beyond the synagogue schools and did not become a disciple of a rabbi. He did receive a (very unorthodox) stamp of approval from John the Baptizer, but not as his disciple. He was known to the people around him as uneducated. Amazed at the depth and power of his words they exclaimed: "How does this man have such learning, when he has never been taught?" (John 7:15). Also, Jesus did not accept disciples upon application, testing them to see if they were "worthy." He personally selected - though not from "the best and the brightest" in his community - those he would especially train. There was a larger outer circle of people who seem to have just showed up in his presence and received training of various degrees (the "other seventy" of Luke 10:1, for example, and the group in the "upper room" of Acts 1:13). Often would-be disciples were subjected to severe discouragement by him (Matt. 8:18-22, Luke 9:57-62 and 14:26-33). He also leveled scalding criticisms at the proud practitioners of the law in his day (Matt. 23:13-33, Luke 11:39-52) and prohibited his followers from being called "rabbi" and using other "respectful greetings" exchanged among those who took themselves to be highly qualified as teachers (Matt. 23:1-12). He was not "one of the boys," nor were his disciples to be.

Nevertheless, the basic nature of the rabbi/disciple relationship of his day was retained by Jesus and his disciples and, arguably, remains normative to this day. That relationship is very simple in description. His disciples were with him, learning to be like him. "With him" meant in that day that they were literally where he was and were progressively engaged in doing what he was doing. Jesus moved about the Jewish villages and towns, primarily around the Sea of Galilee, with occasional forays beyond that and especially to Jerusalem. His main disciples ("apostles") were with him in all of this, and no doubt at considerable hardship to themselves and their families. Peter on one occasion plaintively remarks: "We have left everything to follow you" (Matt. 19:27). It was no doubt a thought that often occurred to his disciples.

As they traveled about he did three things in the synagogues, homes and public areas: He announced the availability of life in the kingdom of God, he taught about how things were done in the kingdom of God, and he manifested the present power of the kingdom by amazing deeds (Matt. 4:23, 9:35, Luke 4:18-44). Then, after a period of training, he set his disciples to doing the things they had heard and seen in him – continuing all the while to evaluate their work and to teach them as they progressed. This continued through his trial and death, and during his postresurrection presence with them when he trained them in how he would be with them after his ascension, without visible presence. His instruction as he left was for his disciples to make disciples of all "nations" – of all types of people – and his promise was that he would be with them always until the end of the age (Matt. 28:19-20).

Dallas Willard, 'Discipleship', T*he Oxford Handbook of Evangelical Theology*, edited by Gerald McDermott, OUP 2010

Being disciples – a group study

'Discipleship is a form of apprenticeship undertaken in community' –
Alison Morgan

1. Volunteers, or disciples?

We were doing some work in the Diocese of Oxford on Mission Action Planning, and as we encouraged people to form parish groups and consider how they wanted to move forward, one woman raised her hand. 'That's all very well,' she said sharply, 'but you have to remember that we are all very busy. We don't have much time, you know – we are just volunteers.' 'We quite understand,' my colleague Martin replied; 'but Jesus is not looking for volunteers, he's looking for disciples.' This led into one of the most fruitful discussions of the day.

So what about you? How do you see yourself in relation to your local church? Are you a volunteer, or are you a disciple? What difference does it make if you see yourself as a disciple, rather than a volunteer?

2. Student, or apprentice?

'I could see absolutely no correlation between the amount of theological complexity and the amount of spiritual vitality, Christ-likeness, or fruitfulness – in my life, or in the lives of others ' – Brian McLaren.

Who in your own fellowship do you particularly respect for the maturity of their faith? What is it that marks them out? What is the experience or the circumstances that have helped them to become like this? Think back over your own faith journey. What has helped you to grow?

Consider the story about the woman in Arusha, desperate to see Jesus heal the sick girl who had been brought to her, and of her regret that although a faithful churchgoer she had not been apprenticed to Jesus much earlier in her life. "You will do the works that I do," Jesus said to

60

his disciples (John 14.12). Do you see yourself as an apprentice of Jesus, learning to do the works that he did?

3. Individuals, or community?

'As in one body we have many members, and not all the members have the same function, so we, who are many, are one body in Christ, and individually we are members one of another' – Romans 12.4-5.

How would you describe your own experience of being part of a community? Think about your family, about your small group or your church. To what extent can you say 'I am, because we are', and 'We are, because He is?'

Have there been times when you have been able to grow in your faith as part of a community, in ways which would not have been possible on your own? What is the particular contribution you have been called to make to the community of faith?

CHAPTER THREE

Following Jesus today

I had been my whole life a bell, and I never knew it until at that moment I was lifted and struck.

Annie Dillard[1]

In January 2014 the Church Growth Research Programme published the results of its long awaited study into the factors influencing church growth in the Church of England. Among the factors strongly associated with growth in churches (of any size, place or context) was a clear focus on discipleship; two thirds of churches running discipleship programmes had experienced growth. Another clear factor was the provision of programmes for children and teenagers; three quarters of churches running such programmes had grown. It is clear that the nurturing of Christian discipleship from childhood onwards is key to the health of the church and the growth of the kingdom.[2]

As we saw in Chapter 2, the Diocese of Carlisle has been quick to grasp this principle, and has placed 'Growing disciples' as the heart of its vision. A few years ago its bishop, James Newcome, invited me to speak to a gathering of archdeacons and rural deans about discipleship, sharing some of the things I have learned through the *Rooted in Jesus* discipleship programme in Africa. Wishing to include both theory and practice in my presentation, I decided to undertake a fresh study of the word 'disciple' in scripture. I began with the Old Testament. The Hebrew word for disciple is *talmidh;* and I found that in the whole canon of scripture before Jesus it appears just once, in 1 Chronicles 25.8, where it refers to the pupils of temple musicians.[3] In the New Testament the word for disciple is *mathetes,* and it is used frequently in the Gospels and in Acts, where it describes the followers of Jesus. But to my astonishment I found that the word disciple is completely absent from the Epistles. Peter, Paul, James and John do not use the word at all. Not even once.

This gave me considerable pause for thought, and eventually I came to two conclusions. The second we will look at in Chapter 5. But the first and most obvious was this: if we are thinking about discipleship, we are thinking primarily about Jesus – not about ourselves, not about church, not even about God, but about Jesus. I remember Colin Urquhart describing his first PCC meeting in the church of which he had just been appointed vicar. He put a single item on the agenda, and it was a question: 'What is a Christian?'. It was greeted with an astonished silence. I remember too reading a book by Martin Down about the unexpected activity of the Holy Spirit in a Norfolk village, and his observation that gradually people began to talk not about the church, but about Jesus.[4] It seems obvious that a disciple of Jesus should focus on Jesus – but how many of us actually wake up in the morning thinking about Jesus? Becoming a Christian disciple is not about joining the church and attending Sunday services; it's about embracing a personal relationship with Jesus, setting out on a journey which will bring change not just to what we do but to the very essence of who we are.

Matthew, Mark, Luke and John tell the story of the three year journey undertaken by the very first disciples of Jesus. What can we learn from their experience? As I reread the gospels with this

63

question in mind, it became clear to me that becoming a disciple of Jesus involves four key things, all of them still made possible for us today by the constant enabling presence of the Holy Spirit:

1. A change of direction
2. Learning on the hoof
3. Learning in community
4. A willingness to embrace pain

We will look at the first of these in this chapter and the remainder in the following chapters.

A change of direction

Every journey has a beginning, and the journey of discipleship is no exception. The beginning is marked by a change of direction, a change which may be slight or may be radical, but which carries us on a path that increasingly determines the kind of people we will become and the kind of life we will lead. Jesus came with a message of good news. Everywhere he went, he proclaimed this message in word and deed, inviting people to accept and respond to it. He expressed it in different ways at different times. In the synagogue at Nazareth he announced "I come to bring good news to the poor, to proclaim the year of the Lord's favour." As he began to travel through Galilee, he would say "Repent, for the kingdom of heaven has come near," or "Repent, and believe in the good news." It's worth noting that the word 'repent' simply means 'rethink' or, in its original Greek form *metanoia*, 'change your mind' – it's not just a reference to the things you may have done, or not done, it's a challenge to reconsider the foundation and direction of your whole life.

To the rabbi Nicodemus Jesus spelt out what was at stake: "Whoever believes in the Son has eternal life." Later he would offer his good news as a simple invitation: "Come to me, all you that are weary, and I will give you rest," or as a promise: "Everyone who acknowledges me before others, I also will acknowledge before my Father in heaven." Sometimes, as we have already seen, he simply said "Follow me."[5] And one by one they did; not just the twelve, but whole crowds of people, all of whom are referred to by Luke and John as his disciples.

So at the most basic level a disciple is a person who has made a decision to commit himself or herself to Jesus and his teaching; a person who has publicly recognised Jesus to be who he said he was, the Son of God, and who is prepared to live in the light of that recognition. After Jesus's death, the term 'disciple' remained the normal word used to designate all those who had placed their faith in him in this way – as we have seen, it was not until the gospel reached Antioch in Syria that ordinary believers were first described as 'Christians'.[6]

From the very beginning, there was no prescribed way of expressing a response to Jesus; for each person it was different. Jesus invited some of these first disciples to enter into a particularly close relationship with him: twelve of them would later be known not just as 'disciples' but as 'apostles' for their specially appointed role as founders of the early church – and indeed this is how Luke always refers to them, distinguishing them from those who responded to Jesus but were not called to such roles. Other disciples also accompanied Jesus on his travels – the women who funded his ministry, and the seventy whom he sent to minister ahead of him.[7] Still others Jesus left to work out their response in their own contexts – the Jerusalem woman brought for stoning after committing adultery, and the Samaritan lepers whom he sent home restored to health; Bartimaeus, a beggar from Jericho whose faith led to his healing from blindness; Zacchaeus, a tax collector from the same town whom Jesus left to rethink his financial affairs; the sisters Mary and Martha and their brother Lazarus who absorbed his teaching at their home in Bethany; Joseph of Arimathea, a 'secret' disciple who would later emerge from anonymity to bury Jesus' body at his own expense, and many more.[8] For all of them, those who travelled with Jesus and those who did not, there was a fundamental change in the direction of their lives, in their priorities, their relationships and even in the way they earned their living.

A multitude of disciples

John and Luke, in contrast to Mark and Matthew who focus on a smaller group, refer to a great crowd of disciples:

- John 4.1, 'Jesus is making and baptizing more disciples than John'

- John 6.66, 'many of his disciples turned back and no longer went about with him'

- Luke 6.13, 'he called his disciples and chose twelve of them, whom he also named apostles'

- Luke 10.1, 'the Lord appointed seventy others and sent them on ahead of him in pairs'

- Luke 19.37, 'the whole multitude of the disciples began to praise God joyfully'

- Acts 1.21, Matthias is chosen from among 'the men who have accompanied us during all the time that the Lord Jesus went in and out among us.'

- Acts 6.1-6, 'the disciples were increasing in number... the twelve called together the whole community of the disciples'

- Acts 14.21-22, 'they proclaimed the good news ... and made many disciples'

66

A couple of years ago a man named Dave Jeal came to tell the students at our local secondary school how his life had changed direction. Dave was brought up in inner city Bristol, and as a teenager he became first a fan of Bristol Rovers Football Club, and then a member of its notorious Young Executives 'firm'. Dave was drawn more and more into the violence at home and hooliganism abroad which characterised English football in the 80s and 90s. Banned from the club, he began to travel to matches abroad. Detained by the police in Rotterdam and involved in violent riots in Stockholm, Dave realised he was heading for prison. "I loved the buzz, and the excitement. It was almost like being a modern day Viking," he said afterwards. "You go to a country, you go berserk, and then you come home again. It's all a bit of fun." Why did he do it? "When I look back on it, I wasn't happy. I don't think happy people want to hurt others. I was not happy at home, not happy at work. I was just angry. I had loads of jobs – on drilling rigs, building sites, in a laboratory, down the sewers – but I kept getting sacked because of my anger. People would say something to me and I'd take offence and tell them to stick it. People just got fed up with me because of my attitude. I was fairly obnoxious."

Volunteering between jobs at a drop-in centre where his mother was working, Dave invited a girl he met there out for a drink. "I'll come for a drink with you," she said, "if you'll come to church with me." Appalled, Dave declined. "You scared, then?" she asked. So Dave went. He hated it, he said. But after the service, two men offered to pray with him. Dave hesitated. "Is there a God, or shall I break this bloke's nose?" he thought. "Just talk to God," one of them said. By the narrowest of margins, Dave did. "From that second on," he said, "I knew there was a God. I felt that all the anger and all the hate and all the pain that I'd carried around all my life had been taken from me. The only way I can describe it is it was like carrying a rucksack around with all of that in it. And it was put down, so it no longer had a hold over my life. I didn't feel these things any more. And I thought, that is it, everything changes from here." Today Dave is married to Nikki, a doctor. He is the pastor of St James, Lockleaze, a church in Bristol, and runs the St James Revolution football club for teenagers on the local estate. He is also – and no one could possibly have foreseen this – Chaplain to his beloved Bristol Rovers Football Club. For Dave, the decision to follow Jesus involved not just a change of direction but a radical reorientation.[9]

Dave's decision to enter into a relationship with Jesus has profoundly influenced not just the direction of his life but the kind of person he has become. Every time we make a choice, CS Lewis remarked long ago, we are turning the central part of ourselves, the part of us that chooses, into something a little different from what it was before; we are moving either towards God, or away from God.[10] We don't do that just once, in the moment of our first acceptance of Jesus, but many times, as we follow him into the changing landscape of our own futures. For Dave, as for Peter and John and the others, there were many other choices to be made after that first choice; but it all started with a single split-second decision which changed the direction of his life.

Stories such as Dave's are common. Over the years I have met bank robbers, fraudsters, drunkards, prostitutes, drug addicts, and many others whose lives were in lesser ways moving through a landscape of pain and hopelessness until they met Jesus. Some, like ex-gangster John Pridmore, drug addict Richard Taylor and armed robber Darrell Tunningley, have published their stories as an encouragement to others; most have quietly set off to find their new identities and build their new futures in the context of their own communities. We should not be surprised at the radical nature of these responses, for Jesus made it abundantly clear that he came to seek and to save not those who were already satisfied with their lives, but those who were not – "the Son of Man came to seek out and to save the lost."[11]

What then, of those of us whose lives have not plunged into such dark places? It's not hard to spot that Dave needed to change the direction of his life; but most of us are not obviously lost in the way that he was. Perhaps the key lies in understanding what Jesus meant by 'lost' – for judged by worldly standards Peter and John, Matthew and Paul were not lost either. And yet perhaps they were, in CS Lewis's sense; for the direction of their lives was not towards God. And if we don't wake up thinking about Jesus, the direction of our lives is probably not towards God either, for we live in a world which fills our minds with other things. "You need to repent of your sins," said a well-meaning evangelist to me when I was trying to find out about God. What does he mean, I thought? I am hard-working and successful; my relationships with friends and family are good; I have never slept around, got drunk or smoked a cigarette, and the only thing I've ever stolen was a small plastic pair of doll's sandals in the girls' cloakroom at my infant school – it wasn't my finest moment but surely he's not talking about that? If he'd said "You are going very successfully in the wrong direction; you need to think not about what is in your life but what is missing from it," then I might have understood. If Dave needed to make a 180 degree turn, perhaps I needed to make a 5 degree turn. 180 degrees is spectacular; 5 degrees is not. And yet if a polar explorer were to set off in the wrong direction by 5 degrees, he would miss his destination by thousands of miles. We all need to change direction; we all need to orient our lives towards God. If we do not disciple people, we can be sure that our culture will; trapped in the false values of a world which does not acknowledge God, our daily choices are liable to lead us ever further from him without our even realising it.[12]

Every society has what is known as a 'framing story', a set of assumptions about the best way to live. In the developed world our framing story is consumerism, a social and economic order and ideology based on the purchase of goods and services, and sustained by sophisticated and persistent advertising. Participation in this story leads us to believe that it is money which will make us happy, for money opens up the possibility of purchase. And so the generation of wealth becomes the guiding principle of our collective life, and never-ending economic growth the priority of every government – borrowing, building, expanding, investing – often at the cost of other factors which cannot be measured in economic terms, and so come to have no value. "You cannot prioritise both God and money," Jesus said. 'Keep your lives free from the love of money, and be content with what you have,' the writer to the Hebrews advised.[13] It seems that they were right, for as borrowing leads us ever further into personal and national debt, as we pursue our endless quest for lower taxes and higher disposable income, survey after survey finds that this is taking us in the wrong direction. It isn't simply that we are greedy – it's far more complex than that. 'What makes our age distinctive,' Alain de Botton notes, 'is our ambition to try and accomplish a variety of complex psychological goals via the acquisition of material goods.' The results can be alarming – witness the now annual 'Black Friday' scenes as shoppers push for pre-Christmas bargains 'like animals fighting over a piece of meat', as *The Times* newspaper described it. "I got a Dyson but I don't even know if I want it. I just picked it up," said Louise Haggerty, a 56-year-old hairdresser and waitress, describing her 1am trip to the Black Friday sales to Rupert Neate of *The Guardian.* "It was mental in there. It was crazy. It was absolutely disgusting, disgusting." Scenes such as these stem from a desire deeper than the thought of saving a few pounds on Christmas presents.[14]

The tragedy is that it doesn't seem to work. Over and above a basic £22,000 annual income (less than the national average), wealth makes no difference to happiness, one study discovered. Another noted that across the UK the wealthiest areas are not the happiest ones: birdsong in Cornwall or Cumbria is, it seems, a better indicator of human wellbeing than the pervasive roar of commuter traffic which cloaks the ears in the relatively affluent South East or West Midlands.[15] A recent research project found that the greatest life satisfaction is reported not by those with the highest income, but by those whose jobs involve meaningful relationships or direct contact with the natural world. And despite the constant media hum of voices encouraging us to boost our self-esteem, increase our social capital or reduce our anxiety levels through the purchase of this or that product, it turns out that however much or little you have, spending money on other people makes you happier than spending it on yourself.[16]

"I came to seek out and to save the lost," Jesus said. 'How does that work here?' wondered Alex Pease as he began his curacy in the wealthy Itchen Valley in Hampshire, where the average house price is £600,000 and most people have everything our culture teaches us to want. Alex took himself off to the local hairdresser, and asked her "where is the pain in this community?" She didn't even hesitate: "Relationships," she said. "Broken marriages, children who never see their parents. It's everywhere." We are encouraged to believe we need more money; and yet 'in our eagerness to be rich we wander away from the faith and pierce ourselves with many pains,' as Paul once pointed out to Timothy.[17]

And so it is that the orientation of our culture towards economic growth and personal spending power places our feet on a path which leads us imperceptibly away from God. Like the polar explorer who has miscalculated his direction of travel, we find ourselves moving further and further away from the kingdom of heaven. As we follow this well-trodden path, we pass other signposts, signposts which invite us to pursue success at work and prioritise personal fulfilment at home; for this is a culture which focusses on self. Some of us follow them, and find that we have created for ourselves lonely and competitive lifestyles; others fail, and find themselves left out of all the things everyone else seems to have. Our progress down this path is charted even by the patterns of our language; increasingly it seems we speak in the first person singular ('I') rather than the first person plural ('we'), using individual-focussed words like 'get' and 'choose' rather than group-focussed words like 'give' and 'obliged' – and the more we do this, the more likely we are to suffer from depression and loneliness.[18] As we grow in our ability to devise new forms of technology, further signposts point to virtual solutions; and yet the growth of apparently welcoming online communities and social networking sites leads us, researchers now suggest, into an ever greater retreat not only from other people but even from ourselves, as human experience is gradually reduced to data that can be posted online. We find ourselves exchanging life for its mirrored and less authentic double; real life becomes 'mere material for the creation of a digital performance.'[19] 'There is a way which seems right to a man, but its end is the way to death,' Solomon wrote. "The gate is wide and the road is easy that leads to destruction, and there are many who take it," Jesus confirmed.[20]

The further we travel down this well-signposted path with its tangle of inviting and confusing side turnings, the more confused and dissatisfied we become. Some seek solace in drink: the number of deaths directly attributed to the consumption of alcohol more than doubled between 1991 and 2005, and over a million adults in the UK now suffer from alcohol dependence. For others, so-called 'recreational' drugs offer a temporary escape from reality; 38% of 16-24 year olds have tried them, some at the cost of their lives. 'There is something going on culturally,' muses Petra Maxwell from the organisation Drugscope – without venturing to suggest what it might be. More and more people are affected by poor mental health: the number of prescriptions issued each year for depression has now rocketed to 50 million; in Blackpool, one in six people are prescribed them every month.[21] The outlook for the young is particularly gloomy: according to a survey undertaken in 2014 by the Prince's Trust, 9% of young people say that their lives are not worth living, and 26% that they have felt suicidal.[22] For many, a new identity seems the best answer; the number of people changing their name each year by deed poll leapt from 270 in 1996 to nearly 60,000 in 2011 – increasingly, it seems, we want to be someone else.[23]

Finally, there is the question of our spiritual lives; signposts for that in our culture are few and far between. 'God,' announced a house-sized poster as I drove down the A1 last week, 'is dead.' That's the

official story, anyway: God, as we are so loudly told, is a delusion.[24] And yet a sneaking suspicion otherwise seems to remain, for whereas just 29,267 people identified themselves as atheist in the 2011 census, some 33 million, 60% of the population, described themselves as Christian. Few of those 33 million Christians are in any real sense disciples of Jesus – at least, most of them do not express their faith in any regular or public way, for only three million are to be found in church on any given Sunday.[25] Some may be among the growing number who no longer expect to find God in church at all, preferring instead to experiment with more contemporary forms of spirituality, which I have discussed elsewhere and which are too numerous and mostly too extraordinary to mention here. Again, the signposts are attractive, but at best misleading and at worst dangerous; for "there is no other way to the Father except by me," Jesus said. We are left with a conundrum: "You go out on a day like this and you're really grateful," remarks moral philosopher Mary Midgley. She adds, "I don't know who to."[26]

So we live in a world which invites us to travel on roads which lead further and further from God. Some, like Dave's, are pitted and rough, full of violence and ambush. Others seem much more pleasant, paved with gold or at the very least adorned with enticing hoardings. Mostly we will get by; but we will not get to God, for to do that a different approach altogether is required. 'It may be that, in the long term, the growth, vigour and beauty of Western materialism will prove to have been not the life-giving dynamism of youth but a malignant cancer in the throat of the world,' Timothy Neat remarks as he compares the Scottish island life of his youth with the reality of consumerist society today.[27] There are winners in the race to life and there are losers, but there are no easy answers, and certainly none which can be bought. As Holocaust survivor Viktor Frankl once observed, 'happiness cannot be pursued; it must ensue, and it only does so as the unintended side-effect of one's personal dedication to a cause greater than oneself or as the by-product of one's surrender to a person other than oneself.'[28] Many have discovered that today – not just those whom our society would regard as failures, but also those who have ridden the waves of success: journalist AN Wilson, geneticist Francis Collins, lawyer Nicky Gumbel, all previously atheists; singers Bob Dylan and Bono, once alienated from religion through their Jewish and Irish backgrounds but finding faith as they grew to adulthood; ambitious politicians Jeffrey Archer and Charles Colson, for whom the bubble burst when they received criminal convictions. All these, and many more, have found their lives changing direction following an encounter with Jesus.

As Jesus prepared to leave his disciples, he tried to explain how it was that their journey with him would continue beyond his death. "I am," he said, "the way, the truth and the life." This single sentence offers a one-line summary of what it means to be a disciple of Jesus. "I am the way to the Father," Jesus said; "I go to prepare a place for you." The first disciples were referred to as 'followers of the Way', and Jesus appointed them in their turn as guides to others, introducing them to him and teaching them to obey everything that he had commanded them.[29] In *The Message*, Eugene Peterson translates his words like this: "Go out and train everyone you meet, far and near, in this way of life." Walk on this path, use this map, and aim at that destination; and all will be well.

Then "I am the truth," Jesus continued; 'I am the one who created reality, and I am the one who created you; I am the one who can set you free from the web of deceit that surrounds you, I can show you what matters and what does not. Forget your status update and throw away your credit card, for I can show you who you are in the sight of God the Father.' "What is truth?" asked Pilate, confused – for like many politicians today, he knew only expediency. Even today most of us aren't sure whether there is any such thing as truth, for we live in a world which celebrates values, and if we recognise truth at all we tend to limit it to what can be tested by science. But Jesus is talking about something bigger than that, something which goes back beyond the creation of the universe itself, something which will change the whole way we think and will shake our whole understanding of who, and why, we are. Christianity is not just a set of things you believe, 'it's a way of seeing and comprehending all reality,' American political adviser Charles Colson wrote after the dramatic change of direction which led him from a prison sentence following his involvement in the Watergate scandal to a life as a prominent Christian thinker and activist.[30] Truth is reality itself.

And finally, "I am the life," Jesus concluded. 'I am the life, because all life comes from God, Father Son and Holy Spirit; it was by the finger of God that life first came into being, and I was there, speaking the words which shaped the world. More than that, I am the life for you – by bringing you back into relationship with God the Father and filling you with the Holy Spirit, I breathe life into the core of your disconnected being, giving you a spiritual life which you will never lose, even when the universe itself decays and dies. And you don't need mantras or crystals; you just need to ask.' The great mystic Thomas à Kempis summed all this up in the fifteenth century: 'Without the way, there is no going; without the truth, there is no knowing; without the life, there is no living.'[31]

We live in a world which impregnates our thoughts with its own understanding of the best way to find happiness, its own definition of truth and its own confusion about what it is that will makes us feel truly alive. Jesus offers another way. 'Discipleship,' Liz West and Trevor Withers suggest, 'is the process by which our belief system is rewritten and our values are changed through an experiential encounter with God.'[32]

Discipleship ... towards a definition

Μαθητές *Discipulus* Learner, trainee, follower, disciple
Μαθετεια *Discipulatus* Following a teacher, discipleship

"Come follow me," Jesus said – Matthew 4.19
"I am the way, the truth and the life" – John 14.6
"Who belonged to the Way" – Acts 9.2

Discipleship is about learning but it is about much more than the acquisition of knowledge. Discipleship is following, walking with, the one we trust. It is centred on this one whom we follow, who we allow to shape our life, whose own life begins to transform our lives, in whom we find our eternal destiny. For Christians this is Jesus, the Christ, the Son of God.

Discipleship is ultimately about transformation, the transformation of every aspect of our lives – how we think, how we behave, how we relate to others and how we understand ourselves. It is very closely related with metanoia, often translated as 'repentance' but really signifying a much more profound total reorientation of our lives towards God.

Discipleship is about BELONGING – becoming part of the community of those who follow Jesus.
Discipleship is about BEHAVING – adopting a lifestyle which reflects the reign of God on earth.
Discipleship is about BELIEVING – accepting the teaching of Jesus and putting all our trust in Him.

Discipleship is not a course, or a stage in becoming a Christian – it is a continuous, life-long, process of allowing God to shape every aspect of our lives – and that will only be completed when we see Him face to face.

Mark Oxbrow, writing in *Anglican Witness,* May 2013

Changing direction in Africa

Canon Jacob Robert Oyange is Dean of the Cathedral of Musoma and Diocesan Coordinator for *Rooted in Jesus* in the Diocese of Mara, Tanzania. Since the first *Rooted in Jesus* conference was held in the diocese in 2011, Jacob has travelled from village to village, visiting the new groups and listening to their stories, stories which echo those reported to us by coordinators in other places.

Alcoholism is common in rural Africa, where home-brewed beer and spirits provide an escape from the harsh realities of a life of poverty and disease, and often Jacob meets people who have been healed of their addiction and restored to their families through the ministry of the groups. Marriages break down there as they do here; men leave their wives for other women, abandoning their children – a serious thing in a society with no state benefits or social care. Mothers in such situations are often forced into prostitution, and children no longer able to go to school. Jacob wrote one day in joy as he met one such man, who had joined a group in the village to which he had moved with his new partner; as he grew closer to them and to God he had been overwhelmed by guilt at what he had done, and had sought their advice. The group prayed for him; he returned to his wife and family 'and started a new journey with the Lord,' Jacob reported.

The family is the mainstay of African life, and so when the family unit is damaged, the consequences can be devastating. On a visit to the village of Masinono, Jacob found himself listening to several members of the *Rooted in Jesus* group there, all of whom were talking about a little girl named Susan. Susan's parents had died of AIDS when she was six years old; now nine, Susan was living with her grandmother and attending a *Rooted in Jesus* group. Susan's grandmother earns her living by prostitution and the sale of alcohol; but she too had recently been diagnosed with AIDS and taken into hospital. Susan continued to attend the group. One of the memory verses is John 3.16, 'for God so loved the world that he gave his only Son, so that everyone who believes in him may not perish but may have eternal life.' Little orphaned Susan realised for the first time that this promise applied to her, even to her. Her response was so dramatic that the news spread round the whole church; seven people gave their lives to the Lord that same day.

Traditional religion continues to play a major part in the lives of millions of people. Many turn in times of illness or difficulty to traditional healers, or witchdoctors, and Jacob often meets people who have suffered as a result of the charms and incantations sold to them as cures. On one occasion, in the village of Nyakiswa, he found himself talking with a group member named Leah. She told him that before she joined the group she herself had been a churchgoer but also a witchdoctor; no one had ever suggested to her that prayer and divination were incompatible, and she had never been invited to give her life to Christ. Leah recounted how at the first group meeting she had been overcome by a sense of great spiritual heaviness, and had heard a voice telling her to give up her life as a witchdoctor. The group leader, who was also the pastor, laid hands on her and prayed. Leah had a sensation of something life-giving entering her; she found herself calling aloud for Jesus. She went home that day feeling, for the first time in her life, completely free – " light in my life and my heart," as she put it. As she finished her story, she looked at Jacob, and said "I have been in this church for seven years. This is the story I never heard."

'This,' writes Jacob, 'is how the Family of One Heart and One Mind in *Rooted in Jesus* (his title for the *Rooted in Jesus* programme) has been working in our diocese. The situation is the same everywhere in many groups. People tell the story of how the Family of One Heart and One Mind has helped to change their lives. This is helping the Church to grow as never before in the history of the Church here in the Diocese of Mara, and many people have been receiving the gospel everywhere in our Diocese.'

In every culture and every society, Jesus invites people to change direction. What we turn from will vary from person to person, now as it did then. Whether it's anger which has erupted into violence, emptiness which has sought solace in materialism or spiritualism, or despair which has led to family breakdown makes no odds. Whether you are rich or poor, outwardly successful or a social failure, whether you live in Africa or England makes no difference. The issue is not where you are coming from; it's where you are going.

Following Jesus today : John Pridmore

Brought up in the East End of London, John Pridmore had become a wealthy gangster involved in drug deals, protection rackets and vicious crime. In May 2013 he told his story at a Catholic Miracle Rally organised by Damian Stayne and the Cor et Lumen Christi community.

"I was born in the east end of London. At the age of 10, my parents got divorced and I made an unconscious decision not to love any more. At the age of 13 I had started stealing. By 15 I was put in a detention centre. When I left home after having been released, my only qualification was stealing, so that's what I did. At 19 I was in prison again and, because the way I dealt with my pain was with anger, I was always fighting. They put me on 23 hour solitary confinement and I came out of there even more angry and bitter. I started bouncing round the east end and west end of London. I liked fighting so I thought I might as well get paid for it! I met some guys who seemed to have everything and I started to work for them. Before long I wasn't working for them, I was working with them. These were the guys who ran most of the organised crime in London. To my shame I was involved in massive drug deals, protection rackets and vicious crime of all sorts. I had what I thought was everything. Money, power, girls, drugs, the lot. But yet there was something missing... This struck me more than ever when I thought I had killed someone outside of a nightclub I was working at. After nearly taking that man's life, something incredible happened and my life began to change." ...

"One afternoon, I drove over to a mate's flat in Kilburn to play backgammon, but he wasn't in. As I sat in the car waiting for him, I found myself thinking about [a conversation I'd had with my mate] Gary and what he had said about leaving the past with God. I couldn't get it out of my mind. I was sipping a can of Special Brew and smoking some dope, but then I saw a policeman coming towards me. I flicked the spliff out of the window and put the can under the seat. The policeman asked me to get out of the car and take a breathalyser test. After I had done this, he told me I was under the limit – just. He suggested that I didn't drink any more, but should go home. Feeling fed up, I took his advice.

Back at my flat I sat alone and found myself thinking how my life was completely messed up. I felt very depressed and empty. It was about 9 p.m. Then I heard what I can only describe as a voice. It was telling me the worst things I had ever done. It must be the TV, I thought, and flicked to the next channel. The voice was still there. I turned the TV off. What was happening? Was I going mad?

Then something clicked inside me: it was the voice we've all heard, sometimes when we've done something good, sometimes when we've done something bad. It was the voice of God, my conscience. The breath was going out of me. It was as if I was dying, and an incredible fear gripped me. I'm going to hell, I thought. I fell to my knees, and tears began to well up in my eyes. 'Give me another chance!' I cried. Suddenly, I felt as if someone's hands were on my shoulders and I was being lifted up. An incredible warmth overpowered me and the fear immediately evaporated. At that moment I knew – really knew, not just believed – that God was real.

I had an overwhelming desire to leave the flat and share this incredible experience with someone. As I closed the door behind me, I looked at my watch and was amazed to see that it was now 1 a.m. Unbelievably, four hours had passed. Then I did something I had never done before: I prayed. 'God, up to now, all I've done is take from you in my life and now I want to give.' What I can only describe as an awesome feeling of love consumed me. This is the most amazing buzz I've ever experienced, I thought. It couldn't have lasted for more than a minute. Then I knew for the first time in my life that I was loved by God. Up until then, I had always thought I was worthless and it didn't matter whether I lived or died."

That turned out to be the beginning of a long journey for John. Today he works all over the UK and beyond with young people at risk, telling them Jesus loves them and helping them to find a different path through life from the one he first took; many of them do. As Daily Record interviewer Brian McIver remarks, 'the man who once went out with a machete and CS gas is armed now with a cross and a message of peace.'

John tells his story on his website johnpridmore.yolasite.com and in his book *From Gangland to Promised Land* (2nd edition xt3media 2008, written with Greg Watts).

Following Jesus today – a group study

1. A change of direction

'Christians in the West have largely neglected what it means to be a disciple of Christ. The vast majority of Western Christians are church members, pew-fillers, hymn-singers, sermon-tasters, Bible-readers, even born-again believers or Spirit-filled charismatics, but not true disciples of Jesus' – David Watson

'Sometimes it's hard to tell the difference between Christians and non-Christians. We do the same jobs, live in the same areas, use our money in the same ways, hold many of the same values. The only difference is that on Sunday mornings we go to church, while they go to a car-boot sale. But being a follower of Jesus, being a disciple, must mean more than doing something different on a Sunday morning. It must transform our entire lives; it must mould everything' – Nick Page

What difference has it made in practice to your life that you are a disciple of Jesus?

Would a visitor to your church notice anything distinctive about the lifestyle and priorities of its members?

2. Discipleship in a consumer society

'Consumerism is the embodied structure and priority within western cultures that shapes our lives. Consumerism functions as a counterfeit experience of assurance. The biblical virtue which puts things back in their place is called contentment' – Graham Cray

'If we don't disciple people, the culture sure will' – Alan Hirsch

To what extent do you think we are shaped by our consumer society? Do you know why you buy what you buy, want what you want? How can we ensure that our values come from Jesus, and not from the advertising industry?

3. Living as disciples of Jesus

In his book Exiles, Michael Frost suggests five promises which flow from a commitment to follow Jesus in the midst of a secular society:

- We will be authentic – in a world of false celebrity and fake experience

- We will serve a cause greater than ourselves – in a world where people are concerned about their own needs

- We will create missional community – in a world of individuality

- We will be generous and practise hospitality – going beyond conventional hospitality to serve the hungry/needy

- We will work righteously – seeing our secular work as an expression of being sent by God into the host empire

How realistic do you think these promises are? How would you implement them in practice? What would be the consequences for your church if you were all to live by them?

David Watson, *Discipleship*, Hodder 1981
Nick Page, *The Jesus-Shaped Life*, ReSource magazine issue 12, *Being Disciples*, 2008
Graham Cray, *Who's Shaping You: 21st Century Disciples*, Cell UK 2011
Alan Hirsch, *The Forgotten Ways*, Brazos Press 2006
Michael Frost, *Exiles – Living Missionally in a Post-Christian Culture,* Baker Books, 2006

CHAPTER FOUR

Learning on the hoof

Discipleship is a life of learning from Jesus Christ how to live in the Kingdom of God now, as he himself did.

Dallas Willard[1]

There are many ways of learning a trade. Jesus's father Joseph was a carpenter, or builder, and it was customary in the first century for a father to teach a son his trade from the age of twelve. It seems likely therefore that Jesus would have spent nearly twenty years working in the building trade, from the age of twelve to the beginning of his public ministry at the age of about thirty.[2] Today we can do what Jesus could not do, and buy a book on carpentry – such as the *Collins Complete Woodworker's Manual,* described as 'the definitive and bestselling woodworker's bible' and 'the one book every woodworker needs.' It explains every stage of the work of a carpenter, starting with the basics of setting up a workshop, and covering all types of joint and all major crafts from veneering to woodcarving.[3]

Impressive though these claims are, I suspect that the most diligent study of the pages of the *Complete Woodworker's Manual* would not turn a young carpenter into a master of his art. Even today, most would-be carpenters recognise that to make real progress they need to train through some form of apprenticeship in which these skills can be learned from an experienced craftsman, one who will set the young carpenter assignments and evaluate his progress – usually over a period of two or three years. Carpentry cannot be learned simply through study; it has to be learned in practical ways.

In 2008 Sue Hope wrote an article for ReSource magazine entitled 'Being a disciple in the power of the Holy Spirit.' She began with the story of a young man named Jacob:

Jacob is the youngest son of close friends of mine. Already showing skill at all kinds of woodwork, he has decided to train as a cabinet maker, and he has been fortunate to have been accepted by the French system of *Les Compagnons du Devoir* to train as a master craftsman. It turns out that this isn't just about 'apprenticeship' – it's about a whole-life change. So, Jacob finds himself living in a French village, in community – a community of people who are willing to put everything aside to become masters of their trade. There are 'house parents' – meals are taken together, there is laughter and companionship – it's 'family'. The apprentices, who are following different trades (stone masons, boiler makers, roofers, and even bakers among them) spend their days working on the shop floor in appropriate factories, or workshops, (carefully selected and monitored by their trainers) and their evenings at base, working at their chosen craft. It's a highly disciplined framework: there are two hours in the workshops after supper, classes all day Saturday and one day off a week to do sport, relax and take time just to be. To be accepted as an 'aspirant' they have to produce their first 'piece', and in evaluating this a humble, teachable attitude is considered as important as the standard of craftsmanship shown. They then start a journey around France moving every six months to another *Compagnons* house, to gain new skills and experience. Each move takes them to a different town and a different job, living with a different group of people, but all with the same aim. To qualify as a master craftsman they must produce a superb piece of original work at the end of several years of living in this way. The training is done in community, it's disciplined, it takes account of the individual (the community leaders worked hard to encourage Jacob into the local rugby team in the village so he could 'connect' with a bit of his own culture). It's loving and fun but also strongly structured and determined to get the person concerned to the end goal – to turn out a master craftsman. To become a *Compagnon* means a world-class training for a world-class goal.

As she thinks about what it means to be a disciple of Jesus, Sue reflects on the training being received by Jacob. 'Jacob's journey is a very good picture of discipleship. To be a disciple is to be a learner. That's what the word *mathetes* means. It means leaning by apprenticeship, but also more than that. It means 'whole life apprenticeship' – not just nine to five. Jacob is discovering that he can't just keep cabinet making in a box (!). If he is going to be a real artisan it has to permeate the whole of his being. His gifting, his chosen trade is about the whole of his life. He's becoming a true journeyman.'[4]

Growing in character

We saw in Chapter 2 that a disciple is an apprentice, that Jesus too was a master-craftsman who expected his disciples not just to listen to him but to follow and imitate him. Perhaps he was influenced by his own background as an apprentice carpenter, an experience very different from that provided by the text-based methodology of the professionally trained rabbis.[5] At any rate, what Jesus offered to those who accepted the invitation to journey with him was remarkably similar to what was offered to Jacob: it involved joining a new community, travelling together and learning in practical ways as they encountered each new situation. It involved not just the acquisition of skills but the formation of character; it was a whole-life assignment. Perhaps, like Jacob, these men and women were chosen not for their accomplishments but for their teachability.

89

And so we watch Jesus travelling from place to place with his disciples, both the twelve future apostles and the wider group mentioned by Luke and by John. We notice that the twelve whose journey we observe most closely had to be willing to become part of a new community bound together not by kinship or affinity but by a shared commitment to Jesus. They had many things to learn – not least, as their rough edges were gently rubbed and smoothed, about themselves; but also about how to relate to those they encountered on the way. And we cannot help noticing that they learned these things not before they set out, but as they travelled – they learned on the hoof. They watched Jesus offer compassion to the poor and searing rebuke to the arrogant. They watched him sidestep the verbal traps of the clever and the powerful; they watched him taking time out to consult his Father in prayer. Eventually, and perhaps most significantly of all, they watched him walk knowingly to his death – a death he knew would be excruciatingly painful, and yet which he accepted as the will of God. And as they watched, they changed. Young John grew older and wiser. Grasping Matthew realised there is more to life than money. Impetuous Peter became the rock on which the church would be built. Zealous Simon discovered that political activism is not the best way to influence society. Uneducated and ordinary they may have been; but as they grew into the futures that God had planned for them, they became people who would change the world. These were not lessons they could have learned in the classroom, bending over their books, memorising texts, discussing theological issues. They were lessons that could be learned only in the midst of daily life, as they encountered new situations and figured out how best to respond.

An apprentice carpenter, Nazareth Village

I am the Way, the Truth and the Life

As these first disciples travelled with Jesus, they learned that he embodied truth, offered them life and showed them the way to live. They found that they were being taught to think differently; they were, as Paul would express it later to the Romans, having their minds renewed. As they listened to Jesus's teaching and watched him interacting with the people they met, they learned to see life in a new way, with a growing understanding of the radical values of the kingdom of God as opposed to the restrictive norms of the society in which they had been brought up. They were being introduced to the truth.

Secondly, they found that they were beginning, through Jesus, to develop their own relationship with God. Jesus taught them to pray. He taught them about the Holy Spirit who was at work among them, and who would come to fill them individually and corporately after his death. He helped them to see themselves as God saw them, and gradually to change, so that day by day, as Paul would explain later to the Corinthians, they would become more and more like Jesus himself. They had, as Jesus promised, received not just life, but abundant life, life in all its fullness.[6]

And thirdly, they found that gradually they were filled with a new sense of purpose. As they moved towards God, they began to recognise who they were in his sight and what it was that he was calling them to. This process would be completed only when the Holy Spirit fell upon them after Jesus's death, for without the resources made available to them by the Spirit they would not be able to minister to others in the powerful way possible when they were working under the direct authority of Jesus. 'How now shall we live?', Charles Colson asked when he gave his life to Christ and began to think more critically about the world in which he had been so successful – in a deliberate echo of the cry of the people of God in exile.[7] 'Differently!', was the answer. 'According to the Word of God,' said Paul to the Roman governor Felix as he explained what it meant to follow The Way.[8] The Way *leads* somewhere.

Growing in skills

What did that mean in practice? For Jacob, apprenticeship to *Les Compagnons du Devoir* meant growing in confidence and character as he travelled from one place to another; but even more importantly it meant actually making pieces of furniture, and doing so to the highest possible standards. Jesus expected his apprentices to grow in faith and in character, but he too had a more practical outcome in mind; he was training them to do certain specific things.

'Everyone knows,' John Coles suggests, 'that to be a Christian involves becoming more like Jesus. My understanding is that this is a process that involves at least three things:

1. Developing the type of relationship with God that Jesus had
2. Having our lives transformed by the Holy Spirit, so that we increasingly reflect the qualities of purity and holiness that characterised Jesus' life
3. Learning to minister to others with the same love and power in which Jesus ministered.'[9]

There is more to be said about all three of these, and we will come back to them. But it's in the third thing that we find the practical outcome, and perhaps it was this aspect of their training which took the most courage. Jesus knew that apprenticeship takes time. First of all comes the invitation – come, follow me. A second stage involves listening and observing; the disciples listen to Jesus teach, and they watch him at work. Once they have done this for a while, Jesus expects his disciples to have a go themselves, and so he moves them into a third stage: he sends the twelve out in pairs, with a very clear set of instructions – they are to teach people about the kingdom of God, just as they have heard him teach; and they are to do the works that they have seen him doing in support of that teaching. These were his exact words, and they leave no doubt as to his intentions:

"Proclaim the good news, 'The kingdom of heaven has come near.' Cure the sick, raise the dead, cleanse the lepers, cast out demons." (Matthew 10.5-8).

Luke tells us that the same instruction was given to seventy others a little later, and after Jesus's death it would form the basis of the ministry of the early church as described in the Book of Acts. It seems that this was to be the normal ministry pattern of Jesus's disciples; that this was how people would know that Jesus was who he said he was. "What sign are you going to give us so that we may see it and believe you? What work are you performing?" the disciples had asked Jesus as they watched him feed five thousand people with five rolls and a few fish. In other words, what's this all about – are you *really* the Son of God, and how can we be sure? "Believe me that I am in the Father and the Father is in me; but if you do not, then believe me because of the works themselves," Jesus had said. Jesus was not just bringing prophetic words or ethical teaching; he was bringing visible, tangible evidence that the kingdom of God was near, that a new world order was beginning, that history was entering a new phase. And as his disciples followed him, as they advanced deeper into their apprenticeship, Jesus explained that these works were not to stop with his death; they were to remain the carrying card of his followers from generation to generation: "Very truly, I tell you, the one who believes in me will also do the works that I do and, in fact, will do greater works than these, because I am going to the Father."[10] The works would act as their ID, the demonstration that they were indeed his representatives, that he had remained with them just as he had promised. Disciples of Jesus are actively engaged in ministry in the name of Jesus – ministry which offers a present demonstration of the power and presence of God.[11]

It is probably this third aspect of becoming more like Jesus that is most commonly neglected in our churches today. We have accustomed ourselves to the academic model of discipleship – and it is of course much easier to *talk* about

The Stages of Discipleship

One of the first scholars to look carefully at the training process offered by Jesus was AB Bruce, who in 1871 wrote *The Training of the Twelve*. Bruce identified just three stages: 'Come and see', 'come and follow me', 'come and be with me'. Bruce's analysis has been expanded by later commentators:

In his 1963 book *The Master Plan of Evangelism* Robert Coleman identified 8 steps in Jesus's training of disciples:

1. Selection of people
2. Association with those selected
3. Consecration – he required obedience and loyalty
4. Impartation – he gave himself away: peace, joy, kingdom, glory, life
5. Demonstration – he showed them how to live
6. Delegation – he assigned them work: Luke 10 the 12, Matt 10 the 70
7. Supervision – he kept checking on them
8. Reproduction – he expected them to make other disciples: praying for workers (Mt 9), making disciples (Mt 28)

In *The Purpose-Driven Life* (2002) Rick Warren picked out 4 stages on the journey of spiritual progress:

1. Committed to membership – knowing Christ
2. Committed to maturity – growing in Christ
3. Committed to ministry – serving Christ
4. Committed to mission – sharing Christ

In *The Complete Book of Discipleship* (2006) Bill Hull adds a 4th stage to Bruce's original three:

1. 'Come and see' – John 1.35-4.46. Introduction: 4-5 months
2. 'Come and follow me' – Matt 4.19, Mk 1.16-18. Basic principles: 10-11 months. Jesus now had 70-120 consistent followers.
3. 'Come and be with me' – Mark 3.13-14. Preparation of a small number for world mission: 20 months
4. 'Remain in me' – John 15.5-7: Learning to rely on the Holy Spirit. The whole church: a few hours, then a lifetime.

things than to actually *do* them. And perhaps we are more than a little frightened – to pray for people expecting them to be cured, cleansed, restored and freed is to take an enormous risk. The potential for looking silly is huge, and the possibility of disappointing people is ever-present. Perhaps this is why we have been inclined to spend more time studying the manual than making the furniture. And yet the commandment is clear; Jesus left his disciples in no doubt that he didn't just want them to hear his teaching, he wanted them to apply it. "Everyone who hears these words of mine and acts on them will be like a wise man who built his house on rock," he said. "And everyone who hears these words of mine and does not act on them will be like a foolish man who built his house on sand." 'This, the crowds murmured, is not what we are used to.'[12]

In 2011 I visited the Anglican Diocese of Toliara in southwest Madagascar. It's a new, missionary diocese, and at that time it had just three priests. One of these is a man called Donné, and Donné's story is a good illlustration of what it means to be a disciple of Jesus. Donné used to be the village drunkard. On coming to Christ, his life was radically transformed. The whole village noticed; and through Donné others too began to commit themselves to Jesus. Soon Donné had planted a church; then another, and another. His ministry was growing so rapidly that Bishop Todd McGregor thought it wise to ordain him; he also enrolled him in a course of theological study. Donné took the course, but failed the exams – not once, but three times. Recognising that Donné was not cut out to be a theologian, the bishop decided that Donné should forget about the study and focus on ministry. By then so many people were coming to Christ that fierce local opposition was growing, Acts 19 style, to Donné's ministry – Madagascar is still only fifty percent Christian, and the other fifty percent follow a particularly strong form of traditional religion. Eventually the bishop had to move him to another place – and people are now coming to Christ there too. Why is this happening? Not because Donné had completed an appropriate course of theological study – though of course theological study is always helpful – but because Donné was doing what Jesus had equipped him to do – he was proclaiming the good news of the kingdom of God, and bringing freedom to others as Christ had brought freedom to him. Ministry is not primarily about study; it's about doing the things which Jesus has commissioned us to do. Donné is now the Diocesan Coordinator for *Rooted in Jesus*, supporting discipleship throughout the diocese.

For these first disciples of Jesus there had been many lessons to learn. They had been apprenticed to Jesus, learning to pray as he prayed, learning to minister as he ministered. And now comes the final stage; now they are to open the door for others to be apprenticed in the same way. 'Now you've grasped all this,' Jesus tells them as they stand on a mountain beside the Sea of Galilee, 'I want you to make more disciples, and teach them to obey all that I have commanded you – all that I have taught you as we travelled together through the towns and villages of Galilee, Judea and Samaria.'

This was not just a new belief system: it was a job description, a commissioning into a new and lifelong task. Here are his exact words:

"All authority in heaven and on earth has been given to me. Therefore go and make disciples of all nations, baptizing them in the name of the Father and of the Son and of the Holy Spirit, and teaching them to obey everything I have commanded you. And remember, I am with you always, to the end of the age." (Matthew 28.18-20)

Travelling with Jesus – James Tissot (1836-1902)

Learning on the hoof today

So what of us? Do we need to set off like Jacob into some kind of full-time training process? The key lies in the last sentence of Jesus's commission to his graduating apprentices: "Remember, I am with you always." Even now that he is leaving them to work independently, Jesus does not require them to

Learning on the hoof...

'Jesus calls us to follow him, and this means following him wherever he leads us. It means "following" in so many different ways. We follow him like we follow a dance partner. We follow his teachings. We follow the leading of the Spirit. We follow in his footsteps to the cross. We follow his example in loving the outcast, praying for the sick, and delivering those who are oppressed by demons. We follow him because he has won us: by his love and his beauty, his power and grace his truth and forgiveness. We find, even in the worst times, that we refuse to follow anyone else, because only he has the words of eternal life. But nobody ever follows perfectly. Learning to follow Jesus is a personal journey and it takes a lifetime.'

Lucy Peppiatt, *The Disciple – On Becoming Truly Human*, Cascade Books 2012.

'Discipleship is not about learning a list of do's and don'ts, ticking the boxes and feeling good about it, or missing out on a few boxes and feeling guilty. That is legal country. Discipleship is moving forward a step at a time, discovering the heart of Jesus, learning to enjoy the presence of God, being helped to live from the Spirit within; and being taught from Scripture what pleases the Lord, as we begin to find God's law written on our hearts and gradually flowing down the slope of personality. Making mistakes, getting it wrong sometimes, but with our hand in his. And surrounded by the body of Christ.'

Tony Pullin, *Making Disciples: How did Jesus do it?* CWR 2014

'Discipleship should be defining quality of the Christian life; we can never move from the primal commitment that is involved in becoming his follower in the first place... The degree that we are living the life laid out by our Master is directly proportional to the degree that we can call ourselves authentic disciples.'

Michael Frost & Alan Hirsch, *ReJesus – a Wild Messiah for a Missional Church*, Hendrikson 2009 perform any of these works under their own authority or in their own strength. He has already told them that he will send the Holy Spirit to them, and it is through the presence of the Spirit that they will carry out this commission to minister the good news and to equip others to do so in their turn. Jesus has not gone; Jesus still walks with us as we seek to live and work as his disciples.

There are a number of ways in which we can join in with this process of apprenticeship. Most of them involve the same kinds of processes that we see Jesus offer to his very first disciples – learning and growing together in small groups or intentional discipleship communities, facilitated by those who have travelled further on the road than we have, and always with the emphasis on application rather than information. We will look at some of the options in Chapter 9. But there are informal ways too, for the key element to discipleship is the presence of Jesus in our lives, and not our participation in this or that programme. Sometimes people stumble into an active ministry almost by mistake.

Graham is an ordinary Christian who had signed up for *Beautiful Lives*, one of ReSource's small group programmes. 'Beauty of life causes strangers to join our ranks,' Roman Christian Minucius Felix had written as people rushed to embrace the gospel in the third century; 'we do not talk about great things, we live them.' *Beautiful Lives* encourages people to develop the confidence to share their faith naturally and effectively, simply by the way they live.[13] After each meeting, group members are given some practical exercises for use during the following week. One week, Graham found that he was expected to spend a day just being nice to people – not worrying about how to share his faith, but just taking the time to chat with those he would come across that day. Graham had chosen a Saturday for this exercise, and he went as usual to his allotment. Turning over the soil, he paused for breath, looked up and noticed his neighbour on the next allotment. Graham hadn't spoken to this man before, but remembered he was meant to be being friendly, so he introduced himself and asked how it was going. It turned out the man had a bad back. "Oh," said Graham, forgetting he wasn't meant to be sharing his faith, "I'm a Christian, I wonder, would you like me to pray for that?" "Er... OK," said the man, looking a bit surprised. Realising with some embarrassment that he had exceeded his brief, Graham prayed. The man gasped. "That's amazing. My back's gone all warm! The pain's gone!" And then, "Hey, you could do that for an awful lot of people!" Graham was learning as he travelled.

A few months ago I was leading a discipleship retreat at Lee Abbey. One of those taking part was Mark, who shared with us what following Jesus was meaning for him. Mark's mother had a best friend whose daughter Sophie needed regular medication. Mark visited his mother one day to find her very upset. A doctor had prescribed Sophie the wrong drug, and she had fallen straight into a coma. Sophie had been admitted to hospital and put in intensive care; her heart and kidneys had stopped functioning. The consultant had said that she was unlikely to survive, and if she did she would be permanently and severely brain damaged. Mark went upstairs to pray. He had no experience of praying for healing; but he felt that God was telling him to go to the hospital. Feeling rather foolish, Mark went. After a long wait Mark was admitted to the intensive care ward. Sophie was unconscious, "out of it," Mark said. Mark felt that God was telling him to pray for her. Mark felt embarrassed; he wasn't used to this, and there were nurses everywhere. He decided to pray quietly. "Pray out loud," God said. So Mark did; and then went home. God told him to go to the hospital again at intervals over the next few months – perhaps thirteen times over the following six months, Mark thinks. Each time he found Sophie a little better. On one occasion God told him to lay hands on her and pray; another time he said "Pray for the dendrites." Mark had no idea what dendrites were, but he looked it up later and discovered they are part of the nervous system in the brain. Once as he prayed he felt an incredible sense of heat; it was like being surrounded by fire, he said. He looked round, and for a moment he saw a figure in white standing at the end of the bed. He finished his prayer and went home as usual. Eventually, against all expectations, Sophie was discharged from hospital fully recovered. Mark responded to these experiences by telling God that if ever he wished him to pray for people to be healed, he is available! He is now part of the Healing on the Streets team in Bournemouth.[14]

It isn't always as dramatic as that; and often the prayers we will offer for others are about everyday things. Jesus was not actively looking for people to heal; indeed, it seems that sometimes he tried to avoid the hordes of sick people brought to him from far and wide. But he always responded to human need, dealing with the situation as he found it, bringing comfort, challenge or forgiveness as the need arose. He expected his disciples to do the same; and that is our brief too. A chance conversation, a willingness to take risks, the desire to be available for Jesus to work through you – these are the attitudes Jesus is looking for in his disciples. Our primary role is to be obedient to him, for tasks great and small.

In the autumn of 2013 I met Steve, who had come to a day conference ReSource was leading for the Diocese of Portsmouth. Steve was an engineer with the Royal Navy, and over lunch he told me of an experience he had had whilst on active service in the Gulf War. He was on a ship carrying 1400 men. Of these 1400, just six were Christians, and these six were in the habit of gathering together each Sunday to worship God. On one particular Monday the ship was due to begin a hundred days of heightened engagement, and on the Sunday the six Christians assembled as usual on the Quarterdeck. It was a peaceful scene, Steve remembers, with a bright horizon, a clear blue sky, and the sound of water lapping gently round the ship. The Captain joined them, as he sometimes did; numbers were usually a bit higher when the Captain came, Steve said, as he had his hangers on. But on this particular day there was a sense of apprehension about what was to come, and no fewer than 400 men turned up for the service. It was Steve's turn to read the lesson. To his surprise, although he had never talked about his faith, he found that for the next hundred days, people would seek him out – usually at a quiet moment, usually in private – and ask him to pray for them and their families. Steve always tried to pray then and there – even when they came to him in the darkened control room, amongst all the screens with ships and planes tracking across them. When all looked quiet on the screens Steve would remove his headphones and pray as requested. It went on like this for the whole of the danger period, Steve said, with one person after another. At times of stress and turmoil people instinctively turn to God – and Steve, a quiet and unassuming man, found that he was able to help them. He had neither expected nor sought this; like Mark, he was simply trying to follow Jesus in the circumstances of his daily life. Back in Portsmouth, Steve is now part of the leadership of his local church.

What all these ordinary disciples had in common was that they were open to the possibility that Jesus might wish to use them to minister to the people they met as they went about their perfectly ordinary lives. We like to have things all settled in advance, but Jesus reveals our mission to us as we travel, just as he did to those first disciples two thousand years ago. Bill Hull suggests in his book on discipleship that many people accept what he calls 'non-discipleship Christianity,' and then agonise over what their mission is. They will never find out, he believes; for we find our own calling, our own particular contribution, not by completing questionnaires or signing up for study courses, but by consciously and humbly following Jesus.[15] Perhaps it's not that difficult – Graham, Mark and Steve did not ask what the plan was; they simply allowed Jesus to accompany them into the allotment, the hospital and the ship.

104

But, difficult or not, it's something we need to give more attention to if we are going to take seriously our apprenticeship to Jesus. We are very good at making things so complicated that we prevent ourselves from doing them; but the decision itself is very simple. George MacDonald puts it like this: 'Instead of asking yourself whether you believe or not, ask yourself whether you have this day done one thing because he said "Do it," or once abstained because he said "Do not do it." It is simply absurd to say you believe, or even want to believe in him, if you do not do anything he tells you.'[16]

We are apprentices of Jesus. We have stepped out of the flawed story of our own culture into a new world, and we are learning together to do the things that Jesus did. Discipleship begins with a change of status; it turns into a journey which rewrites our lives.

Learning on the hoof:
How the mother of a former gang member persuaded others to turn their lives around

Mimi Asher, a Pastor in the Word of Grace Ministries, was terrified to learn that her son, Michael, had joined the local gang on her housing estate at Myatt's Fields. She took matters into her own hands and decided that the best way to end his involvement was by getting the gang, Organised Crime, or the O.C., to dissolve itself. For three years, Pastor Mimi threw open her house to O.C. gang members. She cooked meals for them, washed their clothes and even took them on trips to the cinema and swimming pool. For a time, the leader of the gang, Karl Lokko, or 'General Lokks', as he is now known, lived at the house. He is now a successful musician and acts as a mentor helping young people leave gangs. Mimi has continued to work with a local church group and with parents and ex-gang members to set up a range of activities for young people. Mimi's story was published in ReSource magazine, issue 25, 'Beautiful Lives':

"Myatt's Field estate has been described as a place that not even the devil would walk through because young people living there at the estate were terrorising people. That's the estate I was living in. Young people there were interrogating people, asking them their password before coming on the estate. It was their way of monitoring who came on the estate. I had no idea my son was involved in anything because he was such a good boy. I did not know anything about gangs, nothing to my knowledge at all until I spoke to a police officer.

The young ones look to the older ones as role models and they feel inspired because they see them with cars, and girls, and money. The young ones get recruited or initiated. Everywhere in London it's the same process. What I used to do is I would go out there with my wooden stick looking for him. Random times he would be in conversation with friends and I would just turn up and tell him to come into the house and because he was very respectful he would follow me.

So everybody knew that Michael's mum would come at any time so they felt quite a lot of unease. They would see me on the estate and they would be hiding because they knew Michael's mum was coming. If need be I would turn up anywhere. Two o'clock in the morning I would be driving round the estate looking for him. I was really desperate to save my son because I knew that either he would end up dead or in prison and I couldn't live with that. I then started going through his friends to invite them to my house and cook for them. They would come over and I would try and have a conversation with them.

All the boys on the estate, I generally cared for them. I was seeing them as these young boys that had potential to do well but it's only through things that can happen to them. So it was that drive, that real drive and passion in my heart. I was desperate to save all of them. The little money I had I would share with them. It was a big task. Sometimes I was afraid for my own life. There were times I would get paranoid. I had to hold my faith and keep my head high. But I don't let fear stop me doing what I'm doing."

In 2010 Mimi Asher received a London Peace Award from Mayor Boris Johnson.

Learning on the hoof – a group study

1. Apprenticed to Jesus

Have you ever been an apprentice, or learnt a particular skill through a process of apprenticeship? If so, what was it like? Have you had any similar experience in your Christian life?

2. The stages of apprenticeship

In this chapter we have suggested that Jesus apprenticed his disciples in four stages:

1. They accepted Jesus's call
2. They watched him at work
3. They learned to join in with that work
4. They were commissioned to train others to join in with it too

Which stage do you think you personally have reached?

3. You can't steer a parked car

The first disciples of Jesus learned not in a classroom but on the road with Jesus. And yet so often we seem to want to train people before we let them do anything. Bill Hull puts it well when he points out that you can't steer a parked car.

Think about your own church. Do you teach people to be disciples by putting them in the driving seat, or do you prefer to teach them in the safety of the car park?

4. Doing the things that Jesus did

Read Matthew 28.19-20 and Matthew 10.7-8. What are the implications of these two passages for us today?

5. "I will be with you always"

'I hope your own plans, dreams and aims for this coming year are not so modest that they are achievable in your own strength' – Simon Guillebaud

Read Ephesians 3.20 together. Are you being ambitious in your asking and imagining, or do you find it easier to play safe?

6. Learning on the hoof

Think about the stories of Graham, Mark and Steve. How willing are you to be used by God in your ordinary daily life? What are the implications of this chapter for you, individually and together?

CHAPTER FIVE

The Plural of disciple is church

Christianity is not a school for the teaching of moral virtue, the polishing of our manners, or forming us to live a life of this world with decency and gentility. It is deeper and more divine in its designs, and much nobler ends. It implies an entire change of life, a dedication of ourselves, our souls, our bodies unto God in the strictest and highest sense of the words.

William Law (1686-1761)[1]

A historical perspective

William Law lived in the eighteenth century, at the beginning of a period of extraordinary social change – change which has not been equalled in fact until our own times. Much of England was still a traditional landscape of fields and market towns, each with its own trade in cheese or geese or cloth, and connected to its markets by a network of navigable rivers whose pattern formed the mental map which today is etched on our minds in motorways. No one yet foresaw the Industrial Revolution which would transform the social landscape of the country; but change was nonetheless in the air. Daniel Defoe, travelling through England in the 1720s, writes of his astonishment on reaching Liverpool, previously 'a neat and populous town' but now undergoing rapid expansion, with a doubling of buildings and population in just 28 years, and a magnificent new dock for the import and export of manufactured goods. He finds the same in Manchester, which he can still refer to as 'perhaps the greatest mere village in England', whilst noting that it had lately increased in population from 20,000 to 50,000 due to its burgeoning manufacture of textiles. Manchester was becoming a city of the future; and in 1750 my great-great-great-great grandfather Richard Keymer would be sent there as an apprentice – a far-sighted move on the part of his father, a woollen draper in Suffolk, for the resulting family cotton business was to flourish until the 1930s. Further south, Defoe reports that the city of Bristol had grown to 100,000 inhabitants, all living in a densely populated central area. As trade (much of it connected with the slave trade) flowed in and out through its port, freshly mined coal was transported in by road from the new mining areas – in one of which, Kingswood, John Wesley was, in 1739, to preach his first open air sermon.[2]

Why do I mention all this? Because it is at times of social and cultural change that the opportunity arises for a fresh expression of the gospel, a fresh offering of the call of Jesus to the men, women and children whose lives have been turned inside out by the confusing currents of a changing world. Slums were springing up in the new cities as people moved in from the countryside, and the violent miners of nearby Kingswood were feared even in the disorderly city which was Bristol. Wealth did not bring an increase in godliness to the newly rich trading and manufacturing classes; Jonathan Swift lamented that 'hardly one in a hundred among people of quality or gentry appears to act by any principle of religion; great numbers of them do entirely discard it, and are ready to own their disbelief of all revelation in ordinary discourse. Nor is the case better among the vulgar, especially in the great towns.'[3] This was the context in which John

111

Wesley, then an Anglican minister with a mission 'to spread scriptural holiness throughout the land,' would rediscover the concept of Christian discipleship.

Manchester – 'perhaps the greatest mere village in England',
engraving by Buck Brothers, 1728

What about now?

We too are living in changing times. Not, despite all the hype, times of crushing poverty, and certainly not of virgin industrialisation. But there are for all that similarities between our world and the world which reshaped itself in the second half of the eighteenth century: high levels of social mobility, growing international migration, increasing debt, a widening gap between rich and poor, and a financial sector which by gospel standards falls a long way short of the ideal. Like theirs, our cultural landscape is changing in all sorts of ways, raising new questions and opening up the possibility for us to do what Wesley did, and think again about what it actually means, in practice, to be a disciple of Jesus – not two thousand years ago, but here and now. 'A culture that cannot answer its own questions is a culture open to an answer,' Mark Greene has remarked. My understanding is that, in Jesus, we have such an answer; and it's all to do with this curious word disciple.[4]

In the foregoing chapters I have suggested that Christian discipleship is best seen as a form of apprenticeship undertaken in community. It begins with a personal response to Jesus, involves a change of direction and initiates the disciple into a lifelong process of learning. But there is more to it than that, for it is clear that this learning is not an individual undertaking, but a corporate one. We are called not just to learn from Jesus, but to learn together; we are called to become part of a learning community. And that is the subject of this chapter.

The plural of disciple is church

In Chapter 3 we noted that the word disciple occurs frequently in the gospels and in the Book of Acts, but that it is not used in the Old Testament or, more surprisingly, in the letters of Peter, Paul, James and John. This led us to conclude that if we are thinking about discipleship, we are thinking primarily about Jesus. But a bigger question now rears its head. Why should it be that Peter, Paul, James and John do not use the word disciple in their letters, when the calling and training of disciples is so clearly central to the ministry of Jesus in the gospels? As I thought about this, it occurred to me that there is of course another word which they do use, a word which in turn is rarely used in the gospels. That word is church.[5]

What accounts for this change of vocabulary between the gospels and the epistles? Are we to conclude that discipleship went very quickly out of fashion after the death of Jesus? That would seem odd, given his insistence on the beach in Galilee that he wanted his disciples to make more disciples, teaching them to obey everything that he had commanded them. And we know that they did in fact do this. The teaching and training continued as missionaries were sent out from the first churches – Philip, Peter and John from Jerusalem, and Paul, Barnabas, John Mark and Silas from Antioch. Soon new leaders were emerging from among the new disciples made in these places. Simeon, Lucius and Manaen became teachers of the church in Antioch. Lydia, Phoebe, Chloe, Nympha and Philemon founded churches in their respective homes in Philippi, Cenchreae, Corinth, Laodicea and Colossae. Mary, Urbanus, Tryphaena and Tryphosa, Persis, Clement, Tychicus, Onesimus, Aristarchus, Justus, Epaphrus, Archippus, Titus, Demas, Luke and others whom Paul describes as his co-workers were recruited in the various places he had visited. A disciple called Dorcas devoted herself to good works and charity. Two married couples get special mention: Priscilla and Aquila, who taught and discipled new congregations, and Andronicus and Junia, described as apostles. And there were many others whose names we don't know, appointed as elders in Lystra, Iconium, Antioch Pisidia, Ephesus and the churches of Asia Minor. Meanwhile Paul was pouring his energies into Timothy, instructing him to pass it all on 'to faithful people who will be able to teach others.'[6] The Great Commission to make disciples was clearly being carried out, not just in Jerusalem but throughout the Empire.

How then are we to account for the mystery of the disappearing disciples in the letters of the apostles? It's clearly not that disciple-making was unimportant to Peter and Paul, James and John. Nor is it simply that with the passage of time one word was replaced by another – for although the epistles come in our Bibles after the gospels and Acts, they were in fact written at the same time, or even earlier. Peter, Paul, James and John are writing their letters, without using the word disciple, even as Matthew, Mark, Luke and the very same John are writing the gospels and Acts, using it frequently. The answer lies neither in what they were doing nor in when they were writing.

One simple difference may hold the answer. The word disciple may have vanished from the apostles' writing, but the concept of discipleship is still clearly there. The difference is that the emphasis is now not on the individual, responding to the call of Jesus, but on the group, learning to reshape their lives in the light of that call. Just as Jesus needed a new word to designate his followers, so those followers need a new word to describe the communities to which they now belonged; and they chose the word *ekklesia* – not a religious word, but one commonly used to refer to an assembly of citizens in a Greek city state. In English we translate it as 'church'. It's an interesting choice, for in its Greek form *ekklesia* this word simply means 'those who have been called out' – *ek* means out, and *kaleo* means to call. The emphasis on calling provides another clue linking these two words disciple and church, for whereas in the gospels we are called to be disciples, in the epistles we are called to be church – both Paul and Jude use the phrase 'to those who are called' when writing to a church.[7]

All of this leads us to an obvious conclusion: *the plural of disciple is church*. A church is a community of disciples, a gathering of people who have been called individually and collectively into relationship with God. *Ekklesia* became the accepted term for a group of people bound together by a shared relationship to Jesus, for we are called as individuals but formed through communities. The English word 'church' in fact carries this meaning beautifully: it derives from the Greek *kurios*, or 'Lord'. A church is a group of people who belong to the Lord – *kuriakos*.[8]

If the plural of disciple is church, that of course leads us inevitably to another conclusion: if the church is not about making disciples, it is not church. Discipleship is not something that the church *does*: it is what the church *is*: the church is the community which supports and directs our discipleship in the world. 'Since all true Christians are disciples,' Michael Wilkins writes, 'the ministry of the church may be seen in its broadest sense as discipleship. The church is a community of disciples.' Graham Cray suggests that 'churches have to realise that the core of their calling is to be disciple-making communities, whatever else they do; the primary purpose of Christian community is formation as disciples.' Mark Greene points out that 'the Church's goal is to make disciples'; that is what it is for. Rowan Williams says the same thing in different words: 'Church is what happens when people encounter the Risen Jesus and commit themselves to sustaining and deepening that encounter in their encounter with each other.'[9]

So I find it helpful to remind myself that a church is not a building, or an event, or an institution.[10] A church is a group of people who are helping one another to deepen their relationship with Jesus. A church is, or should be, a community of disciples learning to follow Jesus together, baptising new members in the name of the Father, Son and Holy Spirit, and teaching them to obey everything that Jesus had commanded them. If discipleship is not at the heart of what we do, then we are not a church at all. And that means that the health of the church depends on the depth of our discipleship.[11]

If the word disciple has shrunk over the years, so it seems has the word church.

What is the meaning of the word 'church'?

'The word 'church', and the Scottish kirk and German *Kirche* and Russian *tserkov*, come from the Greek word *kuriakos*, 'belonging to the Lord'. The adjective was first used to refer to the 'Lord's supper' – that is, the Holy Communion – and the Lord's day. But by AD 300 the name began to be used as a noun, *kuriakon*, 'the Lord's place', to mean a church. The word for the congregation was *ekklesia*. This word meant 'the people called out', or 'chosen'. By AD 400 it also began to mean the place where Christian people met, the building.'

Owen Chadwick, *A History of Christianity*, Phoenix Illustrated 1995

'The term Paul employed to describe a gathering of Christians (since there was literally no such collective noun at the time) was the Greek term *ecclesia*. Paul takes this pre-existing term and invests it with a new, distinctly Christian meaning. *Ecclesia* literally means "the gathering of the called-out ones." It comes from two words, ek, meaning "out," and kaleo, meaning "to call".'

Michael Frost & Alan Hirsch, *ReJesus – A Wild Messiah for a Missional Church*, Hendrikson 2009

'The concept of the church began with Jesus Christ, though he may not have used the Greek word, ekklesia. When ekklesia was used, it became what it was because of Jesus Christ; for it became the technical term of that institution which assembled in his name, and which was composed of people who sustained a certain relationship to him, i.e., people "in Christ".'

Roy Bowen Ward, *Ekklesia – A Word Study*, Restoration Quarterly 1958

Discipleship and the church

While we are concerned that people come to the church, we have not thought deeply enough about what they will become in time within the church
– JI Packer & Gary A Parrett[12]

If the plural of disciple is church, what does that mean in practice? The earliest description of church in the New Testament comes in Acts Chapter 2, which describes the coming of the Holy Spirit to the apostles in Jerusalem. Peter preaches, and three thousand people accept his invitation to repent and be baptised in the name of Jesus. These new believers devote themselves to the apostles' teaching and fellowship, eat together, meet daily for prayer, and support one another financially and materially. As the gospel was carried to the towns and cities of the Empire, small groups of believers were formed in each place, meeting in people's homes (the first church buildings were not put up until the third century) and gradually establishing a lifestyle which was markedly different from that of the people around them. The New Testament offers us no blueprint for this process, doubtless because it depended on the context – it is hard to imagine that precisely the same pattern would have been adopted in the crowded Syrian city of Antioch, in small fishing villages in Galilee and in the bustling ports of Cyprus; in Jerusalem with its centuries of Hebrew tradition and Rome with its expansionist political structures; in modest Turkish towns such as Derbe or Lystra and the great city of Athens, famous for its democracy and its philosophy. The letters of Paul, Peter, James and John tell us as much about what these first churches were getting wrong as what they were getting right. But the writers of those letters do seem to have had two key priorities for the new Christian communities.

Their first priority was lifestyle – the new believers were required to live in a way which reflected the teaching of Jesus, and was distinct from that of the surrounding society. In Corinth this meant a radical change in the way they conducted their relationships, particularly with regard to sexual behaviour and the chaotic nature of their meetings. In Ephesus it meant taking a united stand against the forces of evil which dominated the city's pagan heritage. In Colossae and Laodicea it meant rejecting the esoteric philosophies of the local mystery religions. In the cities of Asia Minor it meant standing firm in the face of persecution. In all these places the distinctiveness of the new communities is summed up through metaphor – it's about living not in the surrounding darkness but in the light of the good news of Jesus; it's about putting off an old identity and putting on a new one; it's about being yeast which transforms a whole batch of dough.[13]

The second priority was belief – Paul's letter to the Romans and the circulars of Peter and James offer teaching on the major doctrines of faith: salvation, judgment, life in the Spirit, hope, grace, the Second Coming of Jesus, the importance of demonstrating faith through good works and others. In other words there was both a behavioural and a cognitive dimension to the discipleship of these early Christians.

As the new churches expanded and multiplied far from the religious heartland of Judea, the need for instruction in practical discipleship grew. The gospels were written, starting with Mark, so that new believers could be clear about who it was they were following. We know from the letter to the Galatians that they were assigned to a teacher, and soon they came to be known as catechumens, from the Greek verb meaning to instruct.[14] Within a hundred years of Jesus's death a formal system of catechesis was in place, and this grew into a lengthy process of apprenticeship which demanded a radical change in both lifestyle and belief.[15] There were four main stages, which can be loosely summarised under the headings enquiry, instruction, baptism and spiritual formation. The first stage focussed on transformed behaviour; it involved a change of identity and an allegiance to Jesus and to his kingdom made visible in the church. Once these changes had been made, the catechumens were admitted to the second stage, in which they would be made familiar with the story of the Bible, the teachings of Jesus, and how to live as part of a Christian community. This stage might last for up to three years, after which the new believers entered the third stage, preparation for baptism, during which they received prayer ministry, underwent exorcism, and learned the Lord's Prayer and the Creed. This stage ended with baptism: the new Christians were now accepted as full members of the church fellowship. During the fourth and final stage the candidates were taught the mystery of the sacraments, admitted to communion, encouraged to exercise the gifts and talents identified in the catechetical process – and referred to, for the first time, as 'disciples'. Gradually, as society at large came to identify itself as Christian and people were increasingly brought up in Christian homes, the need for a process as exhaustive as this faded, and the system fell into disuse.[16]

Two features of this early initiation process stand out. Catechesis, based on the teaching of the New Testament, was 'the intentional passing on of the faith, not merely for cognitive apprehension, but for the holistic transformation of individual believers and for the maturing of those believers together as the body of Christ.'[17] So firstly, whereas today we tend to start with belief, the early church started with lifestyle. We would do well, now that once again we live in a secular culture, to recapture something of that, recognising that discipleship may be as much about changing our patterns of living as about learning new facts. And secondly, whereas we tend to focus on the individual, the early church focussed on the formation of a discipling community united by its relationship with Jesus. It is no use believing all the right things if in fact we fail to live them; disciples of Jesus are not those who share certain views, Dallas Willard reminds us, but those who apply a growing understanding of what it means to live in the kingdom of God to their lives.[18] And for that, we need one another.

Identifying a Method

This, as it happens, was exactly the conclusion reached by John Wesley in 1739. As thousands of unchurched people gave their lives to Christ at Whitefield and Wesley's revolutionary open air meetings, Wesley realised that without proper follow-up their newfound enthusiasm would flicker and die. Reflecting on Matthew 28 and the catechism of the early church, he instituted a pattern which would ultimately bring spiritual renewal and social reform to the whole of England. He started by putting the new converts into small groups, devising a system which included both cognitive and behavioural education – but in which these two elements were kept entirely separate. The key unit was the class, a weekly group meeting for 10 to 12 people guided by a (lay) leader and focussed on personal experience (not on doctrinal belief or biblical information). The aim of the class was to bring about behavioural change, and no discussion was allowed which was theoretical, hypothetical or speculative. Membership was open to anyone willing to live by a set of Rules, and admission was by ticket – which was withdrawn if members failed to attend regularly or live appropriately. Class members would also attend a weekly society meeting, held eventually in the new Methodist chapels; this was open to all comers, and consisted of Bible teaching and hymn singing. In addition there was a system of voluntary growth groups called bands, in which people of the same sex, age and marital status met to share their spiritual struggles and pray together.

John Wesley preaching at an open air meeting, from
Selections from the Journal of John Wesley, 1891

Wesley's new method was innovatory; nothing like it had been seen since the catechismal pattern of the early church. It recognised not only that spiritual growth involves both behavioural and cognitive change, but that the latter is dependent on the former. And it recognised that such growth can come about only by personal participation in small groups:

'it was by this means that we have been enabled to establish permanent and holy churches all over the world,' Methodist theologian Adam Clarke would write later that century.[19] Its success has been held up as the primary reason why England did not suffer the revolution which swept France a generation later; Methodist reformers were at the forefront of social change in the newly industrialised communities throughout the country, and ultimately at the heart of the campaign for the ending of the international trade in slaves which had so enriched Bristol, Liverpool and Manchester – and so impoverished Africa.

Rooted in Jesus

If the church would revisit the biblical teachings on discipleship it would revive its life and many of its problems would be rectified. Note that simply teaching the Word is not all there is to discipleship. There must be personal involvement, practical training, practical experience and positive role modelling – Gaspar Kassanda, Diocese of Mara, Tanzania[20]

Many of Wesley's principles are, as it happens, at the heart of the *Rooted in Jesus* discipleship programme now in use in many of those same African countries. Membership of a *Rooted in Jesus* group is normally restricted to 10-12 people, all of whom are there by invitation and all of whom undertake to prioritise attendance at the weekly meetings. Although based on scripture, a *Rooted in Jesus* group is not a Bible study group; its aim is to help members understand and above all apply the teaching of Jesus to their daily lives. Sessions are highly interactive, with a variety of learning methods employed, including discussion, demonstration, drama and practical illustration as well as mutual sharing, prayer and worship – as Wesley recognised, singing scriptural truth is a powerful learning method, of particular value to those who may not be able to read and write. The programme is arranged topically, with a constant emphasis on putting into practice what is being learned. So the opening module, 'What is a Christian?' includes a session in which participants are invited to make a personal response to what they have learned about Jesus; the later session on forgiveness aims not simply to teach the theology of forgiveness, but to identify those whom group members actually need to forgive, and help them to do it (a powerful exercise in countries like Rwanda or Mozambique where few people remain untouched by the traumas of the past). There are teaching topics – for example a module introducing the work of the Holy Spirit, one on learning from the Bible, one on the Church (which covers both preparation for both baptism and communion and also the self-understanding of the Church as the body of Christ, irrespective of kinship or tribal identity). There are lifestyle topics, covering issues such as suffering, self-control, work, money, marriage and family life. Other sessions cover major areas of the spiritual life, learning and then putting into practice what is learned – receiving and exercising the gifts of the Spirit, praying for healing and deliverance, developing in ministry. As group members grow in faith there are modules which help them to share their faith effectively with others, and modules which help them look outwards at the needs of the community. Each session is summarised by a memory verse which members are encouraged to meditate on and put into practice during the week. By the time the group completes the course (this takes two years) all members should be confident to exercise their own God-given ministry – and for some, this will mean leading a group in their turn.

We have heard many remarkable stories from those overseeing the course in each diocese or area where it is in use. Through the support of the groups, alcoholics have been able to turn away from drink and rebuild their lives, prostitutes have given up their trade and set up in business together, and family members have been reconciled to one another. People have prayed about their physical and emotional needs instead of resorting to traditional charms and treatments, and been healed; and attitudes to members of other tribes or communities have been transformed. Bishop Martin Breytenbach tells how a single *Rooted in Jesus* group in his diocese has forged new links between members of different communities: 'St Andrew's Church exists in the very heart of extreme right wing Afrikaner nationalism – some of the strongest resistance to the New South Africa has been in that area. They have formed one group comprising people from the (formerly white) church in Modimolle and the (black) church in Phagameng. The *Rooted in Jesus* material is helping them to find each other and share deeply.'

Group members of all educational levels have become confident in opening the Bible for themselves, and the division of formality between those who know and those who do not gradually disappear – 'the classes are full of friendship, relationship and collaboration,' one diocesan coordinator in Tanzania writes happily; 'it is a great change.' Many nominal churchgoers have entered into a transforming relationship with Jesus – including, in Mozambique, some who were previously both church leaders and local practitioners of traditional religion. Others have come to a first time faith through contact with *Rooted in Jesus* – one Mozambican evangelist, Ramine Joao Martinho, has planted 19 churches among previously unreached people in the remote region of Morrumbala, simply by inviting them to join *Rooted in Jesus* groups. "Before that book, my life was very bad," he told me; "now my life has been completely changed. I want to thank you so much for *Enraizado em Jesus.*"

As people grow in faith and discipleship, their lives change and they begin to understand what it means to be part of a Christian community. 'The opportunity to know the Bible, encourage, pray, share with each other in the Parish and in the Church, it is harmonizing us,' Lukas Saidi reports from Masasi, Tanzania. 'We are starting to see remarkable things in this Diocese as people and congregations are set on fire with the love of Jesus,' Bishop Martin Breytenbach writes from the Diocese of St Mark in South Africa. 'We went to the church at Mmazame,' Linnet Smith relates from the Diocese of Mara in Tanzania; 'they shared with us how now they had confidence in opening the Bible for themselves; now they felt able to share their faith with others; now they had learned the memory verses they could stand against temptation; now they felt able to teach others.' Watching all this often has a profound impact on local people: 'I haven't the words to tell of the many blessings people have received through this programme,' Michael Samuel wrote in the early days from the pioneering Diocese of Kiteto, Tanzania; 'there is wonderful revival in the Church now the Christians know the word of God. The community saw many things from our groups, how they have changed their lives completely. Some of them tried to say really God is great because some people have completely changed their lives from sins, like drink, worship of idols, and witchcraft, and so on.' Meeting with the tripled number of clergy in this diocese some years later, we asked what had accounted for the rapid expansion. "We all came up through the *Rooted in Jesus* groups," they said.

As group members experience the touch of God on their lives, they become confident and active in ministry to others. Lukas Saidi adds, 'Members of groups in different areas witness to me how they have been blessed. One said: "At the present time I have the power of the Holy Spirit. I can stand anywhere to share with other people the good news of Jesus. I can go even to youth groups without a Bible and have dialogue with them, because in my brain I have a lot of verses."' In Arusha, coordinator Charles Unjiro talks about how people in the groups are exclaiming 'God speaks to ME!'. He reports that some of them have gone to new places where they have planted churches and are now working as evangelists. We have heard from Bunyoro Kitara in Uganda how the *Rooted in Jesus* groups have established a healing ministry within every parish, and from Luapula in Zambia and Niassa in Mozambique how they have begun to minister within their communities, providing care for orphans, visiting the sick and raising support for the poor. In addition to this growth in Christian lifestyle and ministry, the teaching component of *Rooted in Jesus* has also been important: in many dioceses it is now used as the standard preparation for baptism and confirmation; in others, it's used to train catechists, evangelists, community workers and community priests; in yet others it has become part of the core curriculum in the Bible Colleges. A new version, *Rooted in Jesus Junior*, has been developed for use with children in Sunday Schools, and this is leading to similar growth in the lives of children, and a great increase in the numbers of children not only attending church but playing an active part in its life and ministry.[21]

Perhaps it's from the Diocese of Niassa in Mozambique that the most remarkable stories come, for there, under the leadership of Bishop Mark and Revd Helen Van Koevering, they have experienced sustained and remarkable church growth in recent years, across an area which makes up half of the country and is three times the size of the United Kingdom. 'We are looking for clues to this grace of God,' Helen mused in 2010 as she reflected on the doubling of the number of churches and church leaders in the region in just five years. 'Perhaps it's through our desire to be the church in new places, a new approach to training leaders as 'training the trainers' to reach and empower more people, offering new life through healing and development, new rootedness for believers and new belonging for communities.' Their determination to place discipleship at the heart of the life of the diocese, she says, has led to an increasing emphasis on *Rooted in Jesus: 'Rooted in Jesus* is the basis for all our ministry and mission training, supporting as it does our diocesan vision to 'become a communion of communities in Jesus', ie small groups studying, discipling one another, church planting and rooting, growing in faith and changed lives together. It is used as the primary study in our Small Christian Communities (midweek family groups of 20 or so people who pray, study and support each other), where we are currently seeing great growth in terms of both participants, healing prayer, and new leadership.' First introduced in 2006, by the end of 2012 there were between seven and twelve thousand members of *Rooted in Jesus* groups across the diocese (it's hard to keep track, apparently), including those using it for confirmation preparation. By the summer of 2013 Helen had reached a simple explanation for the remarkable growth they are experiencing as a diocese: 'Our church is reading the Bible differently.'[22]

However you choose to explain it, it's clear that God is at work in and through the disciples and discipling communities of Niassa. 'Holy Communion in action,' Archbishop Rowan Williams described it when he went there; 'the church is affecting the fabric of society,' another visitor observed. And all this, of course, is exactly what Jesus intended when he told those first disciples to make other disciples, baptising them in the name of the Father, the Son and the Holy Spirit, and teaching them to obey everything that he had commanded them.

Many people, hearing these stories or witnessing them at first hand as part of *Rooted in Jesus* teams, have asked if *Rooted in Jesus* would work here in the UK. It's certainly not, as some suggest, too simplistic – for although the academic challenges it presents are few, the spiritual challenges are enormous. In 2012 I was invited to speak at the first international Anglicans Ablaze Conference in Johannesburg. There I met many people who were using *Rooted in Jesus* – but I was particularly fascinated by two separate conversations. The first was with Zodumo Ndwandwe, using *Rooted in Jesus* with a group in the predominantly rural diocese of Zululand. "When we reached the session on forgiveness," she said, "it took us several weeks, because we had so many people we needed to forgive." The second conversation was with Philip LeFeuvre, a retired bishop leading a group of university lecturers and businessmen in cosmopolitan Cape Town. "When we reached the session on forgiveness," he said, "it took us several weeks, because we had so many people we needed to forgive." The challenges of discipleship are not intellectual; they are spiritual, and they apply to all. 'This course,' writes June from Grahamstown, 'has given me the opportunity of creating bonds with people in an unexpected way. I have become more conscious of how I should conduct myself, how I should treat and respect others. We have delved into the Bible and scriptures at such depth and that has given me a new insight into the meaning of the Word. I can see now what an amazing reference and guideline to life the Bible is – all that we need to know about life and how to live it is right there at our fingertips!'.

And yet despite the fact that we all have the same spiritual needs, there are differences between us too. *Rooted in Jesus* is designed for Africa, where people face particular challenges in their Christian lives; it recognises the reality, for example, of traditional religion, tribal differences and customs, and the pressures of extreme poverty. Here in the so-called developed world the challenges are different – materialism and individualism are much bigger issues for us than they are for our African brothers and sisters. So, keeping the same emphasis on practical discipleship, we created a 'home' version of *Rooted in Jesus*, a three part programme titled *The God Who Is There*.[23] The first part, *Beyond Ourselves*, begins with the fundamental question asked by many here in the western world, but by few in Africa: is there a God? Based on the same principles of small group discussion and participation, it also takes a topical approach, but includes some culturally relevant topics such as science and faith. Many people who come to faith or who deepen

130

their faith through *Beyond Ourselves* continue to the second part, *The New Community*, of which the aim is, as Rowan Williams suggested, to help group members sustain and deepen their encounter with Jesus in their encounter with each other; this part of the programme builds in worship, something which to Africans seems to come naturally, but which here lacks the heartfelt vibrancy which is so widespread there – for the average Westerner it still seems that 'enthusiasm', as the Bishop of Bristol famously said to John Wesley, 'is a very horrid thing.'[24]

The final part of *The God Who Is There* is called *Shining Like Stars*, and it focusses on what it means to live as disciples of Jesus in the midst of daily life, equipping people to live with compassion and integrity as Christians in the community and in the workplace. In all three parts, the emphasis is not on what we know, but on who we are becoming, both in lifestyle and in understanding. If I've learnt one thing in Africa, it's that we need to escape from the near universal approach which thinks we can disciple people by asking them to study a passage and answer the questions. Jesus said, "Go and make disciples, and teach them to obey everything that I have commanded you." I notice that he did *not* say, "Go and make disciples, and teach them to understand everything that I have taught you." We are called to become apprentices of the living God; it's a whole life undertaking.

Rooted in Jesus – the power of community

'I visited Kambwata, where we have planted two Life! Groups. During my visit I met a woman who has been attending the Life! Group, which is using the *Rooted in Jesus* resource. She told me her story. Months ago she was a drunkard, she would insult many people and was a troublesome person in the village. The Life! Group in her village took her in and allowed her to participate in the group. In short, through the *Rooted in Jesus* course, the Lord transformed her life. She is now not a drunkard. She told me that, rather than being a bad mother to her children and a terrible wife, she is now a good mother and a good wife. Her life has changed completely. She now calls herself a committed Christian and is much, much happier as a person. As a result of the startling change in her life, many people have been attracted to the groups and they are growing at a faster rate.' *Augustine, Luapula Impact Team, Dignity Worldwide, Zambia.*

'We met with stories of redemption from people who, through the Family of one heart and one mind in *Rooted in Jesus* groups, met with God. A young boy of 13 years old, Joakim Chacha, whose parents are seriously traditionalists and still believe in the gods of the ancestors, told us a story about his own life before he converted to become a Christian: "My father is a traditionalist god worshipper, he killed my mother and gave sacrifices to local gods. She died into my hands. We are 6 children from my mother's womb. After the death of my mother, I joined Uncle's family where I am still living. My Uncle used take us to church. In church I met with the family of one heart and one mind and I joined them. I heard a lesson about how Jesus was crucified and died and on the third day He rose gain. In the group they said that there is no other Love like this of Jesus to take a cross for our salvation. This touches my life and I committed my life to the almighty God."' *Canon Jacob Robert, Diocese of Mara, Tanzania.*

'I convinced ten girls who are prostitutes who want to join the program. The challenge is they need help to sustain themselves. They want to change, to start a new life. We meet every day at 5 am to 6 am. They propose to do business since others have an idea in business, to start small.' [Two years later] 'They have all now found other means of supporting themselves. Two have got married, and five have returned to their villages to farm.' *Susan Chulu, Canon Missioner, Diocese of Eastern Zambia.*

'Parents saw their children change as a result of being taught the programme and have given thanks to the teachers. The children are now involved and very active in the lessons; they want to put into practice what they have been learning. Now they are smiling and praying all the time. Before we used this programme, praying was a problem and we did not know how to do it with the children. Now they all want to lead the prayer time and serve others, also to read the Bible.' *Jane Nanyonjo, Quality Discipleship Church network, Wakiso, Uganda*

'From the time we adopted [*Rooted in Jesus Junior*], we experienced vibrant exciting Sunday school meetings with the children. The five Sunday school teachers are now more practical during every meeting with the children. This has improved much of the children's zeal and love for Christ. A lot of spiritual gifts were realised like evangelism, worship, preaching, prayer, storytelling, drama, scripture memory verses etc among the children. Some of these children lead worship during the main service and other church meetings. The number of the children which was about 25 at our church, it has now has grown to 150+.' *Pastor Ali Mukembo, New Life Missionary Baptist Church Jinja, Uganda.*

Learning in community

We have nothing to share with the world other than what we are sharing with each other – Jim Wallis[25]

It is natural to human beings to wish to belong to others, to meet together, to share one another's life journeys. It is natural too to look for structure and purpose within those meetings. 'One of the losses modern society feels most keenly is that of a sense of community,' Alain de Botton, our best known contemporary philosopher, observes. He continues, with obvious approval, 'the Church knows about loneliness, it creates community, it invites us to be happy without having to be successful, it deals with our fears and offers us the respect and security we crave through a warm and impressive community which imposes no worldly requirements on us for its welcome.' Alain, however, is an atheist; and the rest of the book from which these remarks are taken addresses the knotty problem of how to import the insights and practices of religion into the secular realm without becoming entangled in the inconvenient demands of its founder.[26] A year after de Botton's non-believer's guide to the uses of religion was published, a man named Sanderson Jones began to host monthly Sunday Assemblies in a deconsecrated church in London, 'with songs and general thoughtfulness but no mention of a higher being,' as *The Sunday Times* put it. "We're happy to take all the best things from religion and leave the bad," Jones said. "We may not believe in God, but we have still got this human need for community." Instead of sermons, there are talks and science lectures; pop songs such as 'Livin' on a Prayer' by Bon Jovi replace hymns. A typical gathering includes time to sit in reflective silence, and ends with tea and buns (I cannot help wondering if they also have green crockery?). The assemblies have proved popular, and later that same year Jones embarked on a world tour to spread the news.[27]

Alain de Botton is undoubtedly right when he observes that human beings are made to live in community. It may be that our understanding of discipleship has shrunk so much that many of our churches model little more than what Sanderson Jones has copied in his Sunday Assemblies – the outward shell of faith with none of the inner dynamic. And yet the need is still there; and it's there perhaps more than it has been at any time since John Wesley noticed that sermons were not enough. I have written elsewhere of the loss of purpose, crisis in spirituality and search for happiness that characterise life at the beginning of the third millennium; secularisation has left a whole generation struggling to know what life is all about.[28] Christians, on the other hand, following Jesus and living as outposts of the kingdom of God, are supposed to live differently, prophetically and invitingly. We need to make sure afresh in our generation that we are fit for purpose. This is what Mark Greene of the London Institute for Contemporary Christianity writes about the church in Britain today: 'We need to return to Jesus' instruction to make disciples, to become lifelong learners and practitioners in learning communities – communities that are focussed on equipping people to go where those who don't know Jesus are. This will require a radical shift in pastoral training, in current pastoral practice and in the readiness of individual Christians to commit themselves to the disciplines of lifelong Christian learning.'[29] Greene's plea is strikingly similar to Gaspar Kassanda's call for a renewed and practical emphasis on discipleship in East Africa: different cultures, same need.

So whether it's here or there, the task is the same: to make disciples of Jesus. It seems odd to suggest that this can be done in any other way than that in which Jesus and the apostles did it: by gathering people together into small fellowship groups and training them to look at life a different way. As we learn from the patterns of growth and decline in the contemporary church worldwide, it is becoming increasingly clear that a healthy church is one which encourages people, whether enquirers or established believers, to deepen their discipleship by becoming part of small, mutually accountable communities in which they can grow in all aspects of their faith. Perhaps the clearest recent demonstration of this comes from China, currently experiencing rapid church growth. Whilst protecting freedom of religious belief, the Chinese constitution places certain restrictions on any unofficial gathering, including the many house churches which are not registered (and therefore remain technically illegal). In particular, meetings of more than 15-20 people are not permitted; meetings may happen only on private premises, not in public buildings; and 'foreign domination' is forbidden, which means that outside leadership or training input is frowned on, not just for unregistered but also for officially sanctioned churches. These conditions would seem to be just what Jesus and the apostles had in mind – small fellowships, meeting in people's homes, under local leadership. It seems to be working; Chinese government figures suggest that the number of Christians has grown from an estimated three million 40 years ago to as many as 110 million today.[30]

The magic ingredient

In Chapter 2 we defined discipleship as 'apprenticeship in community,' and looked at the relationships formed between

Jesus and those who first travelled with him. Jesus drew his chosen disciples into a close and mutually accountable relationship with him and with one another – not simply in order to create the most effective learning environment (though it did do that), but because of the power of the community itself. And he insisted that it was in the power of these relationships that the future of the gospel would lie; there was, as is often noted, no Plan B. As their earthly journey together drew towards its close, he spelled this out beyond any possible doubt: "I give you a new commandment," he said as he washed their feet and ate with them; "that you love one another. Just as I have loved you, you also should love one another. *By this everyone will know that you are my disciples, if you have love for one another."*[31]

The disciples were confused; how would this work? The fishermen among them already knew all about the importance of relationships: Simon and Andrew, James and John had grown up as part of a close-knit, mutually dependent fishing community in which news was readily shared and help was always offered – much as it still is today on the shores of Lake Niassa, where I once watched a whole village help land and distribute the catch of two pairs of fishermen. But those relationships, important though they were for survival, were never going to change the world. And if Jesus wasn't even going to be with them, how would people recognise *him* when they looked at *them*?

Jesus spelt it out for them: "If you love me, you will keep my commandments. *And I will ask the Father, and he will give you another Advocate, to be with you forever. This is the Spirit of truth, whom the world cannot receive, because it neither sees him nor knows him. You know him, because he abides with you, and he will be in you.*" Something new is going to happen, something which will make it all possible: the Holy Spirit will be directly released in and among all those who belong to Jesus – just as the prophets had said he would be. And then Jesus gives them an example they *can* understand: think of a vine, he says. You are the branches, I am the vine. Branches on their own are no good, they just shrivel and die. But branches joined to the vine are alive,

they bear fruit. That's how it will work. The Holy Spirit will be like the sap in the vine, keeping you joined to me. You will, he might have said, be rooted in me.[32]

The Holy Spirit is the magic ingredient which makes everything of which I have been writing possible. Wesley and Whitefield were undoubtedly fine speakers, but it was not the power of their oratory which made ordinary working people want to give their lives to Jesus – it was the voice of God whispering to their souls. Traumatised thirteen year old Joakim Chacha did not simply feel welcomed by the *Rooted in Jesus* group which told him that God loved him; he felt that love touching his heart, and responded to it with astonishment. Ramine Martinho has not planted nineteen churches by the charisma of his personality, for he is a quiet and unassuming man, but by the power of his life, renewed by the Spirit working within him. We respond to the call of Jesus, as the first disciples responded, not because it makes much human sense but because the Holy Spirit himself invites us to draw near to God.[33]

Once we have responded, we are united, drawn together

not by natural affinity but by the shared presence of the Holy Spirit within us. Together, we become different; we grow, we learn to trust and rely on one another. We are made new not just as individuals, but as a community. We learn to forgive one another, to serve one another, to respect one another; we learn to build one another up as we pray for one another. This too is possible only through the presence of the Holy Spirit among us, helping us to become people whose relationships are characterised by love, joy, peace, patience, kindness, generosity, faithfulness, gentleness, and self-control; and working among us through the sharing of wisdom, through healings and miracles, through prophecy, spiritual discernment and answered prayer. It is not through our relationships in themselves that we will make it possible for others to become disciples of Jesus, but through the presence of the Holy Spirit who lives in the spaces between us.[34] Not brought up a Christian, I have been a member of mutually committed, Spirit-dependent communities of this kind ever since I first gave my life to Jesus at the age of twenty-four: this is the context in which I have brought up my children, discovered my calling and prayed through my pain; and supported others as they too do these things. I know no other way to live.

Jesus's teaching about the Holy Spirit may be profound, but it is not complicated. We are called, as disciples of Jesus, to live in the constant awareness that Jesus, through the presence of the Holy Spirit, is still with us, teaching us, helping us and enabling us to make a difference – not individually, as heroes, superstars or experts, but in and through the dynamic of our Christian communities. 'Make disciples of all peoples,' Jesus had said; and he promised, 'I will be with you as you do it.' A community of people dedicated to God and empowered by the Holy Spirit has the potential to become something more significant than any ordinary human community, however good the talks and however tasty the buns. The learning journey of these first disciples is not coming to an end, here on the beach as they prepare to say goodbye to Jesus; it is only just beginning.

'The most important thing to God,' Quaker theologian Elton Trueblood once wrote, 'is the creation of centres of loving fellowships, which in turn infect the world. Whether the world can be redeemed in this way we don't know. But it is at least clear that there is no other way.'[35] The early Christians certainly gave it a go. In third century Carthage, Tertullian described the contrast between the pagan community and the church: '"Look," the pagans say, "how they love one another" (for they themselves hate one another); "and how they are ready to die for each other" (for they themselves are readier to kill each other).' By the fourth century the Christians in Galatia had developed a community life so radically different from the norm that the emperor Julian complained that they were so loving to the poor and the sick that it was very hard to outdo them – 'the religion of the Greeks does not yet prosper as I would wish,' he lamented, 'on account of those who profess it. Why do [we] not observe how the kindness of Christians to strangers, their care for the burial of their dead, and the sobriety of their lifestyle has done the most to advance their cause?'[36] As the new Christian communities learned to live lovingly, counterculturally and spiritually, people flocked to join them; with an average growth rate estimated at 40% per decade, by the middle of the fourth century 56% of the population of the Roman Empire was officially Christian.[37]

A new commandment: love one another

The Church or something like it must be cherished, criticized, nourished and reformed. The Church of Jesus Christ, with all its blemishes, its divisions and its failures, remains our best hope of spiritual vitality. However poor it is, life without it is worse. One of the truly shocking passages of the gospel is that in which Jesus indicates that there is absolutely no substitute for the tiny, loving, caring, reconciling society. If this fails, he suggests, all is failure; there is no other way. He told the little bedraggled fellowship that they were actually the salt of the earth and that If this salt should fail there would be no adequate preservative at all. He was staking all on one throw... One of the most powerful ways of turning people's loyalty to Christ is by loving others with the great love of God... If there should emerge in our day such a fellowship, wholly without artificiality and free from the dead hand of the past, it would be an exciting event of momentous importance. A society of genuine loving friends, set free from the self-seeking struggle for personal prestige and from all unreality, would be something unutterably priceless and powerful. A wise person would travel any distance to join it.'

Elton Trueblood, *The Company of the Committed*, Harper & Row 1961

There is nothing like the local church when it's working right. Its beauty is indescribable. Its power is breathtaking. Its potential is unlimited. It comforts the grieving and heals the broken in the context of community. It builds bridges to seekers and offers truth to the confused. It provides resources for those in need and opens its arms to the forgotten, the downtrodden, the disillusioned. It breaks the chains of addictions, frees the oppressed, and offers belonging to the marginalized of this world. Whatever the capacity for human suffering, the church has a greater capacity for healing and wholeness. Still to this day, the potential of the local church is almost more than I can grasp. No other organization on earth is like the church. Nothing even comes close.'

Bill Hybels, *Courageous Leadership*, Zondervan 2002

141

A personal perspective

When I look back on my own Christian journey, I find that every significant experience has taken place in the context of relationships – both with other people and, through them, with the Holy Spirit. I have learned with others and from others, and it has been in the company of others that I have most closely experienced the presence of God – God who is by his very nature relational, and who made us in his own image.

My Christian journey began in Cambridge, as a postgraduate student. I came to faith through a friend whose world, even as she lay dying, contained so much more than mine. I started going to church, and I joined a Bible study group. Church rather mystified me; it was all family values and unmelodious songs and long sermons. The Bible study group was interesting, but also frustrating; I began to learn more about the Bible, but the discussions were somehow rather unimaginative, and I couldn't quite see the sky or reach this God who had welcomed me a few weeks earlier but didn't really seem to be following through on his initial cloud-bursting communication. It all seemed, in comparison with the intellectually exciting world of my research, rather dull.

A year later Roger and I moved to Corby. As I learned more, I began to pray that I would experience more of the Holy Spirit. Meanwhile in the church we were experiencing some problems: extra-marital affairs between members of the congregation, discontent, bitterness. One by one, people were drawn in to the negative atmosphere; the church began to divide. Unsure what to do, we formed a little prayer group – just eight of us. We had no idea how to pray, so we just sat in silence. And God began to speak – to one a word, to another a picture. None of us knew of such things; but we began to learn, to trust, to follow. The immediate result was that the discontent vanished overnight, without any of us having to say or do anything. For the next five years we continued to meet as a group, praying for one another over issues and needs we would never have thought to share, but which went to the heart of who we each were. We called the group 'Eagles', mindful that 'those who wait for the Lord shall renew their strength, they shall mount up with wings like eagles, they shall run and not be weary, they shall walk and not faint.'[38] All those things became true of us. When I arrived in Corby I was a new Christian with little understanding of the scriptures and no real experience of God. By the time we left six years later I had learnt that faith is about relationships, and that it is through those relationships that we become who God wants us to be.

We left Corby in 1990. Since then I have always been part of a small group of people whose ministry comes out of a shared life of prayer and a shared willingness to be both vulnerable with one another and accountable to one another. We moved to Leicester, and for me the key group there became a community of other women, about twenty of us, meeting just once a month for a meal and an evening which we took it in turn to facilitate – in fact our first meeting went ahead as planned a few hours after my husband was rushed into intensive care after a road accident. All of us were actively engaged in ministry within the church, most with a leadership role; some of us met more frequently as prayer partners. Sometimes we read the Bible together, sometimes we prayed, but often we just talked and laughed, discussed the books we'd read or expressed our circumstances and relationships through art activities. We talked about our children and our marriages and our lives, we prayed for one another and we walked together through the pain which life brings. All of us laughed, all of us cried, and one of us died. We were there for one another.

In 2003 Martin Cavender invited me to be part of what was to become ReSource. Would I join with him and Cesca and a small group of others, he wrote, so that together we might discern God's will for his Church in his mission in his beautiful, singing world, and be obedient to his calling upon us in all of that? And would I hold to myself that this was not just a functional or practical invitation (though it contained both of those) but one which would bind together a fragile group of travellers, with those whom they love, into a pilgrim cell of ministry, a missional community of a kind which has never been seen before? Yes, I said, not knowing what any of that would mean in practice; and again my life changed. Living now in Somerset, we are a small team, but together we do form a little cell of ministry. In addition to our regular working contact with one another, we meet monthly for supper and prayer. We too have found ourselves talking with God about things both professional and personal. We worship together, we share our needs with one another, we wait on the Lord together. In every place I have been, it is through these kinds of committed, accountable and Spirit-filled relationships that I have grown, and it is from these relationships that all of us have gone out in peace to love and serve the Lord. Many of our meetings have not been remarkable in any way – but together they have been the foundation on which my Christian life is built.

It is, however, not just about meeting together. It's not even just about meeting together in the presence of God. There's another factor.

The Plural of disciple is church – a group study

1. 'The plural of disciple is church'

Is this statement an accurate description of the church to which you belong? Are you, in Rowan Williams' words, a group of people who have encountered the Risen Jesus and committed yourselves to sustaining and deepening that encounter in your encounter with each other?

2. Discipleship and the church

'Teaching the Word is not all there is to discipleship. There must be personal involvement, practical training, practical experience and positive role modelling' (Gaspar Kassanda). Thinking about your own Christian community, do you consider that you get the balance right between focussing on what you believe and on how you live?

3. Learning in community

'We need to return to Jesus's instruction to make disciples, to become lifelong learners and practitioners in learning communities. This will require a radical change in pastoral practice and in the readiness of individual Christians to commit themselves to the disciplines of lifelong Christian learning' (Mark Greene). Does that describe your own experience?

4. The magic ingredient

'I will ask the Father, and he will give you another Advocate, to be with you forever. This is the Spirit of truth, whom the world cannot receive, because it neither sees him nor knows him. You know him, because he abides with you, and he will be in you. The Holy Spirit will teach you everything, and remind you of all that I have said to you" (Jesus, John

14). What difference does it make, in your experience, when the Holy Spirit is an active member of your Christian community?

5. Christian community today

'We have nothing to share with the world other than what we are sharing with each other' (Jim Wallis). Thinking of your own context, what are you sharing with each other? How does that shape your lives, and is it attractive to others?

CHAPTER SIX

Community with a purpose

You are a chosen race, a royal priesthood, a holy nation, God's own people, in order that you may proclaim the mighty acts of him who called you out of darkness into his marvellous light.

1 Peter 2.9

When the children were younger, one of our family's favourite days out was to the Cadbury World chocolate factory in Bournville, Birmingham. It was a fascinating place to visit, not only because it involved being given generous samples of chocolate in every conceivable form, but also because of the insight it offered into the history of chocolate consumption and production. On the one hand this meant trying the original Aztec spiced chocolate drink (an acquired taste); on the other it meant learning something of the original vision of George and Richard Cadbury, the factory's founders.

George Cadbury was born in 1839, after a century of industrialisation which had brought hundreds of thousands of people into the new cities first described a century earlier by Daniel Defoe. They came to seek employment in the new workshops and factories, and lived in cramped back-to-back housing with no sewerage or access to clean water. Poet Robert Southey went to visit:

'My head aches with the multiplicity of infernal noises, and my eyes with the light of infernal fires – I may add, my heart also, at the sight of so many human beings employed in infernal occupations. The noise is beyond description; the filth is sickening: it is active and moving, a living principle of mischief, which fills the whole atmosphere and penetrates every where, spotting and staining every thing, and getting into the pores and nostrils. I feel as if my throat wanted sweeping like a chimney.'[1]

The Cadbury Factory at Bournville, from the cover of a Cadbury's booklet, 1925

George Cadbury was a committed Christian, a Quaker who taught adult Sunday school classes every week throughout his working life. As the cocoa business he and his brother had taken over from their father expanded and they looked with horror at the living conditions of their employees, they came up with an innovatory plan: they would buy a site outside the city, and build not only a new factory but also England's first 'garden city' – a new town of houses, gardens and open spaces where their workers could not only live but flourish. They named the site Bournville, and Cadbury's became known as 'the factory in a garden.' As the site expanded, a school, hospital, sports facilities, reading rooms and wash houses were added. Workers were given a half day off on Saturday as well as a Sunday rest day, and enrolled in a pension scheme. A church was built, and morning prayers and daily Bible readings offered; the sale of alcohol was banned – and remains so, by popular local vote, to this day. By the standards of the time this was revolutionary.[2]

Other Christian industrialists were engaged in similar projects.[3] Inspired by their faith and supported by their churches, they had understood something fundamental about what it means to be a disciple of Jesus: it is supposed to make a difference not just to you, but to those amongst whom you live and work – so that they too may be drawn into the kingdom. 'You are,' said Jesus, 'to be salt and light in your communities; let your light shine before others, so that they may see your good works and give glory to your Father in heaven.'[4] John Wesley had known this: he was the first in modern times to recover the idea that growth in discipleship is not achieved simply by paying careful attention to yourself, but by engaging in active ministry to others. True discipleship always has an outward focus.[5]

We have seen that discipleship is a form of apprenticeship, and that it is undertaken in community. Now we must go one further, and grasp that this is not simply because people learn better in community, it is because the aim is to equip not the individual but the community itself. The community has a purpose. The plural of disciple is church – and that is not the end of the story, but the beginning, for the church does not just exist, it is *for* something. We are called, we are trained, and we are sent; purpose is an integral part of discipleship. Church is not about church.[6] It's bigger than that.

A holy priesthood

Centuries of education have predisposed us to think conceptually; whole books have been written about discipleship in which chapter after chapter offers abstract thoughts, theological truths and well-meaning exhortations. In Africa, where life is still rooted in physical experience, I have learnt that polite assent will be given to concepts, but enthusiasm follows practical illustrations, concrete examples, and clear explanation in plain language. This is perhaps not surprising – for every conceptual term, every abstract word we use, derives ultimately from a concrete origin; we understand concepts by thinking about things we can actually see – invisible things, even God himself, are understood by the things which have been made, as Paul pointed out to the Romans.[7] And so when Peter wants to explain that we are called as disciples and formed into communities with a purpose, he does not present the concepts in abstract terms. He hangs them on a metaphor, on something concrete and visible, something which already relates to the common experience of his readers: he talks about temples. 'You are familiar with temples,' he writes to the fledgling Christian communities of Asia Minor. 'Well, churches are like temples, except that we need to think about them organically instead of architecturally.' Churches are temples, built not with stones but with living, breathing people, all linked to Jesus:

Come to him, a living stone, though rejected by mortals yet chosen and precious in God's sight, and like living stones, let yourselves be built into a spiritual house, to be a holy priesthood. (1 Peter 2.4-5)

The cornerstone of the temple, the stone which holds the whole building up, is Jesus. The stones from which the temple is built are the believers. They are living stones because they have been made alive through Jesus, and they have been built together not into a real building but into a spiritual one. So far, so good – the plural of disciple is church. But Peter goes further. 'A temple has a purpose: it is a place where priests lead worship and offer sacrifices. The church too has a purpose,' he says:

You are a chosen race, a royal priesthood, a holy nation, God's own people, *in order that you may proclaim the mighty acts of him who called you out of darkness into his marvellous light.* (1 Peter 2.9)

As disciples of Jesus we are formed into new, living, Spirit-filled communities; but that is not for our own benefit, it is for the benefit of others. We are not just the human components of a new spiritual house, we are a holy priesthood, called to perform not real sacrifices but spiritual ones. We have a job to do – *all* of us, not just our stipendiary minister. We are to tell others about what Jesus has done; we are to shed our light into their darkness, just as George Cadbury tried to do.[8] This too seems natural; as human beings we all have houses, places of refuge and relationship – but if we do not leave our houses each day and go out to play our part in the world, then we are said to be housebound. Churches, like houses, are places from which we go *out*. And this was the key to all three of the small groups I described in the last chapter: in each we were united by our commitment to one another, our commitment to God and our commitment to serving him in the world. None of these groups existed as an end in itself.

We began by defining discipleship as a form of apprenticeship undertaken in community. It starts there, but it doesn't end there: any genuine Christian community also

An anorexic church?

'The church does not exist for the sake of the church. It exists for the sake of the world. Unfortunately, many contemporary churches, unable to bridge this gap of relevance, have either resigned themselves to irrelevance or, even more troublingly, redesigned themselves after two other types of "big ideas." The first is to create a church that meets the needs of its members. Since so many people have such deep spiritual needs, there is much good in this approach. But often it also leads to unhealthy consequences. Needs soon turn to wants. A toxic self-absorption can easily develop. Like a star that has collapsed into a black hole, refusing to release its light, a "need-meeting church" can unknowingly come to exist for nothing bigger than itself.

A second "big idea" driving many contemporary churches is the concept of success. Seeking conformity to a culture dominated by commerce, the "success" mentality is simple: the bigger, the better. Size matters. Numbers count.

More is what is always needed: more people, more facilities, more staff, more money. It is mostly a polite game of Christian Darwinism: the survival of the fittest, or the church with the greatest attendance.

Churches driven by either of these big ideas become islands without bridges. They have nothing to say and no way to say it in the very communities in which they are rooted. The best that can be mustered is the launching of empty words, like deflated balloons, untethered to the community: "Join us this Sunday"…"Jesus loves you'"…"Come to ___ event." For those outside the church, these words float by like leaves in a winter wind.'

Extracts from Robert Lewis, *The Church of Irresistible Influence*, Zondervan 2001, chapter 3.

has a purpose which reaches beyond itself. Michael Wilkins concludes his classic study of biblical discipleship by saying that to be a disciple of Jesus really involves just two things: 'On the one hand, discipleship consists of being moulded by the apostolic teaching, being empowered by an experience with the living God, and being a participant in a community of disciples. On the other hand, it involves both a way to walk and a mission to fulfil.'[9] We are living stones, built into a spiritual house, called to minister as a holy priesthood.

A prophetic community

The question for us is, what does that mean in practice? Jesus talked often about his own purpose, the purpose into which he was seeking to commission others. 'I have been sent,' he announced in the synagogue at Nazareth at the outset of his ministry, 'to bring good news to the poor, to proclaim release to the captives and recovery of sight to the blind, to free the oppressed and to proclaim the coming kingdom of God.' We get our first glimpse of what that means a week later, when we find him forty miles up the road in Capernaum. There he spent the day teaching, healing the sick and delivering the oppressed; he said the next morning that in so doing he had been proclaiming the good news of the kingdom of God.[10] It seems that for Jesus, the good news is to be declared in both word and deed. It is not simply a propositional statement, a set of concepts; it is a doorway into a new world – a world where things will be different. 'I want you too to do all these things,' he would add as he sent them out in pairs for the first time – 'proclaim the good news, heal the sick, cast out demons. As the Father has sent me, so I send you.' In fact, 'I want you to do more than that; you have seen me engage with the forgotten, the despised and the accused, and I want you to do that too – for the kingdom is seen when the hungry are fed, the poor are clothed, the sick are looked after and those in prison are visited.' And then, as he prepared to leave them for the last time: 'Now I am commissioning you not just to do these things, but to train others to do them too: go, and make disciples' – disciples, as Paul would later reiterate to Timothy, who will make other disciples, who will... And finally, a promise: 'I will be with you always, to the end of the age.'[11]

The problem with this is not that it is unclear, but that it seems to cover so many different things; indeed, the gospel writers themselves appear to have different understandings, or at least priorities, in their discussions of discipleship: John places the emphasis on relationships, Luke on ministry, Matthew on society.[12] Can we do all the things they urge us to do? Do we *want* to do them all? To get it into a nutshell, what exactly *is* the mandate? If we don't have a clear understanding of that, we will end up doing nothing, or doing the wrong thing, or even doing the right thing for the wrong reason. We latch onto this, or we latch onto that – but in focussing on the details of what we are being asked to do, we easily forget to ask why it is we are being asked to do them – what's it all for? And so we risk missing the whole point.

Many churches have no real idea of what their purpose should be, other than to meet regularly to worship God and be generally friendly to one another. Mindful of the Johannine command that we should love one another, 'our vision,' they declare, 'is to be welcoming.' Others have a much clearer idea of what they are about; and yet even they can become so busy

Discipleship in the gospels

The unique emphases of Matthew, Luke and John

Matthew

- "Whoever gives even a cup of cold water to one of these little ones in the name of a disciple – truly I tell you, none of these will lose their reward." 10.42
- The Pharisees sent their disciples to him... saying... "You do not regard people with partiality." 22.16
- "I was hungry and you gave me food, I was thirsty and you gave me something to drink, I was a stranger and you welcomed me, I was naked and you gave me clothing, I was sick and you took care of me, I was in prison and you visited me." 25.35-36

Luke

- Then Jesus called the twelve together and gave them power and authority over all demons and to cure diseases, and he sent them out to proclaim the kingdom of God and to heal. 9.1-2
- After this the Lord appointed 70 others and sent them on ahead of him in pairs. He said to them, "the harvest is plentiful, but the labourers are few." 10.1-2
- The whole multitude of the disciples began to praise God joyfully with a loud voice for all the deeds of power that they had seen. 19.37

John

- Then Jesus said to the Jews who had believed in him, "If you continue in my word, you are truly my disciples." 8.31
- "By this everyone will know that you are my disciples, if you have love for one another." 13.34
- When Jesus saw his mother and the disciple whom he loved standing beside her, he said to his mother, "Woman, here is your son." Then he said to the disciple, "Here is your mother." 19.26-27

with the trees that they lose sight of the wood. An increasing number continue in the tradition of the Victorian reformers, faithful to Jesus's warning in Matthew chapter 25, working to bring relief to the poor and to make their neighbourhoods better places to live – but often more because this has become a common secular value than because they see it as a prophetic act, a gateway to a spiritual kingdom which is being foreshadowed here on earth. Social action can so easily become an end in itself – and the invitation, the good news of the kingdom of God, falls between the slats of our absent words.[13]

Others focus on the undoubted need to offer salvation: they proclaim the good news, inviting people to make a personal response and then to join a Bible study group. This is good, of course, but carries the risk that the good news remains essentially one-dimensional – new believers rush over the threshold, only to find themselves in an evening class. I still remember the midnight Christmas service I attended one year, where the message of the incarnation was reduced to an exhortation to spend more time in Bible study – the preacher was undoubtedly right, but I had been hoping for something which might be more of a flowering, a catching of the beginning and end of the universe into this one astonishing moment of human history; 'more Bible study' was not really the message I had stayed awake to hear![14]

For others the key to the kingdom is sacramental, and the purpose of the church becomes to offer a lifelong sacramental journey to its members, who because of our modern concept of ordination remain curiously unable to pass this benefit on to others.[15] "Does it work?" asked statistician Bob Jackson of a priest who suggested that the major and sufficient evangelistic tool of the church is the regular provision of the sacraments; silence was the reply, for invaluable though the sacraments are, their availability in the local church building was not, at least in his context, bringing people to faith in Christ.

For others the primary mandate is the ministry of healing and deliverance which Luke tells us was so often Jesus' own starting point – but if we do not keep constantly in mind that this is a means and not an end, we simply end up with more problems than we started with. The more we convince ourselves that physical healing is available to all, the more complex it becomes when people do not seem to be healed. 'God does not hear my prayers,' a woman wrote to me just yesterday; 'my husband is dying of cancer and he has not been healed – will *you* pray for him?' Jesus referred to healing and deliverance as signs of the kingdom, part of the bigger picture of salvation; powerful signs given as a prophetic demonstration of a new and different world, a world in which there will be no more death, no more mourning or crying or pain. Physical health is always temporary; our ultimate healing comes only through death.

At ReSource we believe firmly that all the above approaches – welcome, social action, personal evangelism, the offering of the sacraments, and prayer for healing and deliverance – are part and parcel of the ministry of the church. Doing any of these is infinitely better than not doing them. The key is to remember that whilst Jesus commended and practised all of them, they were not themselves the main thing. They were all doorways, doorways into the new and redeemed world which is the kingdom of God: the world into which Jesus was inviting his hearers with every parable and every story, the world laid out before them in the unlikely thumbnail sketch of the beatitudes, the world glimpsed by the prophets and painted in the closing chapters of the Book of Revelation. 'Are you the one who is to come, the one who will bring salvation, the one who will open the door – or should we wait for someone else?' John the Baptist asked. 'Look at the evidence,' said Jesus; 'the sick are healed, the dead raised, the poor have good news brought to them.'[16] Jesus pointed to eternal reality in everything he did and said; and he trained and commissioned his disciples to do the same – 'as the Father has sent me, so I send you. Go. Go everywhere. Get on with it. Open the door. Invite them in. Teach them and train them. Then send them; and the whole thing will get bigger and bigger, like a tiny seed growing into a big tree, a tree where great flocks of birds will be able to come and make their nests.'[17] Keep your minds on the big picture, and everything else will fall into place.

We, like Jesus, are people with a purpose. We are to do all of the above, remembering always that these things are signposts not destinations, means not ends. Our purpose is to proclaim the good news of the kingdom of God in our context, bearing constantly in mind that everything we do is prophetic – it speaks of something bigger than itself. This is our task as disciples of Jesus; it is the task of the church. Our church communities are intended not just to keep us afloat in a stormy world, but to point the way to a different one. They are living advertisements for the kingdom of God, places where things are done in a different way; a church is a 'future in advance' community, as Graham Cray puts it, 'a community modelling and ministering an imperfect foretaste of the new heaven and the new earth.'[18]

This is such a radical concept that Michael Frost has coined a new term for it – 'communitas', or community with a purpose. Christian community, he suggests, results from the greater cause of Christian mission; it is a community in action, a community with a mission that lies beyond itself, a community that takes risks. Any community has to be about something if it is to be sustainable; and what the church is about is sharing the good news of Jesus Christ. If we leave out the action, we end up with something more like a support group, a pseudo-community; something which becomes inward-looking, disconnected from daily life, ineffective and, let's face it – boring.[19] This, perhaps, is one of the reasons why people leave churches.

We have known all along that the raison d'etre of the church is mission – sharing the good news of Christ, feeding the hungry, clothing the naked, visiting the imprisoned, working for justice. It is in the service of these goals that we will find communitas with our fellow workers – Michael Frost.[20]

Keeping hold of the why

If we have been trained to proclaim the good news in word and deed, and to do that by living as members of a prophetic and priestly community in our own particular context, we will need to discern what that means in practice in each place. It is no use opening a Messy Church if there are no children living in your village. It would be a pointless gesture to start a Food Bank, as one earnest church member wished to do in her affluent Oxfordshire parish, if there is no one in the community suffering from material hardship. Street Pastors would probably not be perceived as a prophetic ministry in Sidmouth, where the average age is 62 and everyone goes to bed early; and Healing on the Streets is unlikely have the impact in an isolated rural community that it might enjoy in a busy commercial setting. There are many wonderful initiatives out there; but the key question is the one asked by Alex Pease in the materially wealthy but relationship-poor Itchen Valley: where is the pain in *this* community? What is the purpose of the church in this *particular* place among these particular people with these particular needs? What does it mean to live prophetically *here*? How do we get their attention, what would be the doorway that would open up the possibility of the kingdom of God for the people amongst whom we find ourselves living? Perhaps indeed that is the reason for the different emphases of the gospel writers – they were writing for different contexts.

One of the most successful initiatives in the UK in recent times has been the Fresh Expressions movement which developed from the Church of England report *Mission-Shaped Church* published in 2004. Each 'fresh expression of church' has a deliberate outward focus: it is 'is a form of church for our changing culture, established primarily for the benefit of people who are not yet members of any church.' In other words, a fresh expression is not simply a new way of being church for existing churchgoers, it is an intentionally missionary, outward-looking initiative. A fresh expression of church, the website explains, 'will come into being through principles of listening, service, incarnational mission and making disciples,' and 'will have the potential to become a mature expression of church shaped by the gospel and the enduring marks of the church ... for its cultural context.'[21] A fresh expression of church is by its very nature a community with a purpose, aiming to reach out to those with no church background in a way which connects with their own life experience, introducing them to Jesus and inviting them to enter into the kingdom of God. Discipleship is necessarily at the heart of this invitation: 'the salvation we proclaim is simultaneously a call to life-long discipleship because the offer of Christ's salvation is inseparable from his call to follow.'[22] Some fresh expressions of church are short-lived, and many fail to meet the criteria laid down by George Lings of being both missional and ecclesial. But many have become strong, independent fellowships of disciples of Jesus, and since the movement began it is estimated that the equivalent of four new dioceses have been added to the Church of England alone through these new fellowships. Perhaps the most interesting feature of the new churches is that 40% of them are led by lay people with no formal training or diocesan authorisation: they are 'apprentices learning skills as they go,' George Lings notes. Discipleship, we have observed, is a form of apprenticeship undertaken in community. The website tells their stories.[23]

Fresh expressions are at the small and experimental end of the church spectrum. At the other end are the larger, established churches. In such a setting it is not too difficult to remember that our calling is to make disciples; it is less usual to remember that one of the key tasks of a disciple is to recruit and train other disciples. It is easy to feel successful if you belong to a church of hundreds – and yet if it lacks a constant missionary purpose such a church is little more than a religious club, not in real terms a church at all. 'We feel we are making a difference because we are so important to ourselves – but what we've really done is create a ghetto that is easily dismissed by the rest of society,' warns Bob Briner, author of the splendidly titled *Deadly Detours – Seven Noble Causes that Keep Christians from Changing the World.*[24] 'The fill and spill technique won't work,' affirms church leader Alan Scott, 'we need scattered servants – people who carry the anointing awkwardly, insensitively maybe, but carry it.' The key, for members of larger churches as for pioneering missionaries planting new ones, is the one given long ago by Paul to the Ephesians: the primary task of our church leaders is not to minister to church members but to train those members to minister to others, both in the church and in the world – 'to equip the saints for the work of ministry.'[25] Whether you are part of a radical outreach community or an established traditional church, the task is the same – to become a community which makes, trains and sends disciples out into the world to invite other people into the kingdom of God: to be living stones built into a spiritual house, ministering as a holy priesthood.

There are as many ways of doing this, of course, as there are church contexts, and given that contexts themselves change all the time, so must we be prepared to change. When Roger and I first arrived at Holy Trinity Leicester, back in 1990, we found a congregation of some 700 people, including a thriving Sunday school, inhabiting a beautifully and recently reordered building. The church had come a long way – from near closure to stability and growth. Many people had given sacrificially to fund the building project, inspired by vicar John Aldiss's vision of making it fit for a missional purpose – a building which would offer the facilities needed to enable the congregation to reach out to the city. And yet many of the stakeholders of the church, the very people who had funded the building project, were comfortable with things as they were. They belonged to a stable network of home groups, and their children were well taught in Sunday School; they were willing for new people to join, but they had no desire to play any personal part in inviting them to do so – and certainly no desire to see things change. Most had been brought up in Christian families; few had found faith through the ministry of the church.

After a few false starts it was decided that the home group system would be replaced by 'cell' groups – groups whose aim was not simply pastoral but avowedly missional. Instead of the staff sending newcomers to join the existing home groups (usually Christians new to the city, who had found us simply because of our size and location), the cell groups would make their own contacts, taking opportunities to share their faith with friends, colleagues and neighbours.[26] We supported the cell groups in lots of different ways: we provided user-friendly session notes; we ran easy access, multimedia events on life issues of common concern to which members could invite their friends; we expanded our healing prayer ministry training; we put on Alpha courses; we organised creative prayer days at which everyone could pray for some aspect of the church's mission and ministry; we planted a church in a pub. Some of the cell groups began to specialise – focussing on young mothers, on football matches, on students, on people in their twenties, on teenagers and their friends. Fifteen years later nearly everyone belonged to a small group of some kind, and the groups themselves were running a constant stream of Alpha courses, with many coming to faith. The church had become genuinely outward looking – and as a by-product, very diverse.

Meanwhile the city itself was changing. More prosperous, itself more diverse, with whole areas being redeveloped, new people groups moving in, a new football stadium, an expanding cultural quarter and many new opportunities, Leicester is an increasingly vibrant place to live. In 2008 we moved on, and John McGinley took over as vicar, leading the church into yet another new phase in its life. Recognising that the cell groups needed a new challenge, John introduced the concept of 'mission-shaped communities', encouraging each group to identify a particular mission focus – a particular neighbourhood, a network, or a special interest – and to link with others sharing that focus. The church website now lists seventeen mission-shaped communities or MSCs, some of which have grown naturally out of the existing groups, some of which are new, but all of which are 'united around a similar missional heart, focus or calling in life'; each one functions as a form of extended family. Holy Trinity is not alone; missional communities are becoming an established way for larger churches to ensure that they do not become 'anorexic', need-meeting or success-driven: that the discipleship of their members retains an outward focus.[27]

Fresh Expressions and Missional Communities are just two examples of networks which help contemporary churches to overcome the separation which so often exists between the church and the world by engaging prophetically and effectively with their communities. Many community projects have been undertaken by churches in recent years; perhaps the best known are Healing on the Streets, Street Pastors, Food Banks and Christians Against Poverty debt counselling, all now offered by local churches and church networks all over the country.[28] Other projects are constantly emerging: in 2013 a group of churches in Southampton made a joint commitment in to try and find homes for every child waiting for fostering or adoption; within a year seventy families from those churches had come forward as potential adoptive parents, and church networks in Reading and elsewhere have now made a similar commitment.[29] There are many other initiatives, supported by various specialist agencies, which help local churches find ways of engaging prophetically with their communities.[30]

All the signs are that it's working. The media delight in offering us bad-news stories about declining, ineffective and closing churches. But a recent cross-denominational survey, *Church Growth in Britain 1980 to the Present,* states: 'It is a truth almost universally acknowledged that Christianity in Britain is in decline. However, not all universally acknowledged truths are actually true. *Some* churches in *some* regions are declining, but this volume shows that substantial and sustained church growth has *also* taken place across Britain over the last 30 years. This growth is large-scale; it is occurring across a wide geographical range; it is highly multi-cultural in its social reach; and it shows no sign of slowing down.'[31] The model Jesus laid out, of making disciples, forming them into communities and sending them out to share the good news with others still works – if we want it to.

Blueprints or fingerprints?

Fresh Expressions and Missional Communities offer recognised ways of being intentional in our discipleship. But there are lots of surprising one-off initiatives too, things which cannot be categorised, things often which were not planned – things which suggest that perhaps it's not so much blueprints as fingerprints we are after. "This is the finger of God," the magicians warned Pharaoh as they tried and failed to replicate the third plague which came upon the land of Egypt after Pharaoh refused to let the people of God leave the country. "If it is by the finger of God that I cast out the demons," said Jesus, "then the kingdom of God has come to you."[32] We live in a world which likes the simplicity of blueprints, where we are tempted to try here what worked there. Jesus wants us to live more on the edge than that, so that we will be constantly surprised not by the success of our own efforts but by the unexpected involvement of God. Our task is to join in with what God is already doing, to look for his fingerprints in our midst. As Bishop John Taylor wrote more than forty years ago now:

The chief actor in the historic mission of the Christian church is the Holy Spirit. He is the director of the whole enterprise. The mission consists of the things that he is doing in the world ... We must relinquish our missionary presuppositions and begin in the beginning with the Holy Spirit. This means humbly watching in any situation in which we find ourselves in order to learn what God is trying to do there, and then doing it with him.[33]

John Taylor was writing just as a wave of spiritual renewal began through the Church here in Britain, starting in the late 60s and growing through the 70s and 80s. A deepening excitement seized the newly 'charismatic' wing of the church as people began to experience the power of the Holy Spirit flowing through them as they prayed and ministered in new and more immediate ways to others. Richard Hare, the first avowedly charismatic bishop in the Church of England, once told me that even as it was happening, the leaders of the charismatic movement were wondering what exactly God had in mind; why this, why now, after so long?[34] As the years have gone by and the ministry of healing and deliverance has once again become widespread, the answer now seems clear: spiritual renewal is not an end in itself, but a preparation for mission. Those churches which enjoyed the spiritual awakening but failed to connect with their communities have mostly now lost their enthusiasm; those which recognise the gifts of the Spirit as the tools of mission have grown into a new understanding of their calling. "Stay here in the city until you have been clothed with power from on high," Jesus told his disciples as he prepared to leave them; "you will be baptized with the Holy Spirit not many days from now." 'And when you make disciples, you must baptise them in turn, in the name of the Father and of the Son and of the Holy Spirit.' With the Holy Spirit, we are able to discern God's purposes, make wise decisions, pray passionately and faithfully, and minister effectively.[35] Without the Holy Spirit, we are just a movement of men and women, meeting in dead-end communities and striving, mostly unsuccessfully, to run a human recruitment drive. Even godly initiatives such as Alpha and Back to Church Sunday, whilst undoubtedly enabling many people to connect or reconnect with church, often fall short of their potential; mostly, one suspects, because they offer inviting advertisements for a kingdom reality which does not in fact, in the local church in question, yet exist.[36]

Permanently in a pickle

In January 2014 I was invited to speak alongside Mick Ellor at the annual conference of the Fellowship for Parish Evangelism. Mick began by telling his story. Brought up in the backstreet slums of Birmingham, he left school at fifteen, was apprenticed to a pattern maker and eventually qualified as a mechanical engineer. He and his wife Jan became Christians through the baptism of their children, and at the age of forty Mick was called to ordination. Mick is a humble man, constantly surprised to find himself caught up in the purposes of God. But Mick understands about apprenticeship; he learns as he goes along, and he trusts the Lord to lead him.

In 2009 Mick was asked by the Bishop of Stafford if he and Jan would be willing to leave their burgeoning ministry in Stoke and move to the village of Branston, home of the famous pickle.[37] It wasn't an inviting prospect; there were three in the morning congregation and seven in the evening, and the cobwebs in the building told their own story. "If you can't grow it," the bishop said, "we will have to close it." Mick and Jan went reluctantly to visit. "It will be fine, we'll turn it round," Mick heard himself saying reassuringly to the church wardens – alarming himself with his own words. But Mick has experience of trusting God. 'The message of the gospel comes to us not in word only, but also in power and in the Holy Spirit,' Paul had written to the new Christians in Thessalonika; 'God will make you worthy of his call and will fulfil by his power every good resolve and work of faith.'[38] This had been true in Stoke, Mick reflected; and so he and Jan moved to Branston.

Arriving in Branston with no clear plan, Mick found some encouraging signs: the church had just held a holiday club. So Mick and Jan began a children's work. In Stoke, once voted the worst place to live in England, they had seen God grow three churches with a stream of people not just coming to faith but going on to train as ministers themselves. In the process Mick had acquired a rather dynamic understanding of church; and as they settled into Branston he began to wonder what he could do to raise the profile of the church in the village. Church bells, he thought, would be the traditional and obvious answer. Undeterred by the complete absence of either tower or bells, Mick got hold of a recording and a couple of speakers, and soon the village echoed with the rousing sound of amplified bells. Down in The Blacksmith pub one evening for a quiet pint, Mick was disconcerted to find himself being cross-examined by the publican. "Hey, are you that bloody vicar that's got them bloody bells ringing on Sunday morning?" "Yes, I am," said Mick. "Well," said the publican, advancing on him, "let me shake your hand! They're bloody marvellous!" How many complaints have there been, Mick reflects? Just one. People are perplexed about what's going on, and for Mick that's the key. "The question is," he asks, "are people perplexed where *you* are? Doesn't matter how you do it, but get them asking questions about you!"

Mick continued his assault on expectation by preaching thirty minute sermons. He spent time in the pub, spent time visiting people, spent time helping those who came to him. A woman asked him to bless her house – she'd been into witchcraft for ten years, but failed to mention that. They ended up casting various spirits out of her, including once in church when a demon manifested itself and people were understandably alarmed – but it moved them on, they began to grow in their understanding, Mick says, just as the first disciples of Jesus had grown. Another woman attempted suicide during a midweek communion service, taking an overdose just before the service and collapsing as she came up to receive the bread and wine. They got her to hospital, visited her, spent time talking it through.

She's now the church secretary. "It's not easy, growing churches," Mick warns.

Meanwhile they were running Alpha courses and continuing to proclaim the good news of Jesus. An old man called Bill saw what God was doing and left twelve thousand pounds to the church; they took out the pews in an evening, put in chairs, and invited the local school in. It was the first time the children had ever come into the church – they now get all 460 pupils in at Christmas and Easter, in two sittings. From the small number who had helped take out the pews, numbers of men attending regularly grew to thirty; they got hold of a marquee and Frank and Jason began to organise curry nights. A gift day raised a further £23,000; they created an office and a children's area and appointed a youth worker. The congregation continued to grow, mostly through conversion; 78 adults and children now come to the morning service, another 30 or so in the evenings, and they are seeking God's will about enlarging the building. In just five years, five people have undertaken training for lay ministry. Closure, it seems, is no longer on the agenda.

Humanly speaking there is nothing special either about Mick and Jan or about the people of Branston. If you ask Mick about himself he will tell you, 'I'm just a lad from the back streets of Birmingham, trying to work my way to heaven.'[39] What Mick does understand, though, is that as disciples of Jesus we are apprenticed into a community – a prophetic community which exists to invite people into the kingdom of God. "If people come for baptism and they don't stay, it's our fault," Mick says.

Celtic Connexions

In March 2012 I found myself in Langport, Somerset, to give one of a series of Lent talks. There I heard about Celtic Connexions. A few years ago a couple came to visit Hugh Ellis, then the rector of nearby Huish Episcopi: would he take their wedding? It would be good to have it on 1st May, which is the Festival of Beltane, in the picturesque Church-in-the-Field in Low Ham, and would it be all right if their guests came dressed appropriately for the occasion? As Hugh listened he felt a strong spiritual connection with the couple, who turned out to be key figures in the networks associated with the multi-faceted spirituality of Glastonbury. Talking about the love of God and illustrating it through the story of the prodigal son, he asked if he could pray. They assented with enthusiasm; as he completed the prayer one was tearful and the other said 'I feel like I've come home.' The wedding took place, with guests variously dressed as knights templar, green men and druid priests, and of course Hugh in his white cassock alb and colourful stole. It was, Hugh felt, the strongest spiritual marriage service he had ever experienced.

At the reception, which took place in the couple's garden, surrounded by religious symbols of all kinds, the groom invited Hugh into a thatched hut where he saw a cross, images of Jesus and other Christian symbols. Asking again if he could pray, Hugh invited the Holy Spirit to fill the groom and his wife, asking that they might become channels of God's love and grace. Again deeply moved, the groom asked if Hugh would consider holding a fortnightly service in the Church-in-the-Field for them and their friends. They would like the service to include the teachings of Jesus, and not so much talk about God as the opportunity to experience God – with time for questions and prayer. The first Celtic Connexions service took place on 31st August 2008, with the subtitle 'the lost teachings of Jesus'. It was attended by a mix of spiritual seekers and Christians from different traditions; there was a presentation on a Celtic saint, some Christian teaching from his life, and a song from a harpist. As the weeks passed, some from this network of spirituality seekers had mystical experiences – a dream of a being of light, visions of Jesus and the cross, an experience of unconditional love. Some began to talk about 'Christ-consciousness', and to describe themselves as 'intuitive Christians.' The service became more of 'a spiritual event', Hugh says, than a church service. It has grown, with a mix of friends from the network and Christians attending; numbers range from 25 to 55. For the traditional Christians the services have been moving, with some experiencing prophetic visions – including one of the church ceiling being replaced by heaven and a golden waterfall flowing down and out of the door, and one of a well of water seeping up from beneath the flagstones and also flowing out of the door. Hugh has now moved on to a new post in Buckinghamshire; but Celtic Connexions still meets in the Church-in-the-Field.[40]

That of course is not the end of the story, for Langport is part of a team ministry which includes a number of smaller villages, among them Muchelney, scene of the infamous flooding in 2014, when the church became the focal point of the stranded village, acting as a centre for everything from prayer to groceries. Team vicar Jane Twitty explained: "The church has become the real hub of the village, open 24 hours a day, storing the post and food, and offering hot drinks to the firefighters who are manning the boats in and out of the village." Regular Sunday services continued, with an increased congregation; lunch was served after the service so that people could talk and share stories. On the first Sunday of the flooding, villagers made models of all the homes in the village and left them on the altar for prayers. "We've really come together at the church," said Richard England, whom other residents described as an unofficial spokesman for the community, "getting food and post distributed, helping the elderly."[41] In the summer they serve tea and cake; I dropped in after a walk along the banks of the Parrett, and heard one woman explain to another, "I've never really been a regular churchgoer – but during the floods, we all went." One year on cars still line the streets around the church on Sunday mornings.

'I believe a fitting description for the church would be this,' writes Robert Lewis: *a community of people who offer living proof of a loving God to a watching world.*'[42] In Robert's urban, American context that means a network of church-based small fellowship groups engaging in a wealth of community projects. Here in rural Somerset it turns out to mean sharing the lost teachings of Jesus with a network of spiritual seekers, acting as a community hub in times of crisis, or...

Singing God's song

Mission means inviting all the people of the earth to hear the music of God's future and dance to it today – Christopher Wright[43]

There are many ways of imagining what it's like to be part of a living community with a clear purpose. Jesus compared his disciples to the branches of a vine, joined to him and expected to bear fruit. Peter likened the church to a temple, built of living stones and called to minister to the world. Another way of understanding what it means to be disciples of Jesus drawn into community for a purpose which goes beyond the needs of that community is to think of music.

The harmony of music is a constant refrain through the scriptures. The psalms in particular express the relationship between God and his people through the metaphor and practice of song: the singing of praises, of thanks and blessing, of memories, of laments and entreaties. Music was a mark of the early church too: 'Sing psalms and hymns and spiritual songs when you meet together,' Paul urges the disciples of Ephesus and Colossae.[44] Today church remains one of the few places where people still sing together, a tradition which has been preserved not least through the Wesley brothers' insistence on the importance of collective, scriptural, sung worship.

Why should we sing together? I have understood this most vividly in Africa, where music is still something you make, not

175

something you listen to; something which expresses the joys and sorrows of a community; something which can be used to remind the singers of the mercy of God and to help them draw more closely into his presence. I stood once in the darkness which surrounded a fire of leaping flames, as the newly baptised members of a church in a remote area of Zambia sang – they sang the gospel, for being unable to read and write they had set the words of scripture to music. They sang, old and young, not in melody as we sing, but in multi-part harmony; in Africa even the smallest child seems able to sing in harmony. I have paused outside a makeshift tent erected for a Rooted in Jesus conference in a dusty Tanzanian town, listening to the newly reconciled pastors and bishop sing together – a song this time of eerie lament, a song of lilting pain, a song which helped them travel from a divided past into the dawn of a new future. They came late to the session next morning – they had continued singing and praying together until 3 am. Down in Masasi, by the Mozambican border, I have been kept awake by catechists celebrating their first shared meeting by learning a newly composed song from one of their fellows. There too I rejoiced in a closing eucharist where those same, white-robed catechists produced a soaring harmony which rivalled any professional western choir – perhaps the most beautiful singing I have ever heard. I have even fallen asleep to the pounding, rising, jumping singing of the Masai, deep and resonant, both united and yet aggressive, stretching the potential of each man, binding them together into a community and pouring the traditions of their tribe into a public declaration of faith. Song does many things – but always it is about relationships.

Something, we know not quite what, binds our universe together. Often that something has been likened to music, as

Pythagoras suggested long ago when he talked about the music of the spheres; for everything in the universe is held together by the mathematics which also governs pitch and sound. Perhaps the world is a multi-part harmony sung by God, with every creature weaving its own melody into the whole. For us too, music is a way of weaving our individuality into a harmony which becomes far more magnificent than our own contribution, a harmony which is not just there for our own enjoyment but becomes a concert for the benefit of the outsider, another foreshadowing of the kingdom – an eternal kingdom where day and night without ceasing there will be song.[45] Music is a way of acknowledging our limitations, and simultaneously a way of merging with the harmony that holds the world together; it is the thread which weaves individuals into communities and reminds us that we have come together for a purpose – a purpose which is expressive and public and inclusive. We sing because we have something to sing about, and we are called to sing about it together. Pastor Rob Bell talks about living in rhythm with God and the world he has made, each adding our own note to the orchestra of life. Composer James MacMillan talks about an 'umbilical link' between music and the sacred. Scottish Jesuit John McDade suggests that music is the closest we come to the mystery of grace. Music helps us, somehow, to see that we are part of something bigger and more beautiful than we could otherwise imagine.[46]

'That [which] we cal gospel is a greke word, and signyfyth good, mery, glad and joyfull tidings, that maketh mannes hert glad, and makyth hym ssynge, daunce, and leepe for joy,' William Tyndale wrote. William knew what it was to rejoice in the good news of Jesus, singing and dancing and leaping for joy, and he spent his life making that good news available as widely as possible – he was the author of the first complete translation of the Bible from Hebrew and Greek into English. And yet William's singing was not always joyful; William knew that sometimes we sing in pain as well, for nothing comes without a cost, and William paid for his translation with his life. "If any want to become my followers," Jesus had said, "let them deny themselves and take up their cross and follow me." And this brings us to the fourth mark of discipleship: for discipleship is about community and about purpose – but it is also, rather unfashionably, about suffering.

Community with a purpose

Once *Rooted in Jesus* group members have been encouraged to make their own personal commitment to following Jesus, they learn first to apply his teaching to their own lives and then to engage in active, Spirit-dependent ministry to others. They are then invited to think about the needs of their communities, and to begin to pray specifically into those needs. One of the interesting features of the feedback we receive is the wide variety of responses; each group seems to identify its own purpose, its own way of being a prophetic community in its particular context. Here are some examples:

Caring for orphans in Luapula, Zambia

"For quite a while now, a local pastor has been trying to find ways to help the really needy members of his village. As the discipleship groups have been meeting, people have begun to work together. Members of different churches who would previously not even greet each other are coming together and beginning to seek ways to bring hope and relief to their villages. The ideas that one pastor had are all of a sudden becoming reality as many people are motivated to make a difference. Between them, the groups are looking after about 160 orphans, finding ways to raise money to pay for their food and education. New discipleship groups are springing up in the area, some in very remote villages and even one amongst the compound children. Many, many more people are getting the chance to find out more about Jesus."
Jon Paul Witt, Dignity Worldwide, Zambia, June 2011

Tackling street violence in Cape Town

"Recently, I had a conversation with Fr Donny, Rector of the Church of Reconciliation, Manenberg, about how *Rooted in Jesus* was doing in his parish. Fr Donny shared with me the following testimony: "As you know, the gangs were doing warfare and shooting innocent people. As a result, all of our schools in the area were closed. The people of my church, in particularly those leaders who were a part of the RinJ training and the RinJ groups, approached me to do something about the gang shootings. They decided to come together and pray. Then they were going to go out ... to distribute soup and bread, to talk to the gangs and to even pray with some gang members. They took to the streets, demonstrating with placards, singing choruses and praying. The group went on to invite other clergy to join them; and eventually, along with Archbishop Thabo, they held talks with the gang leaders to work out a ceasefire. Now the schools have re-opened. People have the freedom and safety to walk in the community, and RinJ groups have started to meet again." To me, Fr. Donny's testimony is an awesome celebration of what God is able to do when He uses ordinary people to do extraordinary things when they are 'Rooted in Jesus'."

Amanda Ohlsson, Rooted in Jesus Facilitator, Growing the Church, South Africa, September 2013

Providing community support in Niassa, Mozambique

"*Rooted in Jesus* is the basis for all our ministry and mission training, supporting as it does our diocesan vision to 'become a communion of communities in Jesus', ie small groups studying, discipling one another, church planting and rooting, growing in faith and changed lives together. See the guys at the back of this photo? The green caps are 'adeptos' for the Equipa da Vida teams [Life Teams] - growing at a great rate because so active, a real focus for youth to join, and now our integrated mission approach to development around the diocese. One of their jobs as adeptos is to teach RinJ where they are, alongside our Bible study method in small groups, and other pastoral areas. There are now 325 teams in our 504 congregations, and each member of a group looks after 10 families in their community in terms of orphan support, water provision, health, HIV awareness and support of long term sick, etc. Even Muslims have joined in with the community activities in places, and 2 churches have been planted by these teams! In 5 years, our churches have almost doubled to around 500, as have our priests to 45, and there are now around 65,000 members of our church in northern Mozambique! The excitement of being church is palpable."

Revd Helen Van Koevering, Director of Ministry, Diocese of Niassa, Mozambique, September 2010

Priests and 'adeptos' of the Diocese of Niassa

Never doubt that a small group of thoughtful, committed citizens can change the world. indeed, it is the only thing that ever has –
Margaret Mead

Community with a purpose – a group study

1. What do disciples of Jesus do?

Matthew, Luke and John seem to have different priorities in their discussion of what it means to be a disciple of Jesus. Consider the following verses, each of which offers an example of an emphasis unique to that particular gospel:

- "I was hungry and you gave me food, I was thirsty and you gave me something to drink, I was a stranger and you welcomed me, I was naked and you gave me clothing, I was sick and you took care of me, I was in prison and you visited me." Matthew 25.35-36

- Then Jesus called the twelve together and gave them power and authority over all demons and to cure diseases, and he sent them out to proclaim the kingdom of God and to heal. Luke 9.1-2

- "By this everyone will know that you are my disciples, if you have love for one another." John 13.34

Roger Walton suggests that the differences are due to the different contexts for which these three evangelists were writing. He concludes that the commitment to follow Jesus who lived, died and rose again is the constant, but the pattern of discipleship is fashioned by the setting.

Which emphasis best fits your setting, and why? Would it be an effective way of proclaiming the kingdom of God to those who have not heard about it?

2. Five approaches to mission

The Anglican Communion has identified five 'marks of mission' – five pathways for a church to engage in mission to the world:

181

- To proclaim the good news of the kingdom
- To teach, baptise and nurture (new) believers
- To respond to human need by loving service
- To seek to transform unjust structures in society
- To strive to safeguard the integrity of creation

Which pathway is most appealing to you, and why? Can we do one without doing the others? How do we make sure we are doing these things prophetically, so that they are seen not as ends in themselves but as signposts for the kingdom?

3. Community with a purpose

"We can do nothing of any value to God, except in acts of genuine helpfulness done to our fellow men" – George Cadbury (1839-1922). What would Cadbury do if he lived in your village or city?

If you were to ask the members of your church what its purpose is, what would they say?

CHAPTER SEVEN

Take up your cross

The gate is narrow and the road is hard that leads to life, and there are few who find it.

Jesus, Matthew 7.14

Christians have bumper stickers and catchphrases. Believers have creeds and promises. Disciples have scars and stories.

Simon Guillebaud[1]

In Chapter 3 I suggested that four things seem to be true of those who first followed Jesus, and that these can still be taken as marks of discipleship today. Firstly, these men and women responded to Jesus by changing the direction of their lives, reorienting themselves by a different compass. Secondly, they were willing to be apprenticed to Jesus, learning as they travelled and putting into practice the things they learned in their everyday encounters with those they met. Thirdly, they learned not just as individuals but as part of a community, one which existed not for its own sake but for the sake of those who did not yet belong to it. And finally, they were willing to embrace pain, to accept that this was not a ticket to an easy life but a demanding commitment to a cause. "If any want to become my followers, let them deny themselves and take up their cross and follow me," said Jesus, somewhat uninvitingly.[2] For Peter, we know that a cross was exactly what he got. But what about the others? What exactly did Jesus mean, and what are we to make of it today?

Perhaps the best place to start is with the gospel of Mark, for like Matthew, Luke and John, Mark seems to have his own take on what it means to be a disciple of Jesus. If Matthew emphasizes society, Luke ministry and John relationship, Mark seems to be primarily concerned with cost.[3] Having introduced Jesus and the disciples, Mark turns his attention to the future implications of the events he is describing. He begins with the healing of the blind man at Bethsaida, in chapter eight. He ends with the healing of the blind man Bartimaeus at Jericho, in chapter ten. In between these two events he records what Jesus said to his disciples about his own life and death, and what that meant for those who choose to follow him – as if to say, before you did not see, and now you do. The man at Bethsaida had to be prayed for twice; Bartimaeus is healed instantly, and gets up to follow Jesus. Perhaps Mark is asking, 'What about you? How clear is *your* vision, and what is *your* response?'

The first of these uncomfortable conversations comes in chapter eight, where Jesus begins to explain that he will suffer, be rejected, be killed, and rise again. At this point he addresses not just the twelve but the entire crowd, warning that if they want to be his disciples they too must deny themselves, take up their cross and follow him. The incentive? "Those who want to save their life will lose it, and those who lose their life for my sake, and for the sake of the gospel, will save it." The second conversation comes in chapter nine, where Jesus again foretells his death, saying he will be betrayed, killed, and will rise again. The disciples did not understand, Mark says; and they were afraid to ask him – as well they might be, for what has been

184

uppermost in their mind in the meantime is which of them is the greatest. The cost for you, Jesus goes on undaunted, is that it is not status which awaits you, but service; this is not about privilege but about sacrifice, not about rising up the pecking order but about self-imposed deprivation. And then in chapter ten he tells them again, as they walk on the road to Jerusalem, what will happen to him when they get there: he will be mocked, spat at, flogged and killed. OK, think James and John, best to get the request in now, then – can we sit one each side of you when you are raised to glory? And Jesus spells it out again: "Are you able to drink the cup that I drink, or be baptized with the baptism that I am baptized with?" For this, he repeats patiently, is a race not to the top, but to the bottom. Are you ready for that? As they pass through Jericho, Bartimaeus is healed. The disciples now know what the issue is.

Are you sitting comfortably?

When I was little we didn't have a television, but we did listen to the radio, and one of my earliest memories is settling down to 'Listen with Mother.' Each episode started with a rendering of the Berceuse from Fauré's Dolly Suite for two pianos – music which even now settles me into a glow of happy anticipation – followed invariably by the immortal words "Are you sitting comfortably? Then I'll begin." The phrase, apparently coined ad lib by presenter Julia Lang, soaked pleasantly into the subconscious of an entire generation – so much so that

eventually it achieved its own entry in the Oxford Dictionary of Quotations. Sitting comfortably is what we like to do.[4]

We live in a culture which does its best to eliminate pain. Our newspapers are full of articles which encourage us to ensure, by the regular consumption of acai berries, konbu seaweed, beetroot juice, avocadoes, quinoa or pomegranates, that we will live happily and healthily ever after. Exercise of course is also important – fast exercise, or gentle exercise, or wobble-board exercise, will keep us fit, and there are all sorts of treatments available to help us further boost our physical wellbeing, from colonic irrigation to homeopathy to shiatsu. Whilst not attending to our health, we are encouraged to consider our safety. 'Health and safety' has become one of the signature tunes of Western society, so much so that, as one African bishop remarked to me, we have become paralysingly risk-averse. Conkers, yo-yos, Remembrance Day poppies, necklaces – all were banned from my children's primary school on the grounds that the children might hurt themselves; climbing trees is out, sunhats are in. Even in the adult world it is more important to stay safe than it is to enjoy ourselves: recent reports tell of a café in Bedfordshire where staff refused to pour hot strawberry sauce on a customer's ice cream, a dog show in Cumbria where officials outlawed Frisbee catching, and a village in Yorkshire where councillors ordered the removal

of knitted bunting – all for reasons of health and safety. And it's not just physical health which is important, of course; we wish also to live pain-free economically and socially. 'Boost for the economy as families have more to spend,' proclaim the headlines joyfully. 'Equation predicts happiness,' announce researchers.[5] If the equation fails, of course, almost any form of unhappiness can now be treated with medication, including fear of public speaking, a propensity to temper tantrums and, yes, worrying about your health.[6]

The problem is that although we may smile to ourselves at some of the more extreme manifestations of our self-indulgent and cautious culture, these values creep insidiously into our understanding of God. Here in Britain one of the most common questions posed by those thinking about faith is 'How can there be a God when there is so much suffering in the world?' The implication, as George Barna remarks, is that God 'exists for the pleasure of humankind. He resides in the heavenly realm solely for our utility and benefit' – to protect us from pain by keeping us healthy, wealthy and safe.[7] It's a question I have never heard asked in Africa, in fifteen years now of conversations and prayer with people who have suffered all their lives. 'Would you pray for us,' writes James Mayundo from the remote town of Kalémie in DR Congo, a country currently experiencing deep trauma. 'The problems that we are facing [include] the fear that we feel always, the rebellion in different areas of Congo, and the poverty that leads people not to live in peace and always to have a forlorn look and dim face.' On the other hand, he continues, 'we are receiving many testimonies from those who have joined the *Rooted in Jesus* groups – people are being built up in faith, the number of those attending church is increasing, and the love of the church members is becoming greater.' James, who follows a saviour who did not promise freedom from pain, sees no contradiction in these things. I once asked group leaders in Kibaya, Tanzania, how they had got on with the memory verses – was it hard learning them? "Very hard, very challenging," said one woman. Tell me, I said, my heart sinking. "Well," she said, "we were learning James 1.2-4, which says 'whenever you face trials of any kind, consider it nothing but joy, because you know that the testing of your faith produces endurance; and let endurance have its full effect, so that you may be mature and complete, lacking in nothing.' At the time our harvest had failed, we were suffering from famine, and we had only one meal a day to give our children. It was very challenging." I flushed with embarrassment at my naivety in assuming I could help people whose problems lie so far outside my own experience. But before I could say anything, she continued: "But the more we meditated on this verse, the more the Lord gave us peace." Jesus did not promise freedom from pain; he did promise to walk with us through pain.

There seems to be an enormous discrepancy between what Jesus taught his disciples and what we look for today in our determined quest for personal and national well-being. Where did we go wrong? Tom Sine suggests that the imagery of the good life and a better future that pervades Western society is born of the Enlightenment, which not only offered a compelling new myth to make sense of our world, but also offered us new imagery of the better future we are invited to come home to – a new secular salvation. 'Essentially, the storytellers of the Enlightenment took the vertical quest for God's kingdom and turned it on its side. It became the horizontal pursuit of Western progress, technological mastery and economic growth... We call this vision of a better future the Western Dream or the American Dream.' It's a dream, Sine suggests, which has become the driving myth behind a new global economic order; the marketers of our economy have become the brokers of meaning.[8]

This, alarmingly, is becoming true not only here in the Western world but even in places remote from our self-indulgent mindset. A year ago in Madagascar I found myself listening to a woman who wondered if I could explain to her why it was that although she had tried her best to be a good Christian, she still was not wealthy, when it had been preached to her so clearly that God rewards those who place their faith in him with prosperity? What was she doing wrong? We are disciples of Jesus; was Jesus wealthy, I asked? It was a thought that had not occurred to her.

And so it is that the assumptions of the world leak into the church, subtly changing our priorities, inviting us to sit comfortably and Listen with Mother. We have, as we saw in the last chapter, come perilously close to losing our sense of purpose, settling instead for being friendly. Perhaps we need to listen again to Jesus, to consider the possibility that we are to live as a prophetic community pointing the way to a kingdom which is not of this world; and that this may actually hurt. It's a good time to think about it, for there are signs that the Western dream is beginning to fade; even in the famously optimistic US a new pessimism is creeping in. President Barack Obama stumbles his way as he tries to capture the new mood, engendered by economic recession and natural disasters at home and by the daily spectacle of war in Ukraine, beheaded journalists in Syria, Ebola in Africa and dead children in Gaza: "Part of people's concern is just the sense that around the world the old order isn't holding and we're not quite yet to where we need to be in terms of a new order that's based on a different set of principles."[9]

"I came," said Jesus, "so that they may have life. Take up your cross, and follow me."

189

Hearing the bad news first

> Life's but a walking shadow, a poor player
> That struts and frets his hour upon the stage
> And then is heard no more. It is a tale
> Told by an idiot, full of sound and fury
> Signifying nothing.
>
> William Shakespeare

One pastor we spoke to recently estimated that half of those walking through the door of his church each week are in some kind of pain. Perhaps our determination to banish the spectres of ill-health and unhappiness from our lives is driven by the fear that we are not, if the truth be told, the authors of our own destinies; that despite the dutiful purchase of the antioxidant-rich berries, the assiduous pursuit of the exercise programme and the preventative removal of the dangerous knitted bunting, tomorrow could nonetheless bring a diagnosis of cancer, or the threat of unemployment, or the bust-up of a relationship. Humankind, as TS Eliot once remarked, cannot bear very much reality; and so we displace our fears onto something else, and miss the main point.[10] Life, thundered Macbeth as his dreams finally turned to dust, is a tale told by an *idiot*.[11]

Jesus, by contrast, offers no false promises: 'The rain and the floods *will* come, and the winds *will* beat against the walls of your house.' And if the situation is painful, the solution may be even more so: 'the gate is narrow and the road is hard that leads to life, and there are few who find it.'[12] This is not an easy message and, Jesus suggests to his disciples, it is not necessarily going to make you popular. The gospel, points out Frederick Buechner, is bad news before it is good news. Our task is not to cover up the pain and the apparent meaninglessness of life but to acknowledge it; our first message is not to be 'Cheer up,' but 'Yes, I know.' And that means we have to be ruthless with ourselves, acknowledging our own participation in this world of pain and being willing to make friends with our own suffering.

If [the preacher] does not make real to them the human experience of what it is to cry into the storm and receive no answer, to be sick at heart and find no healing, then he becomes the only one there who seems not to have had that experience because most surely under their bonnets and shawls and jackets, under their afros and ponytails, all the others there have had it whether they talk of it or not. As much as anything else, it is their experience of the absence of God that has brought them there in search of his presence, and if the preacher does not speak of that and to that, then he becomes like the captain of a ship who is the only one aboard who either does not know that the waves are 20 feet high and the decks awash or will not face up to it, so that anything else he tries to say by way of hope and comfort and empowering becomes suspect.[13]

This is a far cry from the glitter of the prosperity gospel, from the middle-class desire to have nice Christian friends, from untroubled participation in the fake world of pomegranates and fast exercise. Are we prepared to acknowledge the darkness before we offer the light, expose the void before we locate the life-saving rope, and challenge people to sit a little less comfortably as they consider what it is they are called to? Many people find it's easier to keep the cushions in place. Mark sounds the warning clearly – if it's comfort you are looking for, this is not for you.

Joe is the pastor of a small family church in a friendly but unremarkable English village. Joe has ministered sacrificially and consistently, caring for the church members and their children and running regular Alpha courses. All the original members, and their now adult children, continue to attend the church. And yet few of the many local people who have attended the Alpha courses have found a lasting faith. The problem seems to lie in Joe himself, something which happened to him long ago, something so painful that Joe has buried it and does his best not to think about. Many of those coming on Alpha also carry pain, and sooner or later that pain surfaces in the discussions. But Joe doesn't do pain. When the discussions uncover the angst in people's lives, Joe is the first to offer comfort and support, but he believes it would be cruel to expose the issue which is causing the pain. So he gives them a hug and sends them home. Unwilling to face his own agony, Joe is unable to help other people face theirs. Sooner or later they limp away, carrying their untouched lostness with them.

Bearing fruit in a desert landscape

> Blessed are those who trust in the Lord,
> Whose trust is the Lord.
> They shall be like a tree planted by water,
> Sending out its roots by the stream.
> It shall not fear when heat comes,
> And its leaves shall stay green;
> In the year of drought it is not anxious,
> And it does not cease to bear fruit.
>
> Jeremiah 17.7-8

I have long suspected that if the prophet Jeremiah were to visit his doctor today, he would be put straight onto anti-depressants; 'Jeremiah complains' is one of the more frequent subheadings in my Bible, and he is often referred to as 'the weeping prophet.' The message entrusted to Jeremiah was not a comfortable one, and it did not go down well in Jerusalem. 'This man ought to be put to death,' protested the city officials to the king, 'because he is *discouraging* us.'[14] But Jeremiah persisted, carrying out the Lord's instructions, remaining steadfast even when they burned his words and threw him into prison. "Are you able to drink the cup that I drink, or be baptized with the baptism that I am baptized with?", Jesus would ask his disciples some six hundred years later. Despite the complaints, Jeremiah's answer had been yes; and from his painful text come some of the best known lessons of scripture.

Jeremiah was prepared to deliver the message he was given because he believed it. He knew that the only way to live is to place your trust in God. The image he is given is a vivid one: even in a time of drought, a tree rooted in living water can produce green leaves and bear ripe fruits. The tree stands for each one of us. Pain comes both from the fallen world in which we live, and from the requirement placed upon us to turn away from the illusory comforts of that world and live as disciples of Jesus within it. However it comes, we are promised that we will be given the resources we need to grow.

A friend once gave my book *The Wild Gospel* to an experienced churchwoman. "Do I want to read this," she asked; "has she suffered?" It's a good question, for it is only when things go wrong that we find out who we truly are, only through our suffering that we grow. Out of chaos, God created the world. Out of chaos, he creates me, fashioning me like the potter the clay, refining me like the gold in the fire, chipping away at me like the mason the stone. I hang on

The Practice of the Presence of God

Brother Lawrence of the Resurrection (1614-91) was a lay member of the Discalced Carmelite Priory in Paris. Here he developed a series of spiritual exercises which could be practised in the context of ordinary life by any person, whatever their age, educational experience or social background. He called it the practice of the presence of God, and recommended five simple exercises:

1. Seek God's presence: Guard your heart with extreme care to retain purity
2. See God's presence: Keep the soul's gaze fixed on God by faith
3. Live God's presence: Do all for the love of God
4. Speak in the presence of God: offer short prayers to God
5. Treasure God's presence: value the presence of God more than anything

Brother Lawrence's teaching was written down after his death by Fr Joseph de Beaufort, and is freely available in English online. These five principles are laid out by Michael Frost in his book *Exiles*, pp 64-70.

in there; he comes to meet me, stamping his features into my character, renewing my spirit even as my body weakens and tires, pruning me like the vinegrower who attends to the vine, and so enabling me to grow the fruit of faith – love, joy, peace, patience, kindness, generosity, faithfulness, gentleness and self control (not all of which come naturally to me). He does this, as Jeremiah suggests, through the presence of the Holy Spirit within me, the living water which brings life to the parched soil of my disjointed experience.[15]

'My brothers and sisters,' James had written, 'whenever you face trials of any kind, consider it nothing but joy, because you know that the testing of your faith produces endurance, and let endurance have its full effect, so that you may be mature and complete, lacking in nothing.' James knew that the question is not will we suffer, but what happens when we do – will our pain draw us closer to God, or will it take us further away? 'The deep things of God are learnt in the fiery furnace of the desert,' Simon Ponsonby observes; 'it is here that he digs deep wells of the Spirit into our life.'[16] We are not to be afraid of the desert, but rather to make friends with our own pain and disappointment; for if we do not we will simply pass it on to others.

Once we have grasped these truths, God invites us to work with him, to take an active part in our own growth. He calls us not to be just passive recipients of his loving attention, not merely to cling to him through the vicissitudes of life, but to turn deliberately away from our worldly desire for comfort and actively to embrace the disciplines he commends to us. James had said that it is through suffering and pain that we grow; Paul recognised that this is true whether that pain

195

comes from outside or is imposed from the inside – suffering is not simply the grit in the oyster which forms the pearl, but also the tension in the rowing machine which strengthens the athlete's legs, the field exercises of the soldier which equip him for battle, the daily toil of the farmer which brings forth a harvest.[17] Disciples of Jesus, Dallas Willard suggests, must learn to live in a golden triangle of spiritual transformation – acceptance of life's problems, interaction with God's Spirit, and the exercise of willingly embraced spiritual disciplines – for only then will we shine like stars in a darkened sky, and only then will we bear adequate witness to this Jesus, and his offer of a different world.[18] A life of cushions leads to physical, emotional, moral and spiritual flabbiness; a disciple of Jesus must be willing to live uncomfortably.

Counting the cost

"If any want to become my followers, let them deny themselves and take up their cross and follow me" – Jesus, Mark 8.34

For six years Roger and I lived in a vicarage in Corby. Built in 1957 from the same yellow brick and with the same greened copper roof of the church next door, the house was noticeably different from the redbrick semi-detached and terraced houses which stretched up and down the street to each side of it. We had no immediate neighbours; to our left stood the Anglican church, to our right the Pentecostals, over the road a care home and a row of shops; the house was if nothing else conspicuous. A large delivery van drew up one day. Out got two men. One opened the back of the van, revealing the new double bed we had ordered, shiny in its plastic wrapping. The other, clipboard in hand, looked searchingly in every direction. Clearly bewildered, they paused for a moment in conversation, then eventually one went over the road and into the newsagents. I went outside to ask if there was a problem. "Is that the double bed for number 157?" I enquired, standing beside the gate post which clearly bore the number 157. An expression of astonishment crossed the remaining man's face. "Yes," he said, "but we didn't think it could be for the vicarage!" Was he thinking, I wondered, that we slept on beds of nails?

What did Jesus mean when he said that if anyone would follow him, they must be willing to deny themselves? Over the centuries there have been many different responses to this injunction, including not just sleeping on beds of nails, but wearing hair shirts, never washing, and practising regular self-flagellation. In their determination to escape the alluring comforts of the world, people have fled to the desert, taken up residence on top of columns, and lived as 'anchorites' walled up into single-celled dwellings. Others have eschewed these things – there is no need, CS Lewis once said, to give up the port and the cigars; Jesus himself, as the Pharisees noted to their disgust, was known to enjoy a good party.

If when he said we must be ready to take up our cross Jesus was talking about embracing physical suffering, then CS Lewis was certainly wrong. But although for Jesus self-denial certainly did result in great physical suffering, it was not primarily physical suffering that he was insisting upon. He did not say, 'let them deny their bodies', but rather 'let them deny themselves'; and when he spoke with individuals he spelt out in different ways what this would mean for them – for some their money, for others their family, for others their social status. For Peter it would in fact mean crucifixion, and for many Christians today following Jesus still means accepting the likelihood of physical suffering and even death. But that isn't the primary question. 'Count the cost,' Jesus advised his disciples; 'you must put your loyalty to me before everything – before your family, your possessions, your very life. This is not something to rush into, it's something to think about it very carefully. Imagine you are wanting to build a tower. You need to do your sums before you start, to see if you have enough money to complete it. Or imagine a ruler, facing the threat of invasion – he will be wise to count his troops, and if his enemy has twice as many, to sue for peace rather than declare war.'[19] Jesus is not asking us to manage without the double bed, he's asking us to surrender everything that we have and everything that we are to him. And he promises that, as we lose the safe and secure life we crave, we will gain one which is not only richer but will carry us into another world altogether.

This is a choice which I first made at the age of twenty-four, in a moment of sudden surrender so terrifying that it felt as though I were giving up my very name.[20] But as I look back over the thirty years which have elapsed since then, I find that this pattern of invitation and surrender is one which has recurred again and again. I am a birdwatcher, and God often opens the conversation by showing me birds. 'Do you see that buzzard,' he asked a few weeks before I finally surrendered my life to him, 'and the way it soars high above the earth, the way it can see the pattern of hedge and field, as you cannot? That's the difference between your view and mine – you are going to have to decide this on the basis of your own limited perspective.' And then, eight years later, 'Do you see that red kite, and the way it soars high above the hills, the way it can see the pattern of hedge and field, as you cannot? Are you ready now to come up here with me, and learn to see the world the way that I see it?'

A few months later, as I sat unsuspecting in a conference, I was suddenly overcome with the sweeping, personal presence of the Holy Spirit, and again God seemed to speak directly to me. 'If you would like to – and it really is entirely up to you – I invite you now to sign on this dotted line.' 'But the paper is blank,' I protested in horror. In that moment I realised that God was asking something of me, but wasn't going to tell me what it was; and once again I was terrified. Perhaps that is as good a way as any of thinking about what it means to deny oneself, take up one's cross and follow Jesus: it's the invitation to sign the dotted line at the bottom of a piece of paper which will be filled in only *after* you have committed yourself to it. I signed, and went home shaking with apprehension, thinking perhaps there was some mistake – for after all, I am just an ordinary Christian, not one of those special kinds of ones, ones that get called to things. But perhaps there is no such thing as an ordinary Christian; just ones who say yes, and ones who say no. God kept his side of the bargain: the kite moment led to the writing of *The Wild Gospel*, and the contract I signed

Robert gives up a promising career

Robert Madette is an evangelist and church leader in the Anglican Diocese of Morogoro, Tanzania. He told his story at a *Rooted in Jesus* Conference in March 2013:

"I was born in 1972 in a family which believes and practices traditional religion and at the same time they practice local medicine as witchdoctors. When I was Standard 3 in Primary School my father started to teach me to be a witchdoctor as the way forward for our family heritage. He taught me special medicine which used animal horns and charms called "mauyasa" or "kausha", which means 'dryer'. That kind of medicine has the power to kill, to create disease and to transfer disease from one person to another. If somebody caught the disease there was no possibility for any witchdoctor to give medicine and treat him until a person came to us with lots of money; then we treated. We performed the witchdoctor's traditional dance and I was leader of the team. On 10th November 1991 we were dancing as usual; nearby was a Christian conference which preached the gospel of Jesus. A leader came to us and said, "Why are you continuing to dance while the conference is going on?" We did not respond to him. The leader persuaded us to stop the dance. After the conference we were invited for night prayer in the church. The sermon came from Mark 16:15-16, 'Whoever believes and is baptised will be saved.' I started to cry and when they prayed for me the power of God touched me, then I was baptised. My father heard and became angry. I said Jesus saved me and set me free. His anger came twice, and through traditional gods and his medicine he cursed me. Myself I felt to have joy, peace. He did not want to see me or to communicate. I went up the hill to pray for four days. God anointed me with the power of the Holy Spirit and I was made very courageous. My love of God, my faith and my peace all strengthened. My Pastor gave me a church to lead and we prepared two conferences which God blessed, and 120 people were saved. I have experienced rejection by people, parents and leaders; but nowadays we communicate with my parents."

Robert is not paid for the work he does in the Church.

turned out to be an invitation to work with ReSource, which would not only take me all over the country but lead to the expansion of *Rooted in Jesus* across sub-Saharan Africa. I put in just one request, before I signed: 'Could we please take it just one step at a time?' I thought I might manage that.

Christian discipleship, Rowan Williams has remarked, is about moving into the space that is opened up for us by Jesus.[21] Slowly.

Discipleship in practice

If a commitment to following Jesus involves the willingness to make grand gestures of submission, it is also about the everyday practice of seeking to behave in a way which models the sacrifice of Christ to others. As Rowan Williams writes of Teresa of Avila, 'when you have finally progressed through all the hair-raising mystical experiences that she describes, what it's all finally about is enabling you to do some very ordinary things a little bit better. When you've been through the seventh mansion of spiritual union with God you're better at the washing-up.'[22] God may not ask you to travel as a missionary to the Far East; he may simply ask you to be yeast in the dough of your own ordinary environment.

Evelyn is a pensioner from a poor family in the Midlands, and she spends all her spare cash on family members. When her church had a gift day, Evelyn took her spare jewellery to a shop in town, and sold it. She put the entire proceeds into the collection plate.

Robert works in an office, and was asked to lead a team working on a new project. The team did not gel, and relationships became very tense. As Robert prayed one morning God showed him that if he himself were not willing to change, no one else would be able to do so either. Robert committed himself to pray for the team and for his role within it each morning, and found that he was given a patience and a love for his colleagues that he had not previously experienced. The tension disappeared – and some of the team members later accepted Robert's invitation to attend an Alpha course.[23]

Robin is a trainee evangelist in southern Madagascar. When a cyclone brought devastating winds and floods to the island Robin was forced to flee his home. Returning to a scene of absolute devastation, Robin found looters picking their way between what was left of people's houses, helping themselves to anything they could carry. Approaching his own plot, Robin found a man dragging away one of his roof panels. "That's mine," Robin said. "No," replied the man, "it was outside your boundary." Robin, desperate to rescue his family from homelessness, got into an increasingly aggressive argument with the man. Suddenly Robin remembered that he is a Christian, and that Christians are called to be people of peace – whatever the cost. He stopped threatening the man, and prayed. "Oh well, here you are then," said the man grumpily, instantly relinquishing the roof panel. Robin, like many others, attended a *Rooted in Jesus* conference held, as planned, just two weeks after the cyclone. Some delegates apologised for not bringing their Bibles – they had lost them, along with most of their other possessions, to the floodwaters; others apologised for arriving late – they had been forced to travel for two days along the coast in a sea canoe, the road having been washed away. Recent reports from the diocese (currently the youngest in the Anglican Communion) tell, perhaps unsurprisingly, of remarkable church growth.[24]

Working with *Rooted in Jesus* now in over 70 dioceses across Africa, I cannot help noticing that it is in the places where the pain, the poverty and the sheer danger of living is the greatest that people seem willing to make the greatest sacrifices – and find themselves witnessing the greatest growth. I have not met many English Christians like Georges, the non-stipendiary priest of Ranohira in the diocese of Fianarantsoa, who told us that he prays every day for his *Rooted in Jesus* group – "up there," he said, waving his arm, "on the mountain." On the mountain, we puzzled? "Look," he said, rolling up one trouser leg. Just below his knee was a large round callus, formed where he kneels on the ancient, bare rock to pray. Pain, it seems, is a catalyst for growth, whether it's about the response you make to a cyclone or the discipline you are willing to impose upon yourself.

Sometimes, of course, the ending is not a happy one. In the mid-1990s a fundamentalist Islamist organization gave an ultimatum to all foreign nationals in Algeria: depart or die. Nineteen priests and religious sisters, including eight

Cistercian monks from the monastery of Tibhirine, chose to stay in Algeria. These men and women understood their calling to be to continue to serve and love the ordinary people among whom they lived, themselves oppressed by the new Islamist violence. Each one intentionally committed his or her life into the hand of God, knowing that death was likely, but pledging to remain amongst those to whom they had been sent. Gunned down as they walked to Mass or went about their business helping local people in poor communities, mourned as much by the Muslim population they served as by their brothers and sisters in Christ, these men and women gave their lives as an expression of their Christian discipleship. Fr Chrétien de Chergé, Prior of the monastic community whose monks had made the pledge to stay, wrote these words as he waited for the inevitable abduction and assassination: 'I would like my community, my Church, my family to remember that my life was GIVEN to God and to this country.' Should the Cistercians return to Tibhirine, or would that simply endanger your lives?', the Abbot General asked the local Muslim people afterwards. The answer? 'Our lives were in danger anyway. But when you are absent we live them without hope. If you return we will live them with hope.'[25]

Little sacrifices, big sacrifices; sacrifices on which a new world is built. Would I have had their courage?

Raising the bar

It is clear that anyone considering committing his or her life to Jesus needs to realise that Christian discipleship is not

204

simply a route to a happier and more fulfilled life. If we are apprenticed to Jesus, we must be willing to become like Jesus: to give up our own hopes and plans, to be willing to wear holes in our knees and to go – or stay – where he sends us, and if necessary to die there. It's not just about joining in with the party (although it is that too, as Jesus often made clear) but also about carrying the cross.

What are the implications of all this for our own church communities? As church numbers have declined, often it has seemed sensible to lower the bar of our expectations, to focus on offering sensitive pastoral care, short affirming services and enjoyable social events. We need to make it easy for people to be part of the church, we increasingly feel; we must not place too many demands upon them, for after all they already have busy and difficult lives.

It is certainly true that in our culture people do not readily sign up to be either ignored or bored. And yet it seems that turning a tough option into a soft one does not lead to church growth either. Mick Ellor offers thirty minute sermons to his parishioners. John Wesley expected class members to live by a set of rules. The Chinese government has scarcely made it easy for its citizens to commit their lives to Christ. But in all these situations we see people respond not by leaving but by joining. Increasingly commentators are observing that the key to the growth of the church, and therefore of the kingdom of God, is to be found not in lowering the level of commitment required for membership, but in raising it. Have we, in our desire to make church attractive, in fact imposed unreasonably low expectations on our people and then lamented when they lived down to them, ask Packer and Parrett, as they call for a renewed emphasis on teaching the elements of discipleship?[26] Have our church youth work programmes been offering a great enough challenge to the young people they serve, for example, many of whom still leave church as soon as they reach adulthood – or is there a tendency to offer entertainment as a way of attracting and keeping them, rather than individual mentoring and discipling? Perhaps the answer lies in the observation of Rowan Williams that 'the young will not thank us if we keep them happy and distract them from being left naked before God – and yet that is often exactly what we do in our youth work.'[27]

We need, insists Mick Ellor, to stop selling an easy package; we should, says Neil Cole, founder of a network of 800 'simple' churches, lower the bar of how church is done but raise the bar of what it means to be a disciple of Jesus – if church is simple enough that everyone can do it, and if it is made up of people who take up their cross and follow Jesus at any cost, churches will become healthy, fertile and reproductive.[28] Perhaps instead of helping people to fit God round the edges of their identity we should invite them to recognise that the gate is narrow and the road is hard that leads to life, and there are few who find it, and ask them if they are up for that? And perhaps we should consider the possibility that this will mean that the future lies in the creation not of big impressive churches but of little knots of disciples mixed into the tangled wool of society, knots of people willing to train, to run, to face danger, to labour, toil and lose sleep, and to do all these things while knowing that they have been invited too to laugh, to sing and to dance with joy, for the secret of life is theirs.[29]

"Jesus," said Martin Cavender to a group of church representatives in Oxford, "is not looking for volunteers. He's looking for disciples."

Take up your cross – a group study

1. Embracing pain

As disciples of Jesus we are invited to:

1. Recognise that life hurts and, rather than seeking to deny it, allow the pain we experience to draw us closer to God
2. Be willing to impose pain on ourselves, enabling God to work within us through the voluntary acceptance of spiritual disciplines
3. Submit our lives to God, seeking his priorities and direction rather than our own

Which of these do you find the hardest? Share your experiences with the group.

2. 'Deep End Discipleship'

Greg Downes is the Director of the Centre for Missional Leadership. In an article in the October 2011 issue of Christianity Magazine, Greg proposed four practical outworkings of what it means to be Christ's disciple in the contemporary world:

1. Obedience
2. Holiness
3. Mission
4. Sacrifice

Which of these do you think presents the biggest challenge to us today?

Greg suggests that sacrifice is the missing ingredient in Western discipleship – do you agree?

3. Counting the cost

'If you want to win this world to Christ, you are going to have to sit in the smoking section' – Neil Cole

What does that mean for you?

CHAPTER EIGHT

Living in God's story

Narrative is our culture's currency. He who tells the best story wins.
Bobette Buster

"I'm not a child. I'm a boy called Ebwood," announced our son Edward at the age of two. Long before Ed could speak, we were reading him stories, and long before he went to school, he would sit with his books and read them to himself from memory. So familiar was he with the world of story that he began to see himself as a character in a story, a boy called Ebwood, narrating his own tale as he lived it. By the time he was three he was beginning to read for himself; but in that year between two and three, Edward became his own main character, annotating his part in an unfolding story. He would talk to himself, exclaiming "Oh crikey, Ebwood!" as the door banged, and adding narrative markers to his own observations as he offered them to us: "said Ebwood", "thought Ebwood" or "grumbled Ebwood." As his vocabulary increased, the narrative became more sophisticated: "Oh no, gasped Ebwood!", or "I don't want my coat on, muttered Ebwood!", or "We could have lunch in a tea shop, chuckled Ebwood." Sometimes the narrative was not simply stated but interpreted: "I'm not a bossy boy, spluttered Ebwood!", or "Get off my wall, muttered Ebwood to 'imself in a kind way" – as he addressed an intruding cat. At just two years old, Edward was putting himself into the story.

It comes naturally to us to think of our lives as stories, little stories which form part of the bigger story in which we are all caught up. Stories help us to make sense of life, to impose some kind of order on it, to begin to weave our own distinctive thread through its tapestry. "We tell ourselves stories in order to live," wrote author Joan Didion; "Either our lives become stories," suggested novelist Douglas Copeland, "or there's no way to get through them."[1] We only become who we are if, like Edward, we can somehow write ourselves into the story.

And yet this is not a simple task. "Humans have evolved to be storytellers," says psychology professor Dan McAdams, "but they develop in cultures... and our narratives are almost determined by culture."[2] To find our own part in the story, we have first to familiarise ourselves with the story. And most of us have little say in how that story is told; for the story already exists, penned by the collective voice of the world into which we are born. For us, with the explosion of connectivity which now characterises our society, there are many, many voices contributing to the story, all gathered, communicated and interpreted to us, instalment by instalment, through a constant stream of news bulletins, internet feeds, twitter accounts. The latest updates reach us everywhere: I go into my local bank, and face a television screen while I wait to pay my cheques in. I visit the doctor's surgery, and news is piped out by radio into the waiting room while a constant stream of information appears on the wall. When I receive a new phone, the first thing I have to do is deal with the news feed and decline its offer to keep me connected day and night with 'the things and people that matter most.' Whether we attend or whether we don't, the narrative is there: whispered, urgent, all-pervading. Often, we base our Sunday prayers upon it.

A few months ago Roger and I watched a fascinating programme about the London Blitz. Filled with original footage, it told the story of the bombardment of London, the fight to save St Paul's, the loss of people's homes, the crumbling of the streets and the morale boosting visits of the King and Queen to the East End. I was brought up in London, and my mother, now 87 years old, lived through the war there as a teenager – having chosen, with her brother, not to be evacuated. I told her about the programme. What was it like to live through all that, I asked? Did you know about the night spent by vergers with buckets of water on the roof of the cathedral, extinguishing firebombs one by one, fighting to save the soul of the city? What did that do to morale? Tell me the story. "Well," said my mother, "you have to remember that we didn't have television, so we didn't really know what was going on." And this in Enfield, just eleven miles from St Paul's. How different is our world now: a story that was once local, limited to a single suburb where you were your own newsgatherer, is now global. I know as much about the current outbreak of Ebola in Sierra Leone as my mother knows about the bombing of the City of London on a night she lived through, just eleven miles away.

We tend to welcome this constant media narrative as a good thing. In many ways of course it is – if I know of the crisis in Sierra Leone I am able to contribute in some small way to its resolution, and at the very least I can avoid going there. But in other ways it's not – for the story which is told to us in minute and frequent instalments, the story which presents itself as a factual account of the way things are, is in reality anything but. It carries its own hidden values and perspectives; it is not just a story but an interpreted story. As

210

Alain de Botton has remarked, the news machine 'fails to disclose that it does not merely *report* on the world, but is instead constantly at work crafting a new planet in our minds in line with its own often highly distinctive priorities.'[3]

The way the story is told, whispering not just facts but values, outlooks and judgments, deeply affects not just our own ability to find a meaningful role within it, but even the kind of role we think we are looking for. In silently appointing itself the arbiter of reality, the news has in fact become our Bible – a point elegantly made by de Botton, whose book *The News* comes in a white dustjacket, embossed in gold, with key points highlighted in red letters.

If de Botton is right, and the media narrative insidiously creates a world with its own distinctive priorities – priorities that may be far from those which Jesus wished to impart to his disciples – then what are they? In Chapter 3 I suggested that the consumerist framing story within which we live encourages us to believe that our needs will be met and our identities shaped not by recognising who we are in Christ but through the purchase of goods and services. Few of us are aware, futures consultant Tom Sine suggests, that life is so scripted for us, or that we may in reality be no more free and independent in our choices than the fictional Truman Burbank.[4] In Chapter 7 we looked at the way in which the story seeks to avoid pain and deny suffering, creating a world of self-indulgence and denial which makes it much harder for us to recognise and embrace the calling that God has placed upon our lives. These values creep into the hearts and minds of writers, broadcasters and commentators, emerging as a giant lens through which the events of our time are interpreted: creating, sustaining and constantly reinforcing the narrative of a culture.

Have you noticed, I often ask, the things which are *not* reported in the media (the many good news stories from Africa which do not fit under its typecast heading of 'suffering continent', for example); or why it is that local papers are often full of heart-warming stories of courageous individuals, new initiatives and remarkable accomplishments, while their national counterparts prefer to deal with the fall of celebrities, the decline of the economy and the threat of terrorism?

'Societies become modern, the philosopher Hegel suggested, when news replaces religion as our central source of guidance and our touchstone of authority. In the developed economies, the news now occupies a position of power at least equal to that formerly enjoyed by the faiths. Dispatches track the canonical hours with uncanny precision: matins have been transubstantiated into the breakfast bulletin, vespers into the evening report. But the news doesn't just follow a quasi-religious timetable. It also demands that we approach it with some of the same deferential expectations we would once have harboured of the faiths. Here, too, we hope to receive revelations, learn who is good and bad, fathom suffering and understand the unfolding logic of existence. And here too, if we refuse to take part in the rituals, there could be imputations of heresy.'

Alain de Botton, *The News – A User's Manual*, Hamish Hamilton 2014

And so it is that the consumer narrative becomes not just a force which shapes our individual values and choices but an overarching philosophy by which votes are cast and nations governed. Refracted and filtered through the lens of the media, it becomes a moral and political voice, forming our values and priorities as a society – values and priorities which mostly reflect neither the existence nor the nature of God. As Karl Marx observed long ago, the theologians who used to act as our guides for living have been displaced by the economists whose work now underpins the national and international policies of the Western world. They have, Roman Catholic theologian Tom Beaudouin suggests, created a new religion, one which he calls 'theocapitalism.' This is, he says, a spiritual discipline based on four laws: progress through rapid growth, security through possession and consumption, salvation through competition and freedom to prosper through unaccountable corporations.[5]

It is difficult to find any of these values in the teaching of Jesus. We continue to pay lip service to Christian values, but economic analyst Robert Nelson agrees with Marx: it is 'economists [who now] serve as the priesthood of a modern secular religion of economic progress.'[6] The sadness, of course, is that these faceless modern priests lead us not into a fulfilling and growing role in the grand scheme of things, but into confusion, anxiety and insecurity, into a world in which nothing is certain and where whatever we gain serves only to disguise what we have lost.

What does this look like in practice? Well, failure to examine the story in which we live and measure it against the story Jesus told leads to some puzzling national policies. We find ourselves, for example, in a world in which the supposedly Christian United States, our biggest economy, feels it appropriate to spend up to twenty-one times more on its military budget than it does on supporting the troubled regions from which the threats to its security come – a policy which has been described as 'redemptive violence.' Here in Europe we concrete over our landscape, exploit our environment and allow ever increasing inequalities between the rich and the poor – all in the pursuit of the hallowed economic growth which is by its very nature, in the finite system in which we live, unsustainable. It seems that policies covering everything from the environment to personal taxation are now subservient to the need to foster economic growth and boost individual spending power.

There is, suggests Brian McLaren, 'one great step we can take to dismantle the suicide machine and the framing stories that legitimize it: to stop believing in it, and to believe, in its place, a different story, the story of the kingdom of God.' We do not *have* to live in what's been called 'a 24-hour rolling soap opera where millions of us have a walk-on part.' [7] Jon Alexander, founder of the New Citizenship Project, insists that 'today we have a real choice. We can understand that the Consumer is a powerful moral idea, a pervasive meta role, and not just an inert piece of language. And then we can do something about it. We can reclaim a different morality, a bigger sense of what it means to be human. We can become participants in shaping the context of our lives, working together and expecting more of one another as we do so.' [8]

This is not a new challenge; we are not the first society to have lost touch with God and written our own story – in fact, the most cursory study of history suggests that, all things considered, we have preserved more Christian values than most. But it is the challenge of our times. How, in this context, can we best live as disciples of Jesus?

Living in God's story

*Conversion is not an event but a process, a process of slowly tearing
ourselves from the clutches of the culture*
– Shane Claiborne[9]

The Bible offers us a story, or more precisely a collection of
stories. The story begins at the beginning of time, with the
creation of the world. It ends at the end of time, with the
destruction and recreation of that same world. In between
these two events its pages are crowded with people, with life
and death, with success and failure, agony and ecstasy. Every
human emotion is contained within the story, every possible
response to the demands life throws up is written into its
pages. God speaks constantly into the story, guiding,
rebuking, explaining; and eventually he causes his son Jesus
to be born into the story – Jesus who continues to tell the
tale, and who invites his followers to enter into it in a new way.
It is the story of a people, the people of God.

I've always felt it is important to begin at the beginning,
and God appears to feel the same. The Old Testament starts
with pre-history, with those parts of the story which predate
written records. And a good story, I have always thought,
needs a proper ending. The New Testament ends with post-
history, with John's great visionary painting of the end of time
and the creation of a new world. These parts of the story lie

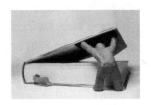

215

outside the reach of historical analysis; they are the endpapers within which the story is contained. In between them comes history, the unfolding of the centuries and a growing understanding of what it means to be, individually and together, called by God. The people of God have not, as is often noted by the critics of religion, always got it right; sometimes indeed they have got it spectacularly wrong. But that is as we would expect, for this is an honest story, a story not of gods and heroes but of ordinary, misguided people, trying (or sometimes not trying) to live by their faith in the midst of a difficult world. Their task is our task; their story is our story.

'To be a Christian,' theologian Stanley Hauerwas once said, 'is to learn to live in a story you haven't chosen.'[10] It has always been so, for the Bible is full of the stories of people who were expecting something else. Joseph, the youngest and favourite son in a family of sheep farmers, abducted and sold by his brothers, finds himself second in command over the whole of Egypt. Moses, who one day would write Joseph's story down, discovers that he is being asked to lead the people of God out of slavery, and then to take delivery of a new law code written on tablets of stone – odd, for Moses was an abandoned baby, a man who had killed another, a fugitive from justice; a man who when addressed directly by God protested that no one would listen to him and that even if they did he wouldn't be able to find the right words. God continues to offer key parts to unlikely people: Gideon, who protests that his clan is the weakest in his tribe and he the least significant member of his family, is appointed to lead an army against the Midianites. David, a boy shepherd, is called from his father's fields to become king of Israel; Esther, a young Jewish woman living inconspicuously with her uncle Mordecai in the Iranian city of Susa, finds herself not only crowned queen of a region which stretches from India to Ethiopia, but expected to speak up for her people after an edict announced their destruction; for "who knows," said her uncle, "perhaps you have come to royal dignity for just such a time as this."[11] Centuries later, both Moses and Esther would be painted by Tintoretto in Venice, surprise on their faces, as the familiar world they had grown up with erupted into new and compelling shapes and their lives took undreamt turnings – almost as if they were actors in a play, ready for the next act, alarmed to find when the curtain rises that the scenery has been completely repainted.

The story of God's people continues in the New Testament. We looked in Chapter 1 at the way in which ordinary men and women were invited to step out of the familiar story they had grown up in, and take an active part in the story of God. Not just the twelve, but others too – Joanna, the wife of King Herod's steward, who supports Jesus financially; a boy who comes to an open air meeting with a few rolls and a couple of fish and finds them being used to feed thousands of people; Simon, a pilgrim from Cyrene in Libya who ends up carrying Jesus's cross. A woman at a well in Samaria, drawing water at the wrong time of day to escape those who disapproved of her lifestyle, rushing back to address her whole community and engineering an invitation to Jesus to spend a couple of days there. The wife of the Roman governor Pilate, given a dream which caused her to warn her husband to have nothing to do with Jesus.[12]

As we read the gospels, we find a constant tension

between the cultural story and the kingdom story. The Old Testament is full of warnings that the Hebrew people should not be drawn into the common narratives of the peoples among whom they lived, but remain distinct in both belief and lifestyle. The events of the New Testament take place in the context of the Roman Empire, one of the strongest framing stories in history – a story of expansion and success, publicised not by radio and television but by the shiny public buildings going up in the new cities, by new roads, new trading opportunities, by a highly trained international army and a common aspiration to citizenship.[13] But for many of its inhabitants, then as now, the story wasn't working: most ordinary people could only watch all this from the outside – for them, reality meant not fame and fortune, but struggling to earn their livings and pay their taxes. Just as it does for most people today.

Everywhere that Jesus went, he offered the ordinary people to whom he spoke an invitation. He told them a new story, or more precisely the next part of an old story. And one by one he invited people into it. To each one he said something like this: 'You are barking up the wrong tree' – literally, in the case of Zacchaeus – 'you are heading in the wrong direction, living according to a lousy set of rules. But you have a choice.' For many, it was the first real choice they'd ever had. And so we watch him, one after another, bringing radical change into people's lives. Blind men and lepers are healed, paralysed men are forgiven and told to get up and go home. People are delivered of demons, children raised from the dead. Tax collectors give away their money and women who have committed adultery go home to live a different way. Ordinary working people leave their homes and livelihoods to follow him. To read the gospels is to see Jesus bursting into one life after another, challenging, changing, creating, undermining. He promised new life, a life more abundant than any life they had known. Not all of them wanted it, but many did, and some of them went on to change the world. Something was on offer that had never been on offer before. 'The story's not working? No problem. Here's a new one, in fact here's the real one. You can have a part in it if you like. Up to you.'[14]

Many accepted his invitation. After his death, they were so filled with the Holy Spirit that they sold their possessions and formed themselves into a new community, deliberately setting out to live a different way from those around them. We find them in the pages of Acts. There are those chosen to serve the community, men with strange names like Prochorus and Nicanor and Parmenas. There are those sent out to travel to faraway places and tell others of the things they had seen and heard, men like Paul and Barnabas and Silas. And there are those caught up into the life-changing ministry of the disciples themselves – a crippled beggar who asked for a donation; a man named Aeneas who found himself commanded to rise from the bed on which he had lain for eight long years; and a girl called Tabitha, raised from the dead. Some were spoken to more directly: Ananias, a Syrian told to pray for the healing of the most notorious persecutor of the new Christians, Saul; and a terrified centurion called Cornelius commanded in a dream to send for Peter, through whose testimony both the people of God and the not yet people of God were invited into the story.[15] These were not the kind of headlines that people were used to. Something new was going on.

As the early Christian community bonded together and began to learn how to live out its own story, Paul began to write specifically to them about the tension between the story of the culture and the story of the kingdom. In each place the pressures were different – a please-yourself-anything-goes society in Corinth, pagan festivals in Galatia, immorality and idol worship in Ephesus, mystic super-spirituality in Colossae. These are the things you need to evaluate and distance yourselves from, he writes to each group; these are the stories in which you no longer live.[16]

In his letter to the Philippians Paul comes up with a new way of explaining the tension we experience as we try to live as kingdom communities within the narrative of our culture. He reminds them that, as followers of Jesus, we may live here on earth, but our true citizenship is in heaven. We live, as Jesus had put it, in this world; but we do not belong to this world.[17] Peter echoes him, and perhaps it's in Peter that we find the most vivid description of the difference between these two stories, or two kingdoms. Now that we have been reconciled to God, we live here as 'aliens and exiles', Peter says; and we need to keep that constantly in mind.[18] The word he uses, *paroikos*, is actually the word from which we get our English word parish. Our parishioners are not, as the media caricature so often suggests, well-meaning, cucumber-sandwich-making ladies; our parishioners are people who belong in a different world, but who are called for the time being to live in this one, in a way which is different and distinctive from those around them. Our parishes, our churches, are meant to be outposts of a different world order, communities of disciples who step out of the pages of a different story in order to advertise it to those caught up in the flawed story offered to us by the voices of our culture. 'The church's main task in society is to be a community that lives out the Christian story for others to see,' the Fresh Expressions website points out.

Living as aliens and exiles

'Christians are distinguished from other men neither by country, nor language, nor the customs which they observe. For they neither inhabit cities of their own, nor employ a particular form of speech, nor lead a life which is marked out by any singularity... They dwell in their own countries, but simply as sojourners. As citizens, they share in all things with others, and yet endure all things as if foreigners. Every foreign land is to them as their native country and every land of their birth as a land of strangers..To sum up all in one word – what the soul is in the body, that are Christians in the world. The soul is dispersed through all the members of the body and Christians are scattered through all the cities of the world. The soul dwells in the body, yet is not of the body, and the Christians dwell in the world yet are not of the world.'

The Epistle of Mathetes ('Disciple') to Diognetus, 2nd century AD, from the American Edition of the *Ante Nicene Fathers*, pp26-27.

Finding our part in God's story

In Chapter 2 we defined discipleship as a form of apprenticeship undertaken in community. A disciple of Jesus is someone who has responded to the call of Jesus, committed his or her life to Jesus, and accepted the invitation to become part of a new Christian community which lives in the world but yet is distinct from the world. This process is made possible by the uniting and empowering presence of the Holy Spirit, and it involves a change of direction, learning on the hoof, learning with others and being willing to embrace pain. It is a process whose purpose is to proclaim the kingdom of God and invite people into it. The question is, how do we, in our ordinary circumstances and our ordinary churches, do that in practice?

Look at the big picture

The first responsibility of a leader is to define reality
– Max De Pree[19]

The first thing we need to do is become expert at reading the story which surrounds us. Most discipleship programmes focus on what the Bible has to say about the spiritual and moral life of the individual; very few do what Paul did in his letters, and help us to evaluate the hidden voices of our culture or assess the validity of the assumptions on which we base our lifestyles. Why *don't* we discuss the influence of the values of the dominant culture, Tom Sine asks? Why don't we talk about the stories we buy into, and their influence on us and our children; why don't we explore the role these stories play in defining our notions of the good life to which we aspire when we come home? We know that Christ wants to transform our spiritual and moral lives, but we rarely talk about how God might wish to transform our cultural values.[20] A disciple of Jesus is someone called out of one world into another, someone who is learning to join with others and live in a different story. If we do not look at the big picture and

222

talk about story, we simply end up with a schizophrenic discipleship which leaves us struggling to live in two worlds at once.

Jesus, of course, was aware of this. The scriptures help us to trace the life stories of many individuals, and the gospels show Jesus engaging with person after person, each in their own way, inviting them to walk out of one story and into another – proclaiming the good news of the kingdom of God, as he put it. But Jesus knew too that stories do not just have characters. They also have a framework of values – and perhaps it is because the characters are attracted by those values that they are willing to enter into the story. For would-be disciples of Jesus, the values are found in the topsy-turvy parables he told, and in the game-changing beatitudes with their vision of a different way of doing things. To the modern eye, the beatitudes read curiously like an anti-news bulletin, creating and celebrating a world of humility, lament, righteousness, mercy, purity and peace-making. Far from celebrating wealth, they dismiss it; far from denying suffering, they promise it.[21] Discipleship is not just about hearing and responding to an invitation; it's about learning to look at the world in a different way. "These people who have been turning the world upside down have come here also," shouted the outraged citizens of Thessalonika, "and Jason has entertained them as guests!" How were Paul and Silas, the people in question, turning the world upside down? They were telling a different story, talking about a new world with different values, a world governed not by the decrees of the emperor but by a king called Jesus.[22]

Working out how to ignore the decrees of the emperor is not easy. Some Christian friends of ours have recently moved to the United States, where life coaching is provided to all young people through their schools. "Follow your dream," the coach urged their daughter Becky. But Becky is just fourteen, and her dream comes not from an assessment of her own gifts or calling but from the voices of the culture which now surrounds her; she has decided she would like to be an actress. She has, her parents feel, no particular ability in this area; but it seems that was not the coach's primary concern – the important thing is to follow a dream, irrespective of where the dream comes from. Writing in just such a North American context, Packer and Parrett observe that

A young person growing up today has their worldview and values powerfully shaped by forces from all fronts. There is the constant influence of all sorts of media, the values inculcation that the schools and educational leaders have devoted themselves to, the political forces that legislate and enforce ever-shifting understandings of morality, the relentless worldview shaping that is driven by forces of advertising and marketing, and much more. The potency of such formative forces is enhanced by the fact that catechumens live among peers who are shaped continually by, and are often deeply committed to, these same things.[23]

It's a situation which prevails all over the world, and it's not just individual spiritual wellbeing which is at stake – the most powerful single word describing what happens when Christians are formed but not discipled is 'Rwanda' – a place where the voices of those who would seek power whispered a new and sinister story, dehumanising a people and legitimising death in a carefully planned radio campaign for months before the events which they eventually unleashed. We, of course, were horrified – but how determined are we ourselves to ensure that our dreams and aspirations come not from the manipulative voices of the culture in which we live but from God, who made us and knows us, who promises that he has good plans for us, and who calls us to find and play the part he has prepared for us in his story?

One of the major purposes of the early catechisms was to help people with just this problem, for then as now every new disciple had to learn to see the big picture, to integrate themselves with the kingdom story. Even for Jewish believers the need was there – Jesus carefully explains to Cleopas and his companion as he walks with them on the road to Emmaus that the recent events in Jerusalem were not a disaster but simply the next stage in an unfolding story. The writer to the Hebrews is at pains to link the new faith in Jesus with the long history of the people of God. John writes his gospel to help those with a Greek cultural background move into the story, inventing a whole new vocabulary in order to do so, and taking great care to start not half way through with Jesus but 'in the beginning' with creation. And the Book of Revelation offers a carefully constructed parody of both contemporary pagan cults and the growing emperor worship; Christians, John says, tell a story which is bigger than all that.[24]

As the gospel spread throughout the empire and was embraced by people with many different cultural backgrounds, this process of induction into the gospel story was achieved through an increasingly sophisticated and formal process of instruction. New believers were gathered together so that they could be introduced to God, Father Son and Holy Spirit, and taught that he speaks to us through scripture. They learned that we are all part of a big, redemptive story, that the gospel is the key to that story, and that our task is to teach one another what that means in practice as we live our lives in this world.[25]

We too need to learn to help people see the big picture. If we do not, they will simply invite Jesus into their story, instead of accepting the invitation to enter his.

Reject the world's offers

The secret of my identity is hidden in the love and mercy of God. Therefore there is only one problem on which all my existence, my peace and my happiness depend: to discover myself in discovering God. If I find Him I will find myself and if I find my true self, I will find Him – Thomas Merton[26]

One of the easiest ways of discerning the divergence between what is available to us in Christ and the counterfeits offered to us by our cultural narrative is to look at advertisements. I prefer not to watch television adverts, for their whole aim is to mess with your head; but posters and magazines fascinate me. A hundred years ago the word 'advertisement' used to mean nothing more than 'announcement'; in today's world it is rather more sophisticated than that. Gone are the days when soap was said to be effective, motor cycles reliable or custard powder tasty; today advertisements promote one thing by subliminally offering another: we are invited to break out of the ordinary with a Volvo, discover our senses with KitKat, or find tranquillity with Commercial Airlines. 'John Lewis is not selling teddy bears and oven gloves,' one commentator mused when the firm's annual Christmas ad came out; 'it's selling love.' In fact few adverts sell their actual product; instead they promise adventure, relationship, fulfilment and a host of other intangible benefits.

An advert from 1920   *An advert from 2012*

For many years I looked after the healing prayer ministry team in our church of Holy Trinity, Leicester. As people came week by week for prayer, we would find that although their pain undoubtedly sprang out of their circumstances, it was exacerbated by their inability to seek God-centred relief – and indeed often arose directly from their uncritical acceptance of the values and perspectives of our society. Members of the prayer team were anxious to help, but often they too were looking at things through the lens of our cultural values. We needed to help people adopt beatitude-shaped responses rather than sticking plaster solutions.

Working from the principle that we cannot take others further than we have been ourselves, we developed a healing prayer training course called *In His Name*. As part of the course we included a session which looks at our basic spiritual needs for security, significance and self-worth, all of which

Jesus urges us to take to God who alone can satisfy them, and all of which lurk unmet behind many of the painful things which cause people to come for prayer. In order to help people identify the ways in which our society encourages us to address these spiritual needs through the purchase of commercial products rather than in the context of a relationship with God, we decided to use the advertising industry. Working with a pilot group of young people, we spread out magazine advertisements on the floor, and looked at the subliminal messages they offered. We found that many of them suggested that by purchasing a particular product one or more of these spiritual needs could be met. Taken together, they functioned as a whole shoal of red herrings, promoting false solutions to real problems.[27]

Many people come in pain for prayer, not because they do not want to live in God's story rather than the world's story, but because they have not been taught to tell the difference. If we don't disciple people, our culture will.

Evaluate your calling

We are what he has made us, created in Christ Jesus for good works, which God prepared beforehand to be our way of life – Ephesians 2.10

Once we have understood the story and begun to live by its values, we need to learn to identify what our particular role within it is meant to be. A story offers an overarching narrative, a framework within which we can find meaning. It articulates and embodies a certain set of values. But of course it also has a plot. The moment I offer my life to Christ, the question arises, 'what is my role in this story to be?' For some of us it will be life-changing and even world-changing – as it was for the first twelve disciples of Jesus. For others it will be more modest and local – most of those whom Luke refers to as disciples of Jesus were not asked to travel the world, plant churches or die for their faith, but simply to go back home and live differently.

Our culture encourages us to dream big dreams, to look for success, to idolise celebrity; faithful, servant-hearted and inconspicuous living is not one of the values of our society. And yet that is what many of us are called to. Helen Keller put it well when she wrote 'I long to accomplish a great and noble task; but it is my chief duty and joy to accomplish humble tasks as though they were great and noble.' She has read, she says, 'that the world is moved along, not only by the mighty shoves of its heroes, but also by the aggregate of the tiny pushes of each honest worker.'[28] God may be preparing us, warns Shane Claiborne, working with the homeless in Philadelphia, 'for something really, really – small.' The Christian revolution, he suggests, will not be televised, broadcast by Fox News with commercial interruptions, sandwiched between ads to accelerate your life or be all you can be. 'The revolution will be cleaning toilets and giving another blanket to Karen.'[29]

How do we do this in practice? We will think about this in more detail in the next chapter – but here are some examples from the lives of people who have tried to find their own part in the story.

A friend told me recently of a farming contractor he knew, a man who toiled not just by day but also by night, hiring himself out by the hour to harvest crops and cut hedges. He asked him why he was doing it. "Well," said the man, "I would really like to be able to take my family on a cruise, so I'm working for that." It seemed that things were not going well at home; perhaps, suggested my friend, your family would be happier if they just saw a bit more of you?

Another man we know works as a contract lawyer, commuting long hours to the city, often staying overnight, rarely taking time off. He's a lovely man, a committed Christian; but his family spend their evenings and weekends without him, and if he does snatch a week's holiday he takes his Blackberry with him. Despite his faith, he has immersed himself unquestioningly in the values of a frenetic, success-oriented, time-poor society.

We can do better than this. The apostle Paul urges us not to be conformed to this world, but to be transformed by the renewing of our minds, so that we may discern what is the will of God. Brian Mclaren says this calls for 'a profound defection from one framing story and a profound investment of trust in another.'[30] Many of us, when we first place our faith in Jesus, fail to do this; we simply add him to what is already in our lives. Attentive listening to our circumstances, to our fellow Christians and to the needs of our communities can all be catalysts which help us to find our own role in God's story.

A young mother, Sue, moved into a country village with her husband and two small children. She found that the local church, like many country churches, had a small, elderly congregation, and no provision for children. Was it interested in children? Sue didn't know how to judge that; but one rainy weekday she decided to do something about it. Bundling one nipper into the pushchair and taking the other by the hand she set out, starting with the terraced row of former labourers' cottages opposite her home. She went to No 1, was welcomed in out of the rain, and explained that she was new to the village but was thinking about starting up a Sunday School – what did her neighbour think? There was a discussion, and then our young mum made her farewells and thanks for the cup of tea and went on to No 2. In the meantime the woman in No 1 had herself gone to No 3 to talk about it so, after another cup of tea, our mum found a prepared welcome at No 3 – and so it went on down the row. By the time she reached No 10 Sue found the house full of neighbours, all very enthusiastic about the Sunday School and asking when it would start and how they could help. With the approval of the priest in charge the Sunday School started a couple of weeks later and began to flourish as the enthusiasm of the neighbours infected the village; single-parent and other families began to appear.[31]

I met Jane on a church weekend. Jane was a musician, and she told us how she had felt her life was at a dead end, offering no opportunities to her to use her gifts. She had attended a prayer event at which everyone present was invited to come and take a card from a basket. Each card had a word and a Bible reference printed on it. Her card simply said 'Door,' and the Bible reference was from

Revelation – 'Behold, I set before you an open door.' This, Jane felt, was such an accurate description of precisely what was *not* happening in her life that she opened her Bible in fury and crossed the verse out. A few days later she received a phone call from a stranger – would she be willing to play the piano in a production of the musical Joseph? The production, it turned out, was in the local prison; and proved to be the beginning of 22 years of prison ministry for Jane.

Stuart Smith lives in Somerset, where he was working as a car salesman. When the villages of the Somerset Levels were flooded in the winter of 2013-14, Stuart gave up his job to help with the flood relief operation. Living off his savings while working with other volunteers, Stuart explained that volunteering had been a life-changing experience. He said: "I didn't know what I wanted to do with my life before and now I do. People were desperate and we were able to help them. This experience has helped me become the person I wanted to be."[32]

We all have a tale to tell, a part to play in a bigger story. We live in a world which offers us a story, a story told for us by the media, a story in which we are invited to find our own part. Don't think too much, is the message which comes as the latest disjointed episode flashes onto our screens – just keep following the story, make sense of it if you can, see if you can't somehow find your way into it. 'We are being sold a narrative,' remarks comedian Russell Brand, 'which keeps us dumb.'[33]

There is much we can do individually to find our way out of this situation. There is even more we can do together.

232

Finding your part in God's story – aged 13

In November 2007 Katy Morgan and Esther Sutherland, both aged 13, joined a *Rooted in Jesus* team to Kibaya, Tanzania. While the adult members of the team worked with the Rooted in Jesus group leaders in the cathedral, Katy and Esther spent a week in the English speaking primary school which forms part of the cathedral compound. It is a boarding school, with many of the pupils children of pastors. Katy and Esther helped in lessons, but also ran, on the Saturday, an open air prayer workshop. Remembering what they had learnt at home in their Pathfinder group, they gathered the children in a circle under a tree, offered some simple teaching about prayer, and helped the children to pray for one another in turn as each came into the centre of the circle. For the children this was the first time anyone had told them that they could bring their own needs to the Lord in prayer, and the first time they had experienced prayer for healing. For Katy and Esther, it was their first nervous attempt at ministering to others. They weren't sure how it had gone, but the head teacher told us the next day that all the children were talking excitedly about it and telling those who had not been present what they had missed.

Two years later, Bishop John Hayden told us what the children had done with what they received that day. They began to meet for an hour each evening to pray. They established a pattern of Sunday prayer, meeting together to pray and praise God for an hour before the service. This deepened the faith not just of the children but also of the English adult volunteers who observed it. Many of the children also returned to their villages and passed on what they had discovered. The result is that in villages all over the Kiteto area children were now to be seen regularly and spontaneously praying with and for one another.

Katy wrote afterwards 'I feel so honoured that God worked through me and pray that He will do so again.' He has, of course. For Katy, this experience proved to be just one step in her ongoing journey as an apprentice of Jesus. A little while later she led a friend to faith and then saw her healed from cancer through prayer. She started a Christian discussion group at her school, and when we moved to Wells was instrumental in setting up and supporting the first Christian Union at the school there. Katy is now a student at Cambridge University, where she acts as Prayer Secretary and member of the Executive Committee for the University Christian Union. She has written for ReSource magazine and is a contributor to our poetry collection *Distilling Life*. Katy is finding her part in God's story.

Living in God's story – a group study

This is whole-life discipleship: your part to be played in the still-to-be-completed purposes of God for His world – Graham Cray.

1. Identifying the world's story

'Humans have evolved to be storytellers, but our narratives are determined by culture' (Dan McAdams). To what extent are we aware of the story we are being told by the spokesmen and women of our culture?

2. Evaluating the world's story

'We are being sold a narrative which keeps us dumb' (Russell Brand). To what extent have your life choices and habits been determined by the values of the story in which we live?

3. Living in God's story

'To be a Christian is to learn to live in a story you haven't chosen (Stanley Hauerwas). How can we best help people recognise that as Christians we are invited to enter into a different story, a parallel story with its own values and plot?

4. Finding our part in God's story

Read Ephesians 2.10: 'We are what he has made us, created in Christ Jesus for good works, which God prepared beforehand to be our way of life' (Ephesians 2.10). What has this meant for you? Can you explain what your own role in God's story is?

5. Depending on one another

We live in a celebrity world, a world where the individual is star of their own show. As Christians we are called into community. What difference does that make to our understanding of the story in which we are invited to live?

CHAPTER NINE

Travelling Together

My conviction is that the journey of discipleship is not intended to be made alone but in the company of others. We are to be disciples together. The form this shared journeying takes is not in itself the most important point. The key thing is that we are not alone in the journey; we need the insights, encouragement, gifts and truth-telling of others along the way.

Roger Walton[1]

In 1999 I went on my first mission trip to Africa. Travelling nervously with four other people, only one of whom I had met before, and with none of whom did I have anything obviously in common except my faith, it was an experience which changed my life. We went to places where no white people had ever been before, driving in a half-repaired vehicle through a country riven with internal conflict, pausing at intervals to converse involuntarily with men with guns. We worshipped with people whose children cried in alarm when they saw our pale skin, we accepted their hospitality and slept on mattresses while rats scurried past our faces. We saw people delivered from demons which spoke in fluent English, we drank water scooped from puddles and boiled for our use, and we exchanged gifts with local chiefs. And we prayed and were prayed for, we relied completely on one another, and God was among us.

Discipleship, I often explain in *Rooted in Jesus* training

conferences, is a journey. A journey which begins when you accept an invitation, respond to a call – just as those first disciples of Jesus did, two thousand years ago. It's a journey which cannot be undertaken alone, for as you travel you need one another – partly because you are a long way from home, partly because none of you has all the resources required by the situations you meet along the way. During that first trip to Africa we learned both to depend upon one another practically, emotionally and spiritually, and to work together at our common task among the people to whom we had been sent. We found that one of us inspired confidence in those we met, one of us had a great gift of encouragement, one of us was prophetic in prayer, one of us was able to charm border guards in French, and another had the ability to produce statements of side-splitting irony: "That," said Laurie as we reassembled one morale-draining morning after being shown, separately and in darkness, to challenging accommodation, "was like travelling in a washing machine, and sleeping in a Paraguayan prison." When we travel, whether it is through Africa or whether it is through life, we need one another to share our joys and burdens, to pool our different gifts and insights. When we travel and minister in community, I discovered, our individual weaknesses vanish, to be replaced by the sum of our strengths – to be constantly added to by the people we meet and engage with, as God brings his blessings to us through them too. It's a good feeling.

Taking part in short-term mission trips is just one way to experience what it means to depend on others, and in depending on them, to depend on God – perhaps it is the nearest we can easily get to the kind of travelling undertaken by the twelve first called to follow Jesus. "I have never felt so part of a team that actually functioned as the body of Christ could," Vic Sekasi wrote on her return from a *Rooted in Jesus* team to Burundi and Rwanda. "Each team member had a role before the trip and during the trip. Every team member was playing to their strengths and was led by the Holy Spirit. If any of the team members were missing either physically or spiritually the team suffered. And after the ministry time I had a beautiful time of prayer with a prophetic catechist who spoke truth into my life, and I felt God's compassion for me afresh." Taking part in a short term mission project is an excellent way of finding out what it means to be apprentices in a Christian community.[2]

The power of Christian community today

Short-term mission trips provide a particularly intense snapshot of what it means to be a disciple of Jesus, learning and ministering as apprentices in a missional community. But what does shared discipleship look like in an ordinary week, as we go about our lives in our twenty-first century Western context? How do we ensure that we are both growing as disciples of Jesus, and training others as disciples of Jesus? The principles may not have changed since Jesus trained his first disciples, but the context is changing all the time.

One thing that is becoming increasingly clear is that traditional sit-in-a-row Sunday services are not an adequate vehicle for making and training disciples in a secularised society. In fact the latest UK research suggests that even committed Anglicans no longer find them helpful: a startling 50% of those who believe, practise and identify with Anglicanism say that they no longer attend church.[3] Dallas Willard insists that 'we must flatly say that one of the greatest contemporary barriers to meaningful spiritual formation into Christlikeness is overconfidence in the spiritual efficacy of regular church services. They are vital, they are not enough, it is that simple.'[4] In a world where Sunday church was the gathering place of a small community of people who lived and worked locally, who knew one another as friends and neighbours and who faced life's challenges together, it made sense to gather in a structured way once a week to anchor all that in the love and worship of God. But as a front-led event for people who come from different networks and communities, do not know one another, and find themselves caught up in the fast-paced story of a hurried and godless world, Sunday services on their own are not enough: vital though they may be as one component of a rhythm of life, disciples are neither trained nor equipped through participation in impersonal gatherings. We need to be more adventurous if we are to be true to our mandate to make disciples of all peoples or, as Paul put it, to 'equip the saints for the work of ministry.'[5]

'I encourage some risk takers,' writes Tom Sine in the United States, 'to consider raising the bar and creating new forms of church as countercultural families giving creative expression to an ancient faith and future hope in a myriad of different ways that are clearly focussed outward. The challenge is finding ways, in our time-stressed world, to actually carve out time and space to be truly known, deeply loved and radically challenged to follow Christ with our entire lives.'[6]

It is time to think about what a church is, how it learns, what it's for and what it does when it meets. And whilst we seem to be falling behind in many respects – or perhaps precisely *because* we are falling behind – the Church in the UK seems to be leading the way in this particular area.

Forming new ecclesial communities

Over the last ten years in the UK, the Fresh Expressions initiative has encouraged churches and church leaders to think more creatively about what it means to be church in our many and varied contexts. This has produced considerable growth – there are now some 3,400 fresh expressions of church all over the country, according to Ben Clymo of the Fresh Expressions team.[7] Over half are led by lay people, and they meet in a wide variety of venues, including cathedral undercrofts, churches and church halls, private homes, a farm; and secular venues such as schools, pubs and cafés, conference centres, garden centres, even soft play centres. It's clear though that just getting people meeting together in new ways and less formal locations does not in itself solve the problem of how they are to be apprenticed to Jesus, for it is self-evident that lots of people enjoying coffee or engaging together in art activities does not in itself constitute church, wherever you do it and whatever you call it. Graham Cray, leader of the Fresh Expressions movement from 2009 to 2014, has put his finger on it in tirelessly reminding us that the big test of any church is not where and how it meets, but the quality of the disciples it makes. He notes that 78% of the new initiatives have taken steps to foster discipleship. Some use published resources, some focus on one-to-one mentoring, others hold regular but informal discussion groups; all engage in mission. Most see themselves as being about relationships rather than events; an increasing number say they are seeking a rhythm to live by rather than an organisation to belong to. Many tell their stories on the Fresh Expressions and Church Army websites.[8]

It is remarkable what happens when churches, new or

established, take seriously the commission to go out and make disciples of all peoples. Here are just a few examples:

In Exeter a monthly worship event called *Holy Ground* offers a rhythm of both worship and service, with participants also involved in weekly work with a homeless café and a pub discussion group; 'Discipleship may be more about changing our patterns of living, than learning new facts,' leader Anna Norman-Walker observes.[9]

In Newton Aycliffe a new church called Life Line has formed unexpectedly through the local work of Christians Against Poverty, an organisation which supports people in debt; most of the members have no prior church experience, but are finding a home in the informal Bible study gatherings which, to the embarrassment of the leaders, keep outgrowing their premises.[10]

In Sheffield an ecumenical community café called Terminus was set up to serve a particularly needy estate after a survey had revealed that most people living there thought that church was irrelevant and had nothing to contribute to their lives. Social activities include discussions and Bible studies, and many of those coming have gone on to join discipleship groups in the café's partner churches.[11]

All of these initiatives have both challenged and deepened the discipleship of the Christians who have given their time to them, and drawn others into the kingdom of God.

Fresh expressions as schools of discipleship

Graham Cray writes: 'Our aspiration is that fresh expressions of church should be communities of disciples, not just gatherings for worship. We have learned that if this is not built in from the beginning it is very difficult to add it in, let alone bolt it on, at a later stage. The initial character of the community being planted often decides the  standard of discipleship that will be obtained. There is no quick fix or easy formula for disciple making, but there are some key principles.

Discipleship is not abstract. It is not a list of rules to be obeyed and sins to avoid. At its heart it is personal and corporate obedience to Jesus by those who have responded to his call to follow. It is not about religion. It is about all of life. It involves a choice to be with Jesus in order to become like him (Matthew 10.25). It is a choice to learn to live our life as he would live our life (Dallas Willard). It is a matter of the will. His yoke may be easy and his burden light but we still have to choose to bear it (Matthew 11.28-30). To become a disciple is to surrender our sovereignty over our personal destiny, and be apprenticed to Jesus, as part of his school of discipleship.

When I was a young Christian all the emphasis was on personal disciplines, particularly of daily prayer and Bible study. Personal disciplines remain important, but I do not believe they are sufficient to form Christian character today. In those early years of faith the Christian story was better known in Britain, and 'Christian' values taken as norms, even if they were not adhered to. Culture reinforced discipleship much more than today. Today culture is more likely to be corrosive of discipleship as supportive. It is corporate disciplines and support which are needed. A Christian way of life – the daily practice of obedience to Jesus – needs a proactive supportive community. The term 'one another' appears frequently in the New Testament and it is persistent, intentional 'one anothering' which will enable lives of discipleship.

Graham Cray, Fresh Expressions monthly bulletin, June 2012

Finding a rhythm of life

Many Christian groups over the centuries have sought to live by a daily rhythm of life, most notably those within the monastic movement; and indeed our Sunday services and seasonal liturgies reflect this tradition within the church. But some are developing the idea in new ways today. Michael Frost is the leader of a church in New South Wales called Small Boat, Big Sea, which structures its discipleship around a rule summarised under the acrostic BELLS. Each member commits each week to *Bless* others through performing acts of kindness, to *Eat* with one another and with those outside the church community; to *Listen* to God through prayer and meditation; to *Learn* from the gospels; and finally to recognise that they are *Sent* into the world to share the grace of God with others.

This approach is becoming more common here in the UK. Ben Edson has helped found a missional community in Manchester under the title Abide, shaped around the shared practice of five 'rhythms of grace': being transformed into the likeness of Christ, being open to the Holy Spirit; setting aside time for prayer, worship and spiritual reading; being a gracious presence in the world, and sharing faith with others. A community named Moot has been formed by people living and working in the City of London, structuring their lives round daily contemplative prayer, meditation, spirituality discussions and a 'Living the Questions' dialogue group.[12] All these represent attempts to break away from a timetabled 'Sunday Christian' pattern and move towards one where members live in shared daily recognition of the fact that they are followers of Jesus.

But it doesn't need to be complicated, or require a great awareness of church history; at its simplest level, it's about orientation, not about structure. Tracy Cotterell writes in the *Beautiful Lives* issue of ReSource magazine about her local primary school: 'Let me tell you about some children in a primary school just down the road from where I live. A little while back, the head teacher invited the whole school – children and staff – to think about what their values should be as a school, what should shape their corporate life, as it were. In amongst those children were a number of Christian kids who decided that being a Christian should actually shape how the school did life together. So they thought and they talked and they prayed and they went to the head teacher with their conclusion: we think that one of the values of our school should be 'what would Jesus do?' As it happens, this is a Church of England primary school. But it also has lots of children from families of other faiths and no faith at all. So the head teacher spoke to the Muslim families about this idea of having 'WWJD?' as a value of the school. Jesus was a prophet, they responded, so that was fine by them. She spoke to the Hindu families and they had no objections. She spoke with families with no particular faith and they agreed this could be voted on. So 'WWJD?' was indeed voted on by the whole school, along with all the other suggestions of what their school values could be, and 'WWJD?' became a value by which that school agreed they would shape their school life and decisions.' Tracy reflects that this small group of ten year old children had pointed to Jesus; they had helped staff and children see that Jesus' way would be good news for their whole school community.'[13]

Maturity in Christ, as Bill Hull observes, is a community project.[14] Even children can do it. In fact, to children it seems to come naturally – as Jesus suggested it would. "But Mummy," our son Edward said to me urgently, aged five, when his bedtime Bible took us to the Ten Commandments, "if those are God's instructions, I must take them to Mrs Teague [his teacher] so that she can read them to the children, because they don't know them!"

Making disciples in small groups

I do not know how discipleship can be sustained without some regular, face-to-face small group for mutual support and challenge – Graham Cray[15]

Although there are many ways of forming and growing disciples, the key learning community remains, as it has been from the time of Jesus, the small group. A small group provides a safe environment in which the Bible can be read, questions asked, struggles shared, and prayer and ministry offered through the exercise of spiritual gifts and the provision of pastoral care; it offers a place of belonging, and enables individual and collective growth. In the informality of a small group, people can explore, question, be challenged, celebrate and fail; they can receive affirmation, mercy, grace and forgiveness. The key to the transformation of England in the eighteenth century was the small group, the key to spiritual and numerical growth in China has been the small group, the key to the success of *Rooted in Jesus* in Africa is the small group, and the key to the evangelistic impact of Alpha is the small group. Small groups have been at the heart of my experience too; the key to the growth of the church Roger and I served for 18 years in Leicester was the small group – as the number of people involved in these groups rose, so the spiritual maturity of the church deepened. By the time we had 650 of our 800 members in small groups, we also had many of their friends coming to faith through the 16 Alpha courses run by those groups each year.[16] For many churches, the small group is the key to both spiritual and numerical growth.

The small Christian group has a long history. The first churches were essentially small, household-sized groups, meeting in homes. In Rome the church met in the home of Priscilla and Aquila; in Colossae it met at Nympha's house; in Philippi it was hosted by Lydia.[17] As more and more people embraced the gospel, new members were put through a careful and thorough small group discipleship process to help them transfer their allegiance from the secular story to the kingdom story. But as numbers grew and public church buildings were erected from the third century onwards, gatherings gradually became less personal, and the new Christian communities became less and less distinctive from the societies in which they were set. Throughout history reformers have called for solutions to this creeping transformation of disciples into churchgoers: the monastic movement of the Middle Ages, the Lutheran Bible study groups of the sixteenth century and the Methodist classes of the eighteenth century are examples.[18]

The twentieth century saw a gradual revitalisation of the small group movement. After the First World War, a 1919 government report called for the increased provision of adult education, to which the Church responded with a new system of theological study groups. In the period following the Second World War many 'house groups' were established, adding the further dimension of pastoral care to the existing emphasis on education. And over the last twenty years or so, influenced by the socially-focussed base communities of Latin America and the mission-focussed cell church model of South Korea, a new form of outward-looking small groups has arisen in this country. These groups are often also called 'cell' groups – not because they imprison their members (!) but because of the capacity of an organic cell to divide and multiply: a cell group has an inbuilt mission focus.[19] Alongside these cell groups are the small groups which have arisen in churches influenced by the charismatic movement, whose growing awareness of the unique, Spirit-led contribution of every individual to a gathering of believers has led to the realisation that corporate worship is not the only setting we need if we are to be and do everything that Jesus is inviting us to be and do. The spiritual awakening experienced by those involved in the charismatic renewal, combined with the mission focus of the cell groups, makes it possible for us (perhaps for the first time in several centuries) to recover a fully biblical model of discipleship.

The small group is fast becoming an established part of the church landscape; by 2001, 37% of English churchgoers said they belonged to one. A cross-section of small group members interviewed by Roger Walton in 2010 found that more than three quarters said their small group experience made them more confident in their faith and their ability to speak about their faith to others, more able to connect their faith and everyday life, more accepting and forgiving of others, stronger in prayer, and closer to God.[20] In 2007 Helen Cameron suggested that small groups are in themselves a new form of church.[21]

Walton suggests that there are three primary formative agents of Christian disciples: participation in mission, participation in worship and participation in intentional Christian communities. If a small group is to become the context in which disciples are made and trained, then probably all three should be true of the small group too. Taking Walton's elements in reverse order, this means that:

1. Group members must be committed to one another.
2. Group meetings must intentionally invite and celebrate the presence of God – Father, Son and Holy Spirit.
3. The group must have an outward focus.

This roughly equates to the traditional shorthand phrase 'inwards, upwards and outwards.' There are many different ways, both formal and informal, of putting these three principles into practice in the life of a small group, and many resources available. At ReSource our three part discipleship programme *The God Who is There*, based on our experience with *Rooted in Jesus*, begins with the nature of God and the call of Jesus; it includes prayer, worship, Bible study and the building of relationships as well as practical exercises to help group members find and play their part in God's story. We have developed a faith-sharing course called *Beautiful Lives*; a healing prayer course, *In His Name*; and a Lent course, *Season of Renewal*, which focusses on the new life brought to us by the Holy Spirit. All of these are elements which help people grow in discipleship and in the active ministry which is an integral part of discipleship. There are many other readily available small group resources, some of which are listed in the bibliography.

Why small groups?

"This is my commandment, that you love one another" (John 15.12).

"Go, make disciples of all nations, teaching them to obey everything that I have commanded you. And remember, I am with you always." (Matthew 28.19-20).

They devoted themselves to the apostles' teaching and fellowship, to the breaking of bread and the prayers (Acts 2.42).

One of the most helpful writers on the practicalities of running a small group is Bill Hull, a pastor and writer who focusses on the formation of Christian disciples. In his book *The Complete Book of Discipleship* Bill identifies four preconditions for the establishment of an effective small group. Firstly, a group which wishes to make disciples must be intentional – that is, every member must be committed to a process of personal growth. Secondly, it must involve a contract – members must make a specific commitment to attend at a specific time and place. Thirdly, it must strive for intimacy between members. And fourthly, it must insist on reaching out to non-members, based on an agreed commitment to reproduce itself. Bill's enthusiasm for a small-group approach to discipleship is clear:

If church leaders want effective platoons of determined believers working together to reach their networks for Christ, small groups are the way. If they want a system that finds and equips other leaders, small groups are the way. If they want to provide the best forum for creating the community necessary for accountability, small groups are the way.[22]

Spiritual direction and Christian mentoring

In the Church Army Research Unit's 2013 study of the Fresh Expressions of church in a number of Anglican dioceses, author George Lings identifies four main means by which Christian fellowships may seek to help their members to grow as disciples of Jesus: small groups, courses, teams and one-to-one mentoring.[23] Whilst some Fresh Expressions still have no strategy for discipleship, most adopt one or other of these four approaches – the illustration shows that in the Diocese of Canterbury they are more or less equally represented. Of these, one-to-one mentoring is the one we have not yet looked at. It can be done formally or informally: coaching, mentoring, spiritual direction and prayer ministry all come under this heading.[24]

Both Jesus and St Paul paid close attention to the individual faith journeys of their disciples. Nathaniel first responded to Jesus not just because Jesus called him, but because he saw into his heart. Peter is constantly guided, rebuked and encouraged by Jesus not simply as a member

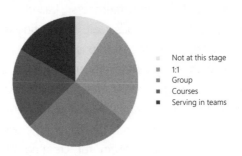

How FxCs disciple people in the Diocese of Canterbury

of the group, but as an individual facing his own particular issues. Wherever Jesus goes, his concern for his disciples' steady growth in ministry goes hand in hand with a concern for their personal development. Jesus knew that it was not enough to impart skills to his apprentices; he also needed to help them deal with their own human weaknesses.

We see the same care for his apprentices in Paul, travelling now with one individual, now with another, assigning tasks according to the different gifts and attitudes of his companions, and providing additional personal input into them as they travel – even to the extent, with John Mark, of temporarily dismissing him altogether. We follow this most closely in Paul's relationship with Timothy, whom he trains in much the same way that we saw Jesus train his disciples – first Timothy watches and listens, then Timothy works in partnership with Paul, and finally Timothy is sent out to work independently, with the further instruction that he is to pass on what he has learned to others who will themselves be able to teach others. But Paul spends as much time addressing the needs of Timothy himself as he does in training him for his role: as he takes him patiently from first steps in ministry through to his eventual position as an independent church leader, he offers him a constant stream of advice and encouragement – know that I love you; remember what has been prophesied about you, do not be shy and do not give up; look after your health.

Every disciple today needs this same care and attention. For most of my Christian life I have met weekly with a prayer partner, a trusted person with whom I can share the concerns of my heart and who helps me bring them to God. In addition to offering individual prayer ministry to others, I have sought it regularly for myself – often finding that God wished to deal with spiritual and emotional issues of which I had been only dimly aware. I have prayed with hundreds of people in this way over the years, usually people already in cell groups within our church, helping them bring their personal issues to God in a deep and focussed time of listening and prayer, and often releasing them into ministry in a way that practical training alone had been unable to do. Without inner transformation of this kind, the urge to ministry and mission becomes little more than a front-led stream of 'oughts' – which, as most church leaders know, is dispiriting for the church leader and guilt-inducing for the church member. I think of the vicar found one day standing by the stream which ran through his village, staring motionless into the flowing water. "What are you doing?" asked a passerby. "I'm just enjoying watching this stream," replied the vicar; "it's the only thing in this village which moves without me having to push it."

There are many ways of making sure that we are receiving not just practical training but also the lifelong spiritual advice and support we need on a personal level. We can look for a spiritual director or undertake guided retreats. We can seek wise and prophetic advice from others, both colleagues and those we encounter at ministerial training events or Spirit-filled gatherings. Church leaders can meet together to share their concerns, join a regional support network or a peer mentoring group. However you do it, make sure that someone, somewhere, knows you and can both challenge and support you.

Paul trains Timothy

1. Apprentice

* Acts 16 – Paul meets Timothy and takes him with him to Derbe and Lystra. Timothy observes Paul, but is given no active role.
* Acts 20.4-5 Paul sends his 7 disciples ahead to Troas and teaches them there.

2. Partner

* Romans 16.21 Timothy is now described as Paul's co-worker
* 1 Philippians 1.1 – Paul and Timothy write jointly to the church
* 1 & 2 Thessalonians – the letter is from Paul, Silvanus and Timothy

3. Equal

* 1 & 2 Timothy – Timothy is appointed to oversee the church in Ephesus.

Paul mentors Timothy

* 1 Timothy 1.2 – Timothy, my loyal child in the faith
* 1 Timothy 1.18 – I am giving you these instructions in accordance with the prophecies made earlier about you
* 1 Timothy 4.7 – Train yourself in godliness; let no one despise your youth; play close attention to yourself and your teaching
* 1 Timothy 5.23 – Take a little wine for the sake of your stomach and your frequent ailments
* 1 Timothy 6.20 – Guard what has been entrusted to you, avoid the chatter and contradictions of what is falsely called knowledge
* 2 Timothy 1.3-7 – I remember you in my prayers night and day.
* Rekindle the gift that is within you through the laying on of hands, for God did not give us a spirit of cowardice, but rather a spirit of power and of love and of self-discipline.
* 2 Timothy 2.1-3 – Be strong, and what you have heard from me entrust to faithful people who will be able to teach others as well. Share in suffering like a good soldier of Jesus Christ.
* 2 Timothy 2.15-22 – Present yourself to God as one approved by him, a worker who has no need to be ashamed. Shun youthful passions, have nothing to do with controversies, be kind and gentle to everyone
* 2 Timothy 3.14-15 – Continue in what you have learned, remember from who you learned it.

Conclusion

"To what then will I compare the people of this generation, and what are they like? They are like children sitting in the marketplaces and calling to one another, 'We played the flute for you, and you did not dance; we wailed and you did not weep.'" Matthew 11.16-17

We have covered a lot of ground in this book, from the way Jesus called his first disciples right through to what that means for us as individuals and communities today. We looked at the way the word disciple, *mathetes*, carries within it the sense of apprenticeship which we observe in the gospels. We noted that for Jesus, apprenticeship must be undertaken within a community, a community which today we call 'church' – for the plural of disciple is church. We saw that this community must have an outward focus if it is to be the kind of community Jesus had in mind. We suggested that if we are to take him seriously we must be intentional about this, setting out to discover what it means in our context and circumstances to live as a prophetic community in a world which does not know God – what it means to find our part, individually and together, in God's story. We reminded ourselves that it is only as we enter into this way of life that we will fulfil Jesus's expectation that we should do the things that he did, living as his body and ministering through his Spirit, so that we too may bring good news to the poor, proclaim release to the captives and recovery of sight to the blind, let the oppressed go free, and announce the kingdom of God. We faced the fact that none of this can be done unless we are willing to overcome our cultural aversion to any kind of risk or pain. And finally, we noted that it is not enough for us to do these things ourselves; we are expected and commissioned to teach others to do them too. Being a disciple of Jesus involves accepting the commission to make disciples of others, baptising them in the name of the Father and of the Son and of the Holy Spirit, and teaching them to obey all that Jesus has commanded us – knowing that he will be with us as we do so.

What does this mean in practice? Well, there are principles but no blueprints. It's a collective endeavour, one in which we will only partially succeed and which still lies outside the experience of most of us. And yet it is not meant to be a burden: "My yoke is easy," said Jesus to a generation of farmers accustomed to getting the most out of their hard-working oxen, "and my burden is light."[25]

Perhaps a better metaphor for us is that of dance. When I visited Mozambique I learned how the Nyanja women of Lake Niassa had sustained the faith of their people through thirty years of war, together developing what Helen Van Koevering calls 'a spirituality of survival' in the face of injustice and violence. Dance is the metaphor Helen has adopted to describe the way in which the faith of these women enabled them to seek healing, build community and gather the strength to carry on through poverty, social turmoil and famine. It is a patient faith, Helen says, drawing on the pagan past but combining it with a sharper sense of female dignity, social purpose and personal piety culled from the Bible and church practice; it is a faith which has enabled the Nyanja to place their hope not in their circumstances but in their status as a community of Christ, and so to win through to a better future. "I came that they may have life, Jesus said, "and have it abundantly."[26] It is never too late, and the circumstances are never too difficult, to accept his offer. We have already seen something of how that better future is now unfolding for the people of Niassa.[27]

My daughter Bethy is studying dance, and for her

teaching diploma she wrote a dissertation on the role of dance in promoting physical and emotional health in people of all ages. Talking with her, I was reminded of John V Taylor's discussion of an interview with Dr Elisabeth Kubler-Ross, a psychiatrist celebrated for her pioneering work among the very old, in which she described an experimental project in a typical residential care home:

They were all sitting half dead in their wheel-chairs, mostly paralysed and just existing, they didn't live. They watched some television, but if you had asked them what they had watched they probably would not have been able to tell you. We brought in a young woman who was a dancer and we told her to play beautiful, old-fashioned music. She brought in Tchaikovsky records and so on and started to dance among these old people, all in their wheel-chairs, which had been set in a circle. In no time the old people started to move. One old man stared at his hand and said, "Oh, my God, I haven't moved this hand in ten years." And the 104-year-old, in a thick German accent, said, "That reminds me of when I danced for the Tsar of Russia."[28]

Reflecting on this story, Bishop Taylor reflects that it is not just an account of a remarkable therapy, but an instance of the effect of the really alive upon the half-dead or upon lifeless situations. It says something about the impact of Jesus Christ upon the people around him, and about the force and impact of the Holy Spirit in our lives. It is never too late to dance.

The Bible is full of people dancing. David was willing to make a fool of himself by dancing before the Ark of the Lord. 'Let us praise him with tambourine and dance,' the psalmist urges. 'There is a time to dance,' says the writer of Ecclesiastes (3.4). 'You shall be rebuilt and restored,' Jeremiah promises to the people of God in exile, 'and then you will praise and sing and dance.' 'I played, and you did not dance,' Jesus reproaches the inhabitants of Galilee.[29]

Perhaps discipleship is like dancing. It's practical, it has to be learned through apprenticeship rather than through study, it is best done together, and it moves those who witness it and become caught up in it. It has to be the right kind of dance, as Robert Madette discovered when challenged by some Christians to stop his witch-doctor's dance. Done properly, dance is all-consuming; it is a form of worship, an offering of our souls and bodies to God. When King David danced before the Lord, to the horror of his wife who was looking for something more stately, more dignified, the Lord responded by inviting David to build him a house, and promising to bless him and all his people. That house became the great temple of Jerusalem, the temple of which Peter was doubtless thinking when he urged the new Christian communities to see themselves as living stones, built into a spiritual house, called to be a holy priesthood who would proclaim the mighty acts of God.

How then do we dance? We dance individually: 'We follow Jesus like we follow a dance partner,' Lucy Peppiatt has told us. And we dance together, as we set forth into the world to accomplish the purpose for which we have been sent: 'Mission means inviting all the people of the earth to hear the music of God's future and dance to it today,' Christopher Wright suggests.[30] The plural of disciple is church; we are invited to dance on our own, and we are invited to dance together: with joy, despite pain, and in hope. "I forget everything else when I dance," Bethy says.

So are we going to sit at home, or are we going to get up and dance our faith in the highways and byways of life? The dancing will not be without pain, for we are invited also to weep. But the outcome is life.

That [which] we cal gospel is a greke word, and signyfyth good, mery, glad and joyfull tidings, that maketh mannes hert glad, and makyth hym ssynge, daunce, and leepe for joy – William Tyndale.

APPENDIX ONE

A Group Study

Called as disciples of Jesus: apprentices in a kingdom community

1. Something new...

Begin this study with Matthew 4.23-24. The point to notice from these verses is that when Jesus came, the kingdom came. This was manifested by a whole series of miracles, mainly miracles of healing.

Jesus could not be everywhere at once. Five miles away from where Jesus was, terrible things could have been happening. But where Jesus was, the kingdom was. Where Jesus was, God reigned. When Jesus returns, the kingdom will be everywhere – but not until then.

How do you feel about being part of God's new kingdom?

2. The mandate of a disciple...

Continue with Mark 3.13-19, Matthew 10.1-10 and Luke 10.1-11. The first disciples were called to be apprentices in this new kingdom world. They saw what Jesus did, and they did what Jesus did. Where the disciples were, the kingdom was. Where the disciples were, God reigned.

Imagine that you are one of the seventy trained and sent by Jesus. How do you feel about the task he is giving you?

3. Depending on the Holy Spirit...

Now look at Acts 2.37-47. A large crowd of people began a new life as disciples of Jesus. As Jesus himself had been baptised with the Holy Spirit, so too are these new disciples. They received him in the person of the Holy Spirit, and the Spirit formed them into a community. Wherever the community was, the Spirit was. Wherever the Spirit-filled community was, the kingdom was. Notice from this passage the various ways in which the kingdom was manifested.

It is the same today: if the church you belong to is a Spirit-filled community, if the people in your church are disciples – that is if they are apprentices in the kingdom – then there will be signs of God's reign all around you. Is this your experience? If not, would you like it to be?

4. Living a different way...

Now look at Romans 14.17, 1 Corinthians 4.20, and Galatians 5.22-23. From these verses, come up with just four words which together characterise kingdom community. Then think back on your life. When have you had the privilege of being a disciple within such a community?

5. Doing the things that Jesus did...

Read Matthew 28.18-20. What would be the mark of the

new disciples? Now look at Matthew 10.7-8. What was it that he had commanded them?

Consider John 14.10-12, where Jesus explains that as he does the things his Father does, so his apprentices will do the things that he does (see also Luke 6.40). What are the implications of this for our own apprenticeship to Jesus?

Read 1 Corinthians 12.4-11. What resources are available to us as we seek to do the things that he did? Notice that these resources are given to us not as individuals but as members of the body of Christ. Does this make a difference to the way you think about them?

6. A new commandment...

Spend some time reflecting on John 13.34-35. Jesus never sent out his disciples on their own – there were always at least two. In the community in Jerusalem, there were 3000 disciples together. What mattered most was the relationship between the disciples. They would have to take the commandment to love each other to heart, or all would be lost and the kingdom would dissipate. Look at the following verses to see how much depended on their adherence to this critical commandment:

- John 14.15-16
- John 14.21
- John 15.9-17

What does it mean in practice for us today, that we should love one another?

7. Living as salt and light...

Read Matthew 5.13-16. What did Jesus mean when he said to his disciples that they are the salt of the earth? What does it mean for us today, in our own contexts?

Jesus also told his disciples that they were like lights shining into a dark world. He said that when other people saw their good works, they would recognise the presence of God. What does this mean in your context?

8. Food for the journey...

Jesus taught his disciples to pray. Communities of disciples do not know how to pray unless they are taught. Look at Luke 11.1-4. What are the lessons in Jesus's prayer school? Does your church community know how to pray? Notice that there is nothing here to suggest that people should pray on their own! Prayer is a fundamental activity of disciples meeting together.

9. Taking stock...

The disciples in Jerusalem had much to learn. Encouraged and motivated by the Holy Spirit, they had to learn to love one other. They also had to be taught to understand their faith. Read through Ephesians chapter 1 and make a list of the things which a Christian community must thoroughly understand together. Do you think that the community which you belong to does understand these things?

10. How easy is it to be disciples of Jesus?...

Joining the kingdom community, becoming disciples of Jesus, was apparently undemanding. Look again at Acts 2.38; you will find that the requirements are simple: repentance and baptism.

But those disciples were to discover that maintaining their discipleship would at times be costly. Look up the following verses to see how Jesus described this cost:

- Matthew 18.21-22
- Matthew 19.21-26
- Luke 6.27-31

- Luke 9.23
- Luke 14.25-33
- John 12.24-26

What has been the cost of discipleship for you? Is this cost made clear to members and prospective members of your church community?

For personal reflection

A meditation on the journey of discipleship

Christianity without discipleship is always Christianity without Christ
– Dietrich Bonhoeffer

What is a Christian disciple?

It's a term we often use, but rarely think about carefully. Like an arrow fired from a distance at a very slightly inaccurate angle, the word disciple somehow seems to have strayed further and further away from its target as the centuries have gone by. What do you think of when you consider the word 'disciple'? Is it a term you would apply to yourself?

Discipleship is the irreplaceable and lifelong task of becoming like Jesus by embodying his message – Alan Hirsch

Student, or apprentice?

Our English word 'disciple' means 'a person who learns', and we often understand discipleship as a process of learning – learning which involves study. So for us, to grow in discipleship often means to grow in knowledge and understanding, particularly of the Bible. But when we read the Bible, we don't actually see Jesus's disciples engaged in study; we see them being trained to do the things that Jesus did. They were more like apprentices than like disciples. Are you learning to do the things that Jesus did?

The one who believes in me will do the works that I do – Jesus

Instead of asking yourself whether you believe or not, ask yourself whether you have this day done one thing because he said, 'Do it,' or once abstained because he said 'Do not do it.' It is simply absurd to say you believe, or even want to believe in him, if you do not do anything he tells you
– George MacDonald

Knowing, or becoming?

When we decide to follow Jesus, we are given the Holy Spirit as our guide and teacher. Through the presence of the Spirit in our lives, we are enabled to grow and change. We become more and more like Jesus himself, and we gradually acquire the inner beauty of a person being made clean from the inside out. Meditate on this thought:

In God we are not condemned or defined, but forever becoming
– Gunilla Norris

Alone, or together?

We are used to thinking about life in individual terms, and this colours our attitude to faith too. But in the New Testament we see something rather different. Jesus did not recruit individuals, he recruited a group – a group who would, for three years, do everything together. He taught them to love one another, to minister alongside one another, to depend on one another. When he left them, he sent the Holy Spirit to be with them instead, and the Holy Spirit equipped them to minister not as individuals but as connected branches of a single vine, as different parts of a single body.

What about you – do you belong to a community which can pray, learn and minister together?

We have nothing to share with the world other than what we are sharing with each other – Jim Wallis

The plural of disciple is church

The word 'disciple' is used throughout the Gospels and the Book of Acts – but never in the Epistles. Why is this? Partly to make it absolutely clear that discipleship is first and foremost about following Jesus. But there's another reason too. Peter, James and John have a new word to talk about discipleship – it's the word 'church'. Church is a group word – it refers to a group of people who have been called to follow Jesus together. Just as we talk about individual houses making up a village, so we talk about individual disciples making up a church. The plural of disciple is not disciples – it's church. This meaning is buried in our language; the English word church means 'of the Lord'.

Would you describe your church as a group of disciples committed to following Jesus?

Church is what happens when people encounter the Risen Jesus and commit themselves to sustaining and deepening that encounter in their encounter with each other – Rowan Williams

A lifelong journey

To be a disciple of Jesus was to travel, and so it has always been. Before the word 'Christian' was invented, the disciples of Jesus were known as followers of 'The Way'. Christian discipleship is not about knowing things, believing things, attending things, or belonging to things – it's about setting out on a shared journey, a journey which will change who we are and the way we live our lives, a journey which begins here but will carry us ultimately into another world. Discipleship is a journey in which we learn gradually to move into the space made available to us by Jesus.

The UK will never be reached until we begin to cultivate open, authentic, learning and praying communities that are focussed on making whole-life disciples who live and share the gospel wherever they relate to people in their daily lives – Mark Greene

It's not meant to be easy...

Whoever does not carry the cross and follow me cannot be my disciple. For which of you, intending to build a tower, does not first sit down and estimate the cost, to see whether he has enough to complete it? – Jesus

What is the cost of discipleship for you?

I long to accomplish a great and noble task, but it is my chief duty to accomplish humble tasks as though they were great and noble. The world is moved along, not only by the mighty shoves of its heroes, but also by the aggregate of the tiny pushes of each honest worker – Soren Kierkegaard

Praying for grace

*My grace is sufficient for you, for power is made perfect
in weakness* – St Paul

Reflect on the things you have been praying about as you
have considered your own journey of discipleship –
apprenticeship, becoming, community, journey, cost. What is
the key element for which you need to ask for God's grace?

ENDNOTES

Introduction

[1] These were probably originally intended as paired scenes, each Old Testament scene standing alongside the New Testament scene it prefigured, and all designed to show God's consistent saving intervention in human history; but the order may have been changed, and the exact intention remains something of a mystery.

Chapter One

[1] For Jesus' calling of the first disciples see Mark 1, Matthew 4, Luke 5 and John 1; for Matthew see Luke 5/Matthew 9. For lists of the 12 see Matthew 10, Mark 3, Luke 6 and Acts 1. For the calling of the 70 (or 72) see Luke 10. For the 120 see Acts 1. Simon would later be known as Peter; Matthew is also called Levi, Nathaniel is also called Bartholomew, and Thaddeus is also called Judas son of James. See pp11-12.

[2] The vocabulary of discipleship is most comprehensively discussed by Michael Wilkins, *Following the Master – A Biblical Theology of Discipleship,* Zondervan 1992: 'The disciples of Jesus, therefore, were all those who responded to Jesus' call to follow him. It was a call to salvation, a call to the kingdom of God, a call to believe on Jesus for eternal life. The term disciple designated a believer in Jesus.' In both his gospel and in Acts Luke calls all those who followed Jesus 'disciples'; among this wider group are the Twelve, to whom Luke refers, in recognition of their particular commission, as 'apostles'.

[3] Mark 16; Matthew 28.

[4] I am indebted to Martin Cavender for this insight.

[5] Mark, or John Mark, is first mentioned in Acts 12.12; his mother had a house in Jerusalem, and he travelled widely with Barnabas and Paul (eg Acts 13; 1 Peter 5.13).

6   Acts 9 (Saul), Acts 10 (Cornelius), Acts 16 (Lydia).

7   Tony and Kevin's stories are told in my book *The Word on the Wind*, Monarch 2011, pp31 & 23.

8   The imam told his story to Martin Cavender, who relates it in John Woolmer's book *Encounters*, Monarch 2007, pp43-45.

9   For more information see rootedinjesus.net/kenya.php, or maasaimissions.org.

10   John 20.25.

11   Acts 9 (Joppa), Acts 14 (Lystra), Acts 19 (Ephesus). For a contemporary example, see the experience of Amorim Rocha, a pastor in Mozambique, related in my book *The Word on the Wind*, pp203-04.

12   Luke 4.18; John 10.38.

13   *The Word on the Wind*, Monarch 2011, pp117-19.

14   I heard a first hand account of these events from Clyde Thomas, once a drug addict but now a pastor at Victory Church, at the Charismatic Leaders' Conference in December 2014. David Pike's blog is at daibach-welldigger.blogspot.co.uk/2013/04/outpouring-in-cwmbran-2013.html, and bigissue.com/features/2977/victory-church-cwmbran-hands-if-you-really-believe. For an interview with Paul Haynes and others watch the 30 minute CBS broadcast on vimeo.com/69160227.

15   John 6.30; John 14.11.

16   1 Peter 3.2.

17   Acts 13 (Cyprus and Antioch Pisidia), Acts 17 (Beroea and Athens). In both Ephesus and in Corinth Paul stays for months, running lunch time classes in the school of philosophy in Ephesus, and in the house of Crispus in Corinth (Acts 18 and 19).

18   Frank Morison, *Who Moved the Stone?* Authentic Media 2006.

19   Frost was quoting from an essay on 'Style' by the 19th century essayist Thomas De Quincey; *Selected Essays on Rhetoric*, edited by Frederick Burwick, Southern Illinois University Press 2010: 'Time must be given for the intellect to eddy about a truth, and to appropriate its bearings.'

20   Mark 1.14-15.

Chapter Two

1   *The Forgotten Ways*, Brazos Press 2006, p103.

2   See John 6.66, 'many of his disciples turned back and no longer went about with him.'

3   So named from the sustained tree imagery of both Old and New Testaments: Jeremiah 17.7-8, Psalm 1, Ephesians 3.17, Colossians 2.7. See rootedinjesus.net.

4   See our website resource-arm.net for more details. For *Rooted in Jesus* see rootedinjesus.net.

5   The attendance statistics for the year 2011 show that of the 44 dioceses, 20 are now growing. See churchofengland.org/about-us/facts-stats/research-statistics.aspx.

6   Graham Cray, *Who's Shaping You? – 21st century disciples*, Cell UK Ministries 2010; Mark Greene, *Imagine*, licc.org.uk/imagine-church/; Michael Frost and Alan Hirsch, *ReJesus – A Wild Messiah for a Missional Church*, Hendrikson 2009 p42; Dallas Willard, *The Spirit of the Disciplines – Understanding How God Changes Lives*, Harper SanFrancisco 1999, p259.

7   Compare Luke 5.1-11 with John 21.1-14.

8   Compare John 21.9-19 with the accounts of the Last Supper, particularly in Luke 22.19 and Matthew 26.26.

9   Luke 24.

10 For an analysis of the ways in which our society is changing see my book *The Word on the Wind*, Monarch 2011.

11 Michael Wilkins, *Following the Master – A Biblical Theology of Discipleship*, Zondervan 1992 p25. See Luke 11.26.

12 Dallas Willard, *The Great Omission – Reclaiming Jesus' Essential Teachings on Discipleship*, Monarch 2006 p53.

13 According to Michael Wilkins the word disciple is used to refer to followers of Jesus 230+ times in the gospels, 28 in Acts; according to Dallas Willard the word disciple is used 269 times in the NT. Wilkins, *Following the Master*, p40; Willard, *The Great Omission*, p3. For 'Christian' see Acts 11.26, Acts 26.28, 1 Peter 4.16.

14 The survey was conducted by Richard Tweedy. Respondents identified these, in this order, as the top markers of discipleship: Bible study, prayer, worship, service to others, Christian beliefs, evangelism and sacramental observance. See gloucester.anglican.org/church-outreach/discipleship2/discipleship-survey/. A Methodist local preacher in Somerset asked the question another way: "if it were illegal to be a Christian, what evidence would there be to incriminate

you?" Answers included 'possession of a Bible', 'your bookshelf' and 'going to meetings.' But after that they were strikingly, if rather randomly, practical: Jesus stickers, emails, bank statements, internet history and the practice of forgiveness were all identified as things which would mark you out as a Christian.

[15] Michael Wilkins, *Following the Master*, p22.

[16] TW Manson, *The Teaching of Jesus – Studies of its Form and Content*, 2nd edition CUP 1935, pp239-40. Manson also suggests that Jesus used a specific Hebrew/Aramaic term, *shewalya*, to designate his disciples, instead of the usual rabbinical term *talmidh*. This is the word which in Greek becomes *mathetes*.

[17] Michael Wilkins, *Following the Master*, p93.

[18] Eg Luke 4 and Luke 6.17-19 (watch); Luke 9.1-6 (the 12 sent out) and 9.10 (reporting back and withdrawing to a quiet place where they could discuss it); Luke 10.1-12 (the 70 sent out); Luke 10.17-20, Mk 9.14-29 (further evaluation); Matt 28.18-20 (the command to teach others to do these things too).

[19] See freshexpressions.org.uk/guide/about/principles/disciples. For a helpful discussion of this point see Alan Hirsch & Dave Fergusson, *On the Verge – A Journey into the Apostolic Future of the Church*, Zondervan 2011 pp177-79: 'The prevailing paradigm of church laced throughout the West has tended to try to make disciples primarily through the transfer (mainly) of doctrinal information about the Trinity, church, salvation, eschatology, and so on. Often, it has tried to track cultural trends and engage in apologetics and evangelism, but again it has done this mainly on an intellectual level, in classrooms and Sunday school sessions. Please don't misunderstand me here; we certainly do need serious intellectual engagement with the key ideas of our time. What is concerning, however, is that such engagement largely takes place in the disengaged and passive environment of the classroom. This is simply not the way Jesus taught us to develop disciples.' Elsewhere Alan links this approach with the abandonment of the holistic Hebraic understanding of faith, involving every aspect of life, physical, emotional and spiritual. 'Hear O Israel, the Lord our God, the Lord is one; love the Lord your God with all your heart, soul, strength', the Law begins (Deut 6.4-9); it covers all aspects of life, from the rules of the temple to what you do when your

donkey falls into a pit. See Michael Frost & Alan Hirsch, *The Shaping of Things to Come*, Hendrikson Publishers 2003, chapter 7.

20   Brian McLaren, *Naked Spirituality – A Life with God in 12 Simple Words*, Hodder 2012, p29. Shane Claiborne, *The Irresistible Revolution – Living as an Ordinary Radical*, Zondervan 2006, p71.

21   Ezekiel 2.8-3.4; Hosea 1.2-8; Mark 12.24; Hebrews 4.12. Dallas Willard, *The Great Omission*, Monarch 2006, p173.

22   Alan Hirsch, *The Forgotten Ways*, Brazos Press 2006 p24.

23   Amiel Osmaston, Ministry & Training Officer, at a seminar on discipleship at Church House in London, May 2012.

24   Dietrich Bonhoeffer, *The Cost of Discipleship*, SCM Press new edition 2001, p59.

25   Danish philosopher Kierkegaard used a different image to express this loss: it's as if we are trying to make a cup of tea from a scrap of paper once used to wrap up a few dried tea leaves from which tea had already been made three times, he said. Or, to use a more modern image, it's as if we are taking a photocopy of a photocopy of a photocopy. The tea is tasteless and the photocopy illegible; what we have ended up with bears no resemblance to what we started out with. See Michael Frost & Alan Hirsch, *ReJesus – A Wild Messiah for a Missional Church*, Hendrikson 2009, pp52, 69.

26   Matthew 23.2-11 (NB the NRSV inaccurately translates 'students' but the Greek word Matthew uses is 'brothers' – as in the NIV). Luke calls Peter and John 'uneducated, ordinary men' – *agrammatoi idiotae* (Acts 4.13).

27   John 15.1-17; John 17.20-23.

Chapter Three

1   *Pilgrim at Tinker Creek*, Canterbury Press 2011, p34.

2   *From Anecdote to Evidence – Findings from the Church Growth Research Programme 2011-2013*, churchgrowthresearch.org.uk.

3   For a full discussion of the concept of discipleship in the Old Testament see Michael J Wilkins, *Following the Master – A Biblical Theology of Discipleship*, Zondervan 1992, ch 3.

4   Martin Down: *Speak to these Bones*, Monarch 1993.

5   Luke 4.18-19; Mark 1.15/Matthew 4.17; John 3.36; Matthew 11.28;

Matthew 10.32; Mark 2.14.

[6]   Acts 11.26. According to Michael Wilkins, the term disciple is used in this simple sense at least 230 times in the gospels and 28 times in Acts (see Chapter 2 note 13).

[7]   For the women see Luke 8.2-3: Mary Magdalene, Joanna the wife of Herod's steward Chuza, Susanna, 'and many others'. For the 70 see Luke 10.

[8]   John 8.11 (the woman) and Luke 17.11-19 (the lepers); Mark 10.46-52 (Bartimaeus); Luke 19.2-10 (Zacchaeus); John 11 (Mary, Martha & Lazarus); Mark 15.43 & Matthew 27.57 (Joseph).

[9]   For a live BBC interview with Dave see bbc.co.uk/ sport/0/football /22079178. To read his story visit football-league.co.uk/ features/20120216/real-football-no-more-the-wild-rover_2293307 _2612728. For the church visit stjameslockleaze.co.uk.

[10] *Mere Christianity*, CS Lewis Signature Classics, William Collins 2012 p92.

[11] Luke 19.10. John Pridmore with Greg Watts, *From Gangland to Promised Land*, xt3media 2008; Richard Taylor, *To Catch a Thief*, New Wine Publishing 2006; Darrell Tunningley, *Unreachable – One Man's Journey through Drugs, Violence, Armed Robbery and a Miraculous Encounter with God in Prison*, Sovereign World 2011 (see also Darrell's testimony in Chapter 1). These are just some recent examples among a whole host of books telling dramatic stories of changed lives following an encounter with Jesus.

[12] I've written elsewhere (Alison Morgan, *The Word on the Wind*, Monarch 2011) about how we are shaped by our environment, by the culture into which we are born; the further I journey with Jesus, the more aware I become of the false directions in which we are so invisibly encouraged to travel instead. The classic writer on this topic is Walter Brueggemann, *The Prophetic Imagination*, Fortress Press 1978; or *Finally Comes the Poet*, Fortress Press 1989; see also Brian McLaren, *Everything Must Change – Jesus, Global Crises, and a Revolution of Hope*, Thomas Nelson 2007; or Michael Moynagh: *Changing World, Changing Church*, Monarch 2001.

[13] Luke 16.13; Hebrews 13.5.

[14] Alain de Botton, *The News – A User's Manual*, Hamish Hamilton 2014 p227. See the articles by Danielle Sheridan in *The Times*, and by Rupert Neate in *The Guardian*, 28.11.14.

15 See 'A Reassessment of the Relationship Between GDP and Life Satisfaction,' Eugenio Proto & Aldo Rustichini, published in the open access journal *PLOS ONE*, July 2013; 'Personal Well-being Across the UK,' Office for National Statistics, October 2013. For a map of life satisfaction by UK county see opendata communities.org/wellbeing/map.

16 Reported in 'Vicar or publican – which jobs make you happy?' Mark Easton, BBC 20th March 2014. 'Prosocial Spending and Happiness: Using Money to Benefit Others Pays Off,' Elizabeth W. Dunn et al, University of Columbia, January 2014. In July 2014 the BBC screened a three part series presented by Jacques Peretti entitled 'The men who made us spend', which offered a fascinating exposé of consumerism and the way in which the public's appetites have been shaped by the advertising industry.

17 1 Timothy 6.10.

18 See the study by Patricia Greenfield, a psychology professor at the University of California, who found that our language has slowly shifted to focus on individualism and material gain. For a summary see popsci.com/science/article/2013-08/usage-self-centered-words-get-and-choose-are-increasing-over-time.

19 Anthropologist Kathleen Richardson argues that digital technology is shifting the focus away from our physical lives towards a virtual existence; see her article 'Me2', Cam Magazine, issue 71, 2014.

20 Proverbs 14.12 (NB the NRSV has 'person'); Matthew 7.13.

21 Drug figures from the Crime Survey for England and Wales 2011-12; see drugscope.org.uk and news.bbc.co.uk/1/hi/uk/4229470.stm. British Medical Journal report quoted in *The Week* 22.03.08. In August 2013 the Health and Social Care Information Centre published data showing that more than 50 million prescriptions for anti-depressants were issued in 2012, the highest ever number and 7.5% up on the year before – see the BBC report on bbc.co.uk/news/uk-23553897

22 Youth index 2014: princes-trust.org.uk/PDF/YOUTH_INDEX _2014.pdf

23 1996 statistics reported in *The Times*, 13.1.07; for 2011 statistics see Caroline McClatchey, 'Why are more people changing their name?', bbc.co.uk/news/magazine-15333140. Dr Julia Cresswell, an authority on names, comments, 'there's a stage in most people's lives when they want to be something else. It is a way of emancipating yourself from your past, particularly if you have unhappy associations.'

24 *The God Delusion* is the title of the well known book by Richard Dawkins published by Bantam Press in 2006.

25 For the 2011 census see ons.gov.uk. Weekly attendance in the Church of England stands at about 1 million (churchofengland.org/about-us/facts-stats/research-statistics.aspx), and attendance in all churches at just over 3.1m (English Church Census 2005, eauk.org/church/research-and-statistics/english-church-census.cfm).

26 John 14.6. Mary Midgley was interviewed for *The Observer* on 23rd March 2014.

27 *When I Was Young – Voices from Lost Communities in Scotland: The Islands*, Birlinn 2000, pxi.

28 In his book *Man's Search for Meaning – The Classic Tribute to Hope from the Holocaust,* first published 1946 in German, English edition Rider 2004, p12.

29 John 14.6; see Acts 9.2; 22.4; 24.14.

30 Charles Colson & Nancy Pearcey, *How Now Shall We Live*, Marshall Pickering 2000, p14. Colson tells the story of his conversion in his book *Born Again*, Chosen Books 2008.

31 *The Imitation of Christ*, III.56.1, quoted by JI Packer & Gary A Parrett, *Grounded in the Gospel*, Baker Books 2010, p117.

32 Liz West & Trevor Withers, *Walking Together – Making 21st Century Disciples*, Cell UK 2007.

Chapter Four

1   *The Great Omission*, Monarch 2006, p62.

2   Joseph is described as a carpenter, or builder (*tekton*) in Matthew 13.55 and Mark 6.3. We read in Luke 2.51 that Jesus continued to lived with his parents in Nazareth and to be obedient to them after he reached the age of 12, the beginning of adulthood. Luke 3.23 tells us that Jesus began his public ministry when he was 'about thirty years old.' Most scholars date his birth to 6-4BC, and his baptism by John to 28-29AD, which was the 15th year of the reign of Tiberius (Luke 3.1). So from about 8AD to about 28AD Jesus would have been living and working in Nazareth with his father.

3   By Albert Jackson and David Day, Collins 2005.

4   From 'Being a disciple in the power of the Holy Spirit' by Sue Hope, ReSource magazine issue 12, *Being Disciples.*The full

article can be found on resource-arm.net/pdf/suehope.pdf. To find out more about Les Compagnons du Devoir visit compagnons-du-devoir.com.

5 Jewish scholar Claude Montefiore remarks: 'Discipleship such as Jesus demanded and inspired (a following, not for study but for service – to help the Master in his mission, to carry out his instructions and so on) was apparently a new thing, at all events, something that did not fit in ... with usual Rabbinic customs' – CG Montefiore, *Rabbinic Literature and Gospel Teachings*, MacMillan 1930 p218.

6 John 10.10.

7 Ezekiel 33.10 – taken as the title of Colson's book.

8 Acts 24.14.

9 John Coles, *Learning to Heal*, Authentic Media 2010, p3.

10 John 6.30, John 14.11-12. To the religious leaders who demanded furiously to know by what authority he claimed to be the Son of God, Jesus had given the same reply: You have a problem with me saying I am the Son of God? "Well, If I am not doing the works of my Father, then do not believe me. But if I do them, even though you do not believe me, believe the works, so that you may know and understand that the Father is in me an I am in the Father." John 10.33-38.

11 For a fuller exploration see Alison Morgan, *Doing What Jesus Did*, ReSource 2009.

12 Matthew 7.24-29.

13 Minucius Felix (160-240AD), *Octavius* 31.7, 38.5, quoted in Alan Kreider, *Worship and Evangelism in Pre-Christendom*, Grove Books 1995. Roger Morgan, *Beautiful Lives – Sharing our Faith with Friends and Neighbours*, ReSource 2010. 1 Peter 3.2-4 speaks of the beauty and reverence which should characterise our lives as Christians, and Roger believes that it is beautiful lives, lived in the power of the Holy Spirit, which lead others to faith. Names have been changed.

14 This story was shared with me by Mark Shell. Some names have been changed.

15 Bill Hull, *The Complete Book of Discipleship – On Being and Making Followers of Christ*, NavPress 2006, ch 4, 'The distinguishing marks of a disciple.'

16 Quoted by Bill Hull, *The Complete Book of Discipleship*, p117.

Chapter Five

1   From 'Christian Perfection 2', *The Works of the Rev William Law*,
     vol 3 p263; quoted by Bill Hull, *The Complete Book of
     Discipleship*, NavPress 2006 p26.
2   Daniel Defoe, *A Tour Through the Whole Island of Great Britain*,
     published in 3 volumes, 1724-1727, reprinted by the Folio
     Society in 1983.
3   Quoted by Michael Henderson, *A Model for Making Disciples –
     John Wesley's Class Meeting*, Warner Press 1997, p20.
4   Mark Greene, *Imagine How We Can Reach the* UK, LICC 2003,
     p7. For an analysis of the ways in which our culture is changing
     see my book *The Word on the Wind*, Monarch 2011.
5   The only gospel to use the word church (*ekklesia*) is Matthew,
     where it occurs just twice: Mt 16.18 & 18.17; in all it occurs 114 times
     in the New Testament, of which 23 times by Luke in Acts, and 62
     times in the letters of Paul. In the English Old Testament the word
     church does not appear either, but in the Septuagint, the Greek
     translation of the original Hebrew text made in the 3rd century BC,
     the word *ekklesia* is sometimes used for the Hebrew words *qahal*
     (also translated synagogue) and *'edhah*, (denoting the people of
     God). See note 8.
6   Simeon, Lucius and Manaen (Acts 13); Lydia (Acts 16), Phoebe
     (Romans 16), Chloe (1 Cor 1.1), Nympha (Col 4); Mary, Urbanus,
     Tryphaena and Tryphosa, Persis, Clement, Tychicus, Onesimus,
     Aristarchus, Justus, Epaphrus, Archippus (Rom 16, Phil 4, Eph 6,
     Col 4; Dorcas (Acts 9.36, where Luke uses *mathetria*, the
     feminine form of the word disciple, to describe her); Priscilla and
     Aquila (Acts 18, Romans 16, 1 Cor 16, 2 Timothy 4); Andronicus
     and Junia (Romans 16). For missionaries and elders see Acts
     chapters 8-14, Ephesians 4 & 1 Peter 5; for Paul and Timothy see
     1 Thess 1.3 and 2 Timothy 2.2.
7   As in Romans 1.6-7 (also 8.28), 1 Cor 1.2; Jude 1.1.
8   For an exhaustive analysis of the New Testament use of the word'
     ekklesia see Ray Bowen Ward, 'Ekklesia: a Word Study',
     Restoration Quarterly 1958 pp164-79 – also available online at
     acu.edu/sponsored/restoration_quarterly/archives/1950s/vol_2_
     no_4_contents/ward.html.
9   Michael Wilkins, *Following the Master – A Biblical Theology of*

Discipleship, Zondervan 1992, p44 & 271; see chapters 14 and 15; Graham Cray, Fresh Expressions ebulletin September 2013; *Making Disciples in Fresh Expressions of Church*, Fresh Expressions 2013 p32; Mark Greene, licc.org.uk/imagine-church; Rowan Williams, Foreword to *Mission-Shaped Church*, CHP 2004 pvii.

[10] For a full discussion of the nature of church see Alison Morgan, *The Word on the Wind*, Monarch 2011 ch 13 'Reimagining church.'

[11] This in fact is reflected in our growing understanding of the need to look again at what we mean by church. 78% of the innovatory 'fresh expressions' of church now place a deliberate focus on discipleship, rather than simply on attendance.

[12] *Grounded in the Gospel – Building Believers the Old-Fashioned Way*, Baker Books 2010, p72.

[13] See Ephesians 4 and 5; Colossians 3; Galatians 5.

[14] Galatians 6.6 – the first use of the words catechist and catechumen occur here (in the Greek text).

[15] Catechesis is a word which comes from the Greek verb *katecheo*, teach; it is 'the process by which persons are initiated into the Christian community and its faith, revelation, and vocation; the process by which persons throughout their lifetimes are continually converted and nurtured, transformed and formed, by and in its living tradition' – JH Westerhof, quoted by JI Packer and Gary A Parrett, *Grounded in the Gospel*, p28.

[16] The best discussion of early catechesis is given by Packer & Parrett, *Grounded in the Gospel*, pp54-57. See also Martyn Atkins, *Resourcing Renewal – Shaping Churches for the Emerging Future*, Inspire 2007 pp174-185; the Catholic Encyclopaedia online, 'Catechumen' (newadvent.org/cathen/03430b.htm); and Michael Moynagh & Philip Harrold, *Church for Every Context – An Introduction to Theology and Practice*, SCM Press 2012 ch 17.

[17] JI Packer and Gary A Parrett, *Grounded in the Gospel*, p29.

[18] *The Great Omission*, Monarch 2006 pxi.

[19] For Wesley's class system see Michael Henderson, *A Model for Making Disciples – John Wesley's Class Meeting*, Francis Asbury Press 1997 p30.

[20] Gaspar Kassanda, unpublished dissertation, 'An exegetical analysis of some Luke-Acts passages on discipleship and its relevance to the contemporary East African church as remedial

model to the current discipleship crisis,' George Whitfield College, South Africa 2005.

21 All these stories and more can be found on rootedinjesus.net.

22 For the full story and many testimonies see rootedinjesus.net/ mozambique.php, or read Helen's article in New Wine magazine, Summer 2013 (also available on the same page)

23 Edited by Roger Morgan and published by ReSource; see resource-arm.net.

24 A remark attributed in various forms to Bishop Joseph Butler, referring to those who claimed to have experienced special revelation or engagement with the Holy Spirit.

25 Quoted by Graham Cray, *Who's Shaping You? – 21st Century Disciples*, Cell UK 2011 p67.

26 Alain de Botton, *Religion for Atheists – A Non-Believer's Guide to the Uses of Religion*, Hamish Hamilton 2012

27 'Church minus God' and 'Congregation growing fast at the Sunday Assembly, the church that is not a church', *The Times* 16.9.13; 'Atheist meetings livin' on a prayer', *The Sunday Times* 22.9.13.

28 Alison Morgan, *The Word on the Wind*, Monarch 2011, chapters 3&4.

29 Mark Greene, *Imagine How We Can Reach the UK*, LICC 2003 p4.

30 Chris Hancock, 'Expert Report: Risks to Christians in China today', Wolfson College, Oxford, February 2013. See also Alan Hirsch, *The Forgotten Ways*, pp19, 77-78, 188-89.

31 John 13.34-35.

32 John 15.1-17. Jesus is building on the image of Israel as the unproductive vineyard in Isaiah 5; and the added implication in his use of this illustration is that outside stock, people not of Israel, will be grafted onto the vine.

33 I say 'himself' to reflect the fact that the Holy Spirit is a person, not to attribute gender; the word 'spirit' is in fact feminine in Hebrew (*ruach*), neuter in Greek (*pneuma*) and masculine only in Latin (*spiritus*) – which is why we in turn say 'he'.

34 See Galatians 5 and 1 Corinthians 12-13.

35 Elton Trueblood, *The Company of the Committed*, Harper & Row 1961, p113.

36 *Epistle of Mathetes to Diognetus*, quoted in Johannes Quasten,

Patrology 250, 2nd century; Tertullian, "Apology", Chapter 39.7 (circa 200AD); Julian the Apostate, *Letter to Arsacius*, AD 360.

37   Rodney Stark, *The Rise of Christianity*, Princeton University Press 1996, ch 1.
38   Isaiah 40.31.

Chapter Six

1   From a passage in *Letters from England*, a work purporting to be a translation of a visiting Spanish nobleman, Don Manuel Alvarez Espriella, published in 1807. Reprinted by Nabu Press, 2013; or online at euppublishing.com/doi/abs/10.3366/vic.2012.0056.

2   George Cadbury became active nationally, campaigning for old age pensions and humane working conditions. He also ran a summer camp each year for 25,000 children from deprived areas of the city. For more information see cadbury.co.uk, birmingham.gov.uk and bournvillevillagecouncil.org.uk.

3   Another Quaker, William Clark, founded a factory village in Street, Somerset; its open air swimming pool remains in regular use today. In 1888 William Lever, a Congregationalist, built the garden village of Port Sunlight for his soap factory workers. Methodist Titus Salt, a cloth manufacturer and by 1853 the biggest employer in the city of Bradford, built the model village of Saltaire, hoping to create an environment where people could lead 'healthy, virtuous and godly lives.' In 1859 Edward Akroyd, an Anglican, built a model housing scheme for workers at his Halifax textile factory; like George Cadbury he introduced a school and a pension scheme, built churches for his workers, and helped found a penny bank to encourage workers to save. Both he and Cadbury were active nationally, Cadbury as a campaigner for social reform, Akroyd as MP for Huddersfield and then Bradford.

4   Matthew 5.13-16.

5   Wesley was influenced by the French Catholic Monr de Renty, who also focussed on personal growth through ministry to others; most Anglican groups at the time focussed on personal growth through careful attention to oneself. See MH Henderson, *A Model for Making Disciples*, Warner Press 1997, p50.

6   Remark by Graham Cray, Fresh Expressions Bulletin September 2013, freshexpressions.org.uk/news/main-thing.

7   Romans 1.20. For the concrete origin of conceptual vocabulary see Steven Pinker, *The Stuff of Thought*, Allen Lane 2007. Abstract concepts are expressed using metaphors which began in the sense world – eg 'independence' means 'not hanging from'; a 'station' is a 'standing place'; to 'respect' means to 'look back'. Once vivid, they gradually become disembodied concepts – and often lose their impact.

8   The metaphor is the more effective because it works on at least two other levels – not only is Peter quoting scripture (Isaiah 28.16, Psalm 118.22, Isaiah 8.14-15), he is also reminding them of Jesus's teaching that he himself is the temple of God, and the implication that the old religion has been completed and superseded by a new one (eg Mark 14.58, John 2.19-21). Paul uses the same metaphor (eg in Eph 2.19-22).

9   Michael J Wilkins, *Following the Master – A Biblical Theology of Discipleship*, Zondervan 1992, p342.

10   Luke 4.16-21 and 31-44.

11   Matthew 10.7-8, John 20.21; Matthew 25.34-40; 2 Timothy 2.2; Matthew 28.19-20. See also Matthew 5.13-16, on being salt and light in our communities through the doing of good works.

12   Roger Walton notes: 'if you had only Luke's Gospel you would think immediately that following Jesus was about mission and outreach... If you had only John's Gospel you might think that discipleship hinges on a personal relationship with Christ, knowing, believing and abiding in him.. The reasons of these contrasting views of discipleship are manifold but a key factor is the life situation of the intended hearers.' *The Reflective Disciple*, SCM Press 2012, pp13-14.

13   Ann Morisy warns against projects which become separated from church community and allow themselves to be driven by a society agenda that emphasizes needs meeting rather than mission; not simply because these miss the main point, but because they create relationships of superiority-inferiority, and prevent the 'givers' from growing in faith and discipleship through their contact with the 'receivers.' See *Journeying Out – A New Approach to Christian Mission*, Continuum 2006.

14   Roger Walton points out that 20th century writers on discipleship

(eg Leslie Weatherhead, *Discipleship*, SCM Press 1934; David Watson, *Discipleship*, Hodder & Stoughton 1981) emphasize prayer, study, fellowship and the nurture of Christian virtues, and that this is clearly helpful but no longer sufficient – 'every attempt to sketch out a concrete pattern of Christian discipleship will only be effective if it is appropriate for its age; but, as a result, it may not work in the next,' *The Reflective Disciple*, SCM Press 2012 p113). A changing cultural context places new demands on our discipleship – Walton cites the new trends of post-nationalism, post-modernity and post-Christendom as influential new factors.

[15] Many of our difficulties about who should or should not be ordained, and the roles of the ordained minister, go back to the redefinition of ordination which took place in the 12th century as the church struggled to win a distinctive voice in counterpart to the increasingly powerful secular authorities. In particular, the offering of the sacrament of the eucharist was redefined as an exclusive ministry of ordained priesthood. Prior to the 12th century ordination had been conceived much more broadly, as an appointment (of a man or a woman) to a particular office in the church or in society – you could be ordained as a queen or even as a doorkeeper! See Gary Macy, *The Hidden History of Women's Ordination*, OUP 2008. For a summary see alisonmorgan.co.uk.

[16] Luke 7.19-20.

[17] Matthew 13.31-32.

[18] Graham Cray, 'Remembering the main thing', Fresh Expressions Bulletin September 2013; and *Who's Shaping You? – 21st Century Disciples*, Cell UK 2011 p24.

[19] Michael Frost, *Exiles – Living Missionally in a Post-Christian Culture*, Hendrikson 2006, ch 5. See also Alan Hirsch, *The Forgotten Ways*, Brazos Press 2006, p25. For a fuller discussion of the nature and purpose of the church see Alison Morgan, *The Word on the Wind*, Monarch 2011, ch 13 – a church, I suggest, is a community centred on Jesus; a united community; a missional community; and a community shaped and formed by the Holy Spirit. The dangers of an inward-looking church are helpfully discussed by Roger Walton, *The Reflective Disciple*, SCM Press 2012, chapter 4 'The rhythm of discipleship'.

[20] *Exiles* p126.

21 *Mission-shaped Church – Church Planting and Fresh Expressions of Church in a Changing Context*, CHP 2004. Website freshexpressions.org.uk. The phrase 'fresh expression of church' was originally coined by Archbishop Rowan Williams.

22 Graham Cray, *Making Disciples in Fresh Expressions of Church*, Fresh Expressions 2013, p33.

23 George Lings, *Snapshots – Stories from the Edge*, issue 2, states that the Church Army Research Unit's survey of all the known fxC in 10 Anglican dioceses make up on average 15% of the church communities in each diocese (see churcharmy.org.uk/sheffieldcentre). In his presentation at the 2014 Anglicans Ablaze Conference in Johannesburg, Graham Cray estimated this as corresponding to the addition of 4 new dioceses to the Church of England.

24 Zondervan 1996.

25 Ephesians 4.11-13. Alan Scott is the founder of Causeway Coast Vineyard in Coleraine, Northern Ireland; he was speaking at the New Wine Leaders Conference 2014 (new-wine.org). Bob Briner was quoted by John Tyson, speaking at the same conference.

26 In making this transition we were helped, among others, by Laurence Singlehurst and Cell UK (celluk.org.uk).

27 There is a dedicated missional communities website, missionalcommunities.co.uk. For Holy Trinity see holytrinity leicester.org/missionshapedcommunities.html. St Thomas Sheffield has served as a helpful model for Holy Trinity: stthomaschurch.org.uk/our-communities.

28 See healingonthestreets.com, streetpastors.org, trusselltrust.org /foodbank-projects, capuk.org.

29 See eauk.org/idea/southampton-churches-set-the-bar-on-adoption.cfm (see also homeforgood.org.uk/local-movements). Life Church, Newton Aycliff: freshexpressions.org.uk/stories /lifechurch.

30 Eg Hope (hopetogether.org.uk) encourages churches to work together in mission, using both words and actions; ROC (Redeeming our Communities, roc.uk.com) helps churches to engage prayerfully with their communities through forging partnerships with the Police and other agencies; Faithworks (oasisuk.org/what/faithworks) seeks to help Christians and churches develop their role at the hub of their local community

and to change public perception of the church by engaging with government and the media; Prayer 24/7 (uk.24-7prayer.com) aims to reconcile the world to God in Jesus Christ by mobilising the Church in prayer, mission and justice, and so on. Mission Action Planning, Growing Healthy Churches and Natural Church Development programmes all help churches to begin the process of discerning how to grow in discipleship and mission in their particular contexts.

[31] David Goodhew (ed) : *Church Growth in Britain 1980 to the Present*, Ashgate Publishing 2012, p3. For a summary see alisonmorgan.co.uk.

[32] Exodus 8.19; Luke 11.20.

[33] John V Taylor, *The Go-Between God – The Holy Spirit and the Christian Mission*, SCM Press 1972 (reprinted 2010).

[34] For a fuller discussion of the history and purpose of the renewal movement see Alison Morgan, *Renewal, What Is It and What Is It For?* Grove Books 2006.

[35] Luke 24.49, Acts 1.5. And see 1 Corinthians 12, and for a discussion of the role of the Holy Spirit in the life of the church today, Alison Morgan, *Doing What Jesus Did – A Fresh Look at the Gifts of the Spirit,* ReSource 2009.

[36] Roger Walton points out that if Alpha does not resonate with a church's ethos and convictions it is unlikely to be effective; 'it can also make for dispirited people and undermine confidence for other ventures.' 'A quick fix, ready-made programme is attractive but should be cautiously avoided; making disciples is more than getting people into a first time commitment or experience of God. In post-modern culture seeking experiences is a common desire but translating that into long-term committed discipleship may require more thought.' *The Reflective Disciple*, SCM Press 2012, pp159, 173.

[37] First made in Branston in 1922; production continued until 2004, when it moved to Bury St Edmunds.

[38] 1 Thessalonians 1.5; 2.11.

[39] Mick told his story at the Fellowship for Parish Evangelism, January 2014. For a short bio see fpe-network.org/Documents/MickJanbio%20.pdf

[40] This story is told mostly in Hugh's own words, from a longer written account which he produced before he moved on in 2012. He retells it in ReSource magazine issue 31, *The Paraclete*. For

more information visit langport-somerset.btck.co.uk/About%20us or langport-team-ministry.org.uk/elements/celtic-connections.

41 See churchtimes.co.uk/articles/2014/31-january/news/uk/church -gives-vital-support-in-somerset-floods-crisis; or independent. co.uk/news/uk/home-news/villagers-tire-of-island-life-on-flooded-somerset-levels-9084105.html

42 Robert Lewis & Rob Wilkins, *The Church of Irresistible Influence*, Zondervan 2001, p41.

43 Christopher JH Wright, *The Mission of God – Unlocking the Bible's Grand Narrative*, IVP 2006. See also his later book *The Mission of God's People – A Biblical Theology of the Church's Mission*, Zondervan 2010, which contains the oft repeated statement 'God doesn't have a mission for his church, he has a church for his mission.'

44 Ephesians 5.19, Colossians 3.16.

45 Revelation 4.8.

46 Rob Bell, *Rhythm*, in his Nooma DVD series (nooma.com); James MacMillian, 'The Divine Spark of Music', Sandford St Martin 30th Anniversary lecture, 1st October 2008; John Dade, quoted by Leonard Sweet, *Nudge – Awakening Each Other to the God Who's Already There*, David C Cook 2010, p152.

Chapter Seven

1 *Dangerously Alive – African Adventures of Faith Under Fire*, Monarch 2011, p30.

2 Mark 8.34.

3 See Ernest E Best, 'Following Jesus – Discipleship in the Gospel of Mark', *Journal for the Study of the New Testament*, 1981. Mark's emphasis on cost is discussed by Roger Walton, *The Reflective Disciple*, SCM Press 2012, pp9-12.

4 So comforting had the programme become that there was an outcry in 1982 when the BBC announced the decision to axe it on the grounds that just 2% of those listening were actually under the age of 5. An audience survey in the mid-70s had revealed that there were as many long-distance lorry drivers as young children listening (presumably sitting comfortably in their cabs). See andywalmsley.blogspot.co.uk/2011/08/are-you-sitting-comfortably.html

5   bbc.co.uk/news/science-environment-28592838 – Melissa Hogenboom reports on a study published in August 2014 in the Proceedings of the National Academy of Sciences under the title 'A computational and neural model of momentary subjective well-being,' by researchers at UCL. The equation in question is

$$\text{Happiness}(t) = w_0 + w_1 \sum_{j=1}^{t} \gamma^{t-j} CR_j + w_2 \sum_{j=1}^{t} \gamma^{t-j} EV_j + w_3 \sum_{j=1}^{t} \gamma^{t-j} RPE_j.$$

6   All of these conditions are covered in the latest edition of the standard psychiatric reference work, the *Diagnostic and Statistical Manual of Mental Disorders*. Fear of public speaking is a form of 'social anxiety disorder', temper tantrums are a symptom of 'disruptive mood dysregulation disorder', and worrying about your health is a result of 'somatic symptom disorder'. 'Social phobia is under-recognised and undertreated,' one helpful website explains; but 'adjunctive use of benzodiazepines can facilitate the treatment response of patients who need initial symptom relief', and it should not be forgotten that 'the use of beta blockers as needed has been found to be helpful in the treatment of circumscribed social and performance phobias.' See aafp.org/afp/1999/1115/p2311.html.

7   Quoted by Michael Horton, *The Gospel Commission – Recovering God's Strategy For Making Disciples*, Baker Books 2011, p 254.

8   Tom Sine, *The New Conspirators*, Paternoster 2009, p79 et passim.

9   For Obama's speech in Seattle in July 2014, see washingtonpost.com/blogs/the-fix/wp/2014/07/23/the-most-important-sentence-president-obama-uttered-on-Tuesday/. For the new sense of unease see the results of a poll conducted in June 2014: washingtonpost.com/blogs/the-fix/wp/2014/08/06/the-single-most-depressing-number-in-the-new-nbc-wall-street-journal-poll/.

10 'Burnt Norton', the first poem in his series *Four Quartets*.

11 William Shakespeare, *Macbeth*, Act 2 scene 5.

12 Reading from Matthew 7. 24-27 and 13-14.

13 Frederick Buechner: *Telling the Truth – The Gospel as Tragedy, Comedy and Fairy Tale*, HarperOne 1977, pp40-41.

14 Jeremiah 38.4.

15 Isaiah 64.8 (potter), Zechariah 13.9 (fire), 1 Peter 2.5 (stones); 2 Cor 3.18 (transforming), 2 Cor 4.16 (renewing), John 15.1-11 (vine), Gal 5.22-23 (fruit).

16 Simon Ponsonby, *More – How You Can Have More of the Holy Spirit When You Already Have Everything in Christ*, David C Cook 2004, p185.

17 2 Timothy 2.3-6.

18 Dallas Willard, *The Great Omission*, Monarch 2006 p124.

19 Luke 14.25-33.

20 I have written about these experiences more fully in *The Wild Gospel*, p242. See also, for the buzzard, p318.

21 In a talk at a Fresh Expressions Conference held in Lincoln on March 5th 2010.

22 In a talk given at a Fulcrum Conference in St Mary's Islington, 27th April 2007, and printed in ReSource magazine issue 12, *Disciples*, Summer 2008 (see resource-arm.net).

23 Evelyn and Robert are not their real names. Robert's story is told by Roger Morgan in *Beautiful Lives – Sharing our Faith with Friends and Neighbours: Course Member's Booklet*, ReSource 2010, p11.

24 Robin came to the second *Rooted in Jesus* conference in Toliara, just two weeks after the cyclone. The diocese, inaugurated in 2014, has already planted 60 churches now attended by over 6000 worshippers; Bishop Todd McGregor has baptised hundreds of new Christians; he writes, "I can't figure it all out but what I do understand is that God is doing something and I want to be part of it." See peoplereaching.org, and rootedinjesus.net/reports/Madagascar%202013%20report.pdf.

25 The story is told by Martin McGee, *Christian Martyrs for a Muslim People*, Paulist Press 2008. In 2010 it was the subject of a film, *Of Gods and Men*, directed by Xavier Beauvois, and reviewed by Martin Cavender in ReSource magazine issue 26, *Intentional Communities*.

26 JI Packer and Gary A Parrett, *Grounded in the Gospel – Making Believers the Old-Fashioned Way*, Baker Books 2010 p175.

27 Speaking at the Fresh Expressions conference, Lincoln, March 5th 2010.

28 Neil Cole, *Organic Church – Growing Faith Where Life Happens*, Jossey-Bass 2005, pp26-27.

29 Images from Paul: 1 Cor 9.24-27, running; 2 Cor 11.23-29, working, facing danger, labouring, toiling, losing sleep; Gal 4.19, suffering pain as severe as childbirth; Phil 3.12-13, pressing on and straining; Col 1.29, labouring and struggling. See also 2

Timothy 2.1-7, the athlete, the soldier, the farmer. For celebration and party see Jesus's repeated comparisons of being with him to being invited to a wedding banquet (eg Matt 22 & 25; his own participation in parties and dinners (eg Luke 5, John 2 & 12); his promises of abundant and fruitful life (John 10, 15); the imagery of the kingdom being like a harvest, a treasure, a pearl, rising dough, a full catch of fish (Matt 13).

Chapter Eight

1   Joan Didion, *The White Album*, Farrar Straus Giroux 2009 (first published 1979). Copeland was interviewed in *The Church Times*, 14.11.08.
2   McAdams is Professor of Psychology at Northwestern University and author of *The Redemptive Self – Stories Americans Live By*, OUP 2007. He was interviewed in November 2013 by Carolyn Gregoire for the *Huffington Post*, huffingtonpost.com/2013/11/18/how-your-life-story-is-a-_n_4284006.html.
3   Alain de Botton, *The News – A User's Manual*, Hamish Hamilton 2014, p11.
4   Subject of the 1998 film *The Truman Show*, in which he gradually discovers that the world he thinks lives in has been artificially created by a television company. See Tom Sine, *The New Conspirators – Creating the Future One Mustard Seed at a Time*, IVP 2008, p87.
5   See Brian McLaren, *Everything Must Change – Jesus, Global Crises, and a Revolution of Hope*, Thomas Nelson 2007, pp190-198. Marx followed his denunciation of the capitalist story with the invention of a communist one – but that is now history.
6   Robert H Nelson, *Economics as Religion*, Pennsylvania State University Press 2001, pxv. He continues: 'this new religion 'serves many of the same functions in contemporary society that Christian and other religions did in their time.' Discussed by Tom Sine, *The New Conspirators*, pp68-69.
7   Brian McLaren, *Everything Must Change*, p275. The figures referred to for the US are quoted by McLaren and relate to the year 2006. Helen Lewis describes our culture as a soap opera in *The Observer*, 23.11.14.
8   BBC News Magazine 28.10.14; see newcitizenship.org.uk.

9   *The Irresistible Revolution – Living as an Ordinary Radical*, Zondervan 2006, p150.

10   Stanley Hauerwas, in an interview by Christopher Landau in the Grand Committee Room of the Houses of Parliament, 21.10.2010.

11   Genesis 41 (Joseph), Exodus 3-20 (Moses), Judges 6 (Gideon), 2 Samuel 5 (David), Esther 4 (Esther).

12   Luke 8.3 (Joanna), Matthew 14.19 (the boy), Mark 15.21 (Simon), John 4.1-42 (Samaritan woman), Matthew 27.19 (dream).

13   For a fuller analysis see Alison Morgan, *The Wild Gospel*, reprinted Monarch 2009, Chapter 1 'Jesus and the culture of his day.'

14   For a more detailed discussion see Alison Morgan, *The Wild Gospel*, reprinted Monarch 2009, Chapter 2.

15   Acts 6.5 (Prochorus, Nicanor, Parmenas), Acts 15.22 (Paul, Barnabas, Silas), Acts 3.3 (beggar), Acts 9.33 (Aeneas), Acts 9.40 (Tabitha), Acts 9.12 (Ananias), Acts 10.4-5 (Cornelius).

16   This was to be a constant process – John later wrote along similar lines to the churches in Pergamum and Thyatira, who had not managed to disentangle themselves from idol worship and sexual immorality, and Laodicea, a city whose pride in its wealth was preventing it from noticing its spiritual poverty (Revelation ch 2-3). See also Chapter 5, 'Discipleship and the church.'

17   Philippians 3.20; John 17.14-16.

18   1 Peter 2.11.

19   Max De Pree, *Leadership is an Art*, Currency 2004.

20   Tom Sine, *The New Conspirators*, IVP 2008, p77.

21   I have written at much greater length about the radical nature of the parables and the beatitudes in *The Wild Gospel*, reprinted Monarch 2009, especially Chapter 3: 'Jesus's teachings – a new vision.'

22   Acts 17.6-7.

23   JI Packer & Gary A Parrett, *Grounded in the Gospel*, Baker Books 2010, p162. Their remarks are applied to the North American context, but apply to the whole of the Western world.

24   See Nick Page, *Revelation Road*, Hodder and Stoughton 2014, eg the discussion of Revelation 7 and the cult of Cybele in Rome (p68), and the discussion of Revelation 2 and the cult of Domitian (p142).

25   See Chapter 5.

26 *Advent*, 1964.
27 *In His Name, A Training Course for Healing Prayer Teams*, by Alison Morgan and John Woolmer, ReSource 2008, Session 4. Two of the young people involved in that session are now, some ten years later, in full time Christian ministry, helping others to learn to live in God's story and not the world's story.
28 *Optimism – an essay*, Wilder Publications 2012, p7.
29 'The Marketable Revolution', *The Simple Way Online Newsletter*, March 2006; thesimpleway.org, quoted by Tom Sine, *The New Conspirators*, p23. See also Shane's book, *The Irresistible Revolution – Living as an Ordinary Radical*, Zondervan 2006.
30 Romans 12.2. Brian McLaren, *Everything Must Change – Jesus, Global Crises, and a Revolution of Hope*, Thomas Nelson 2007, p139.
31 The village was Winterbourne Monkton, the young mother Sue Richardson. The Sunday School grew and now works alongside five local village Sunday Schools in the Dorchester team, attended by 120 children each week.
32 Stuart was interviewed by Simon de Bruxelles, *The Times*, 6.3.14.
33 In a BBC Newsnight interview with Jeremy Paxman, October 2010: youtube.com/watch?v=hYM7SzJMKns.

Chapter Nine

1 Roger Walton, *Disciples Together – Discipleship, Formation and Small Groups*, SCM Press 2014, pxi.
2 For more comments by team members who found a short term mission trip profoundly impacted their faith see the team page on rootedinjesus.net. I have written of the difference that first trip made to my own discipleship in *The Wild Gospel*, Monarch 2004. My travelling companions were John Woolmer, Martin and Cesca Cavender and Laurie White. Martin, Cesca, John and I all went on to be part of ReSource. Laurie continued to grow in faith during his retirement; he died in 2013.
3 Statistics from a YouGov survey commissioned by Linda Woodhead in 2013 – see brin.ac.uk/news/2013/profile-of-anglicans-and-other-news.
4 Dallas Willard, *Renovation of the Heart*, NavPress 2002, p250.
5 Ephesians 4.12.
6 Tom Sine, *The New Conspirators*, Paternoster 2008, p261.

7   Fresh Expressions developed from the Church of England report *Mission-Shaped Church* published by CHP in 2004. See the earlier discussion in chapter 6.

8   Graham Cray, *Making Disciples in Fresh Expressions of Church*, Fresh Expressions 2013; *Who's Shaping You? – 21st Century Disciples*, Cell UK 2011. See also freshexpressions.org.uk/guide/discipleship. Findings from the Church Army's Church Growth Research Programme (2011-2013), published in the report *From Anecdote to Evidence*, are available on churchgrowthresearch.org.uk – 'being intentional in nurturing disciples' is identified as one of the key features of growing churches. Fresh Expressions are now springing up in many other countries.

9   churcharmy.org.uk/Publisher/File.aspx?ID=138306

10 Life Church, Newton Aycliff: freshexpressions.org.uk/stories/lifechurch.

11 Terminus café, Sheffield: freshexpressions.org.uk/stories/terminus.

12 Small Boat, Big Sea – see ReSource magazine issue 26 *Intentional Communities:* resource-arm.net/pdf/Frost%20issue%2026.pdf; Abide – freshexpressions.org.uk/stories/abide. Moot – moot.uk.net/.

13 See resource-arm.net/pdf/beautifullivescotterell.pdf. The BELLS rhythm of life has been adopted by another new faith community – see freshexpressions.org.uk/stories/bells. For Tracy's article see resource-arm.net/pdf/beautifullivescotterell.pdf.

14 Bill Hull, *The Complete book of Discipleship – On Being and Making Followers of Christ*, NavPress 2006, p165.

15 Fresh Expressions monthly bulletin, June 2012, freshexpressions.org.uk

16 We had 65 small groups, or cell groups as we called them, for adults and teenagers; most of the 150 people who were not in groups were children – who met in Sunday school classes each week. See also chapter 6. A free short guide to 'Growing a church through small groups' by Roger Morgan is available from the ReSource office and website.

17 Romans 16.3-5; Colossians 4.15; Acts 16.40.

18 In the preface to his German Mass and Orders of Service Luther recommends that 'those who want to be Christians in earnest.. should meet along in a house somewhere to pray, to read, to baptize and read the sacrament, and do other Christian works' – quoted by Steven Croft, *Transforming Communities*, DLT 2002, p97.

19 A helpful outline of the history of the small group is given by

Roger Walton, *Disciples Together – Discipleship, Formation and Small Groups*, SCM Press 2014, chapters 6 & 7. CellUK, founded by Laurence Singlehurst, has been at the forefront of the development of the cell group in this country. See celluk.org.uk.

[20] *Disciples Together*, SCM Press 2014, p107.

[21] Helen Cameron, *Resourcing Mission: Practical Theology for Changing Churches*, SCM Press 2010, pp24-37.

[22] Bill Hull, *The Complete Book of Discipleship* 2006, chapter 9. Quote from p229.

[23] Church Army Research Unit, August 2008, churcharmy.org.uk.

[24] 'Coaching' is the secular term for what we in the church call 'mentoring'; it involves one person coming alongside another to help them discern and follow their own chosen pathway. 'Spiritual direction' is more directive, involving regular short meetings and set exercises or recommended practices. 'Prayer ministry' is a term sometimes used simply to denote prayer for another in the context of a church service, but is more commonly used to describe a longer period of prayer, listening and discernment focussed on the needs of the individual concerned – usually offered by two people.

[25] Matthew 11.30.

[26] John 10.10.

[27] Helen Van Koevering, *Dancing their Dreams – The Lakeshore Nyanja Women of the Anglican Diocese of Niassa*, Kachere Series 2005, pp114-15. See the discussion of the Diocese of Niassa in chapter 5.

[28] The interview was broadcast on BBC Radio 4 on 18 April 1984 and printed in *The Listener*. It is quoted by John V Taylor, *A Matter of Life and Death*, SCM Press 1986, p35.

[29] 2 Sam 6.14 (David), Psalm 150.4, Ecclesiastes 3.4, Jeremiah 31 4-14, Matthew 11.17 (Jesus).

[30] Lucy Peppiatt, *The Disciple: On Becoming Truly Human*, Cascade Books 2012, p151 (see ch 4); Christopher JH Wright, *The Mission of God – Unlocking the Bible's Grand Narrative*, IVP 2006 (see ch 6).

Books

Full references for all works quoted, cited or referred to are given in the chapter notes, including articles and websites. Full length publications to which I have referred are listed below.

Atkins, Martyn: *Resourcing Renewal – Shaping Churches for the Emerging Future*, Inspire 2007

Bonhoeffer, Dietrich: *The Cost of Discipleship*, SCM Press new edition 2001

Botton, Alain de: *Religion for Atheists – A Non-Believer's Guide to the Uses of Religion*, Hamish Hamilton 2012

Botton, Alain de: *The News – A User's Manual*, Hamish Hamilton 2014

Briner, Bob: *Deadly detours – Seven Noble Causes that Keep Christians from Changing the World*, Zondervan 1996

Bruce, AB: *The Training of the Twelve*, reprinted CreateSpace Independent Publishing Platform 2012

Brueggemann, Walter: *Finally Comes the Poet*, Fortress Press 1989

Brueggemann, Walter: *The Prophetic Imagination*, Fortress Press 1978

Buechner, Frederick: *Telling the Truth – The Gospel as Tragedy, Comedy and Fairy Tale*, HarperOne 1977

Cameron, Helen: *Resourcing Mission – Practical Theology for Changing Churches*, SCM Press 2010

Chadwick, Owen: *A History of Christianity*, Phoenix Illustrated 1995.

Claiborne, Shane, *The Irresistible Revolution – Living as an Ordinary Radical*, Zondervan 2006

Cole, Neil: *Organic Church – Growing Faith where Life Happens*, Jossey-Bass 2005

Coleman, Robert: *The Master Plan of Evangelism*, reprinted Revell 2006

Coles, John: *Learning to Heal*, Authentic Media 2010

Colson, Charles & Nancy Pearcey: *How Now Shall We Live*, Marshall Pickering 2000

Colson, Charles: *Born Again*, Chosen Books 2008

Cray, Graham: *Making Disciples in Fresh Expressions of Church*, Fresh Expressions 2013

Cray, Graham, et al: *Mission-Shaped Church – Church Planting and Fresh Expressions of Church in a Changing Context*, CHP 2004

Cray, Graham: *Who's Shaping You? – 21st Century Disciples*, Cell UK Ministries 2010

Croft, Steven: *Transforming Communities*, DLT 2002

Defoe, Daniel: *A Tour through the Whole Island of Great Britain*, published in 3 volumes, 1724-1727

Down, Martin: *Speak to these Bones*, Monarch 1993

Frankl, Victor: *Man's Search for Meaning – The Classic Tribute to Hope from the Holocaust,* Rider 2004

Frost, Michael: *Exiles – Living Missionally in a Post-Christian Culture*, Hendrikson 2006

Frost, Michael & Alan Hirsch: *Rejesus – A Wild Messiah for a Missional Church*, Hendrikson 2009

Frost, Michael & Alan Hirsch, *The Shaping of Things to Come – Innovation and Mission for the 21st-Century Church*, Hendrikson Publishers 2003

Goodhew, David (ed) : *Church Growth in Britain 1980 to the Present*, Ashgate Publishing 2012

Greene, Mark: *Fruitfulness on the Frontline – Making a Difference Where You Are*, IVP 2014

Greene, Mark: *Imagine How We Can Reach the* UK, LICC 2003

Guillebaud, Simon: *Dangerously Alive – African Adventures of Faith Under Fire*, Monarch 2011

Henderson, Michael: *A Model for Making Disciples – John Wesley's Class Meeting*, Warner Press 1997

Hirsch, Alan & Dave Fergusson: *On the Verge – A Journey into the Apostolic Future of the Church*, Zondervan 2011

Hirsch, Alan: *The Forgotten Ways*, Brazos Press 2006

Horton, Michael: *The Gospel Commission – Recovering God's Strategy for Making Disciples*, Baker Books 2011

Hybels, Bill: *Courageous Leadership*, Zondervan 2002

Hull, Bill: *The Complete Book of Discipleship – On Being and Making Followers of Christ*, Navpress 2006

Jackson, Albert & David Day, *Complete Woodworker's Manual,* Collins 2005

Kreider, Alan: *Worship and Evangelism in Pre-Christendom*, Grove Books 1995

Lewis, CS: *Mere Christianity*, William Collins 2012

Lewis, Robert & Rob Wilkins: *The Church of Irresistible Influence*, Zondervan 2001

Lings, George: *From Anecdote to Evidence – Findings from the Church Growth Research Programme 2011-2013*

Macy, Gary: *The Hidden History of Women's Ordination*, OUP 2008

Manson, TW: *The Teaching of Jesus: Studies of its Form and content*, 2nd edition CUP 1935

McGee, Martin: *Christian Martyrs for a Muslim People*, Paulist Press 2008

McLaren, Brian: *Everything must Change: Jesus, Global crises, and a Revolution of Hope*, Thomas Nelson 2007

McLaren, Brian: *Naked Spirituality – A Life with God in 12 Simple Words*, Hodder 2012

Montefiore, CG: *Rabbinic Literature and Gospel Teachings*, MacMillan 1930

Morgan, Alison: *Doing What Jesus Did – A Fresh Look at the Gifts of the Spirit,* ReSource 2009

Morgan, Alison: *Renewal, What Is It and What Is It For?* Grove Books 2006.

Morgan, Alison: *The Wild Gospel – Bringing Truth to Life*, Monarch 2004, reprinted 2009

Morgan, Alison: *The Word on the Wind – Renewing Confidence in the Gospel*, Monarch 2011

Morison, Frank: *Who Moved the Stone?* Authentic Media 2006

Morisy, Ann: *Journeying Out – A New Approach to Christian Mission*, Continuum 2006

Moynagh, Michael: *Changing World, Changing Church*, Monarch 2001

Moynagh, Michael & Philip Harrold: *Church for Every Context – An Introduction to Theology and Practice,* SCM Press 2012

Neat, Timothy: *When I Was Young – Voices from Lost Communities in Scotland – The Islands*, Birlinn 2000

Nelson, Robert H: *Economics as Religion*, Pennsylvania State University Press 2001

Packer, JI and Gary A Parrett: *Grounded in the Gospel: Building Believers the Old-Fashioned Way*, Baker Books 2010

Page, Nick: *Revelation Road*, Hodder and Stoughton 2014

Peppiatt, Lucy: *The Disciple – On Becoming Truly Human*, Cascade Books, 2012

Pinker, Steven: *The Stuff of Thought*, Allen Lane 2007

Ponsonby, Simon: *More – How You Can Have More of the Holy Spirit When You Already Have Everything in Christ*, David C Cook 2004

Pridmore, John, with Greg Watts: *From Gangland to Promised Land*, xt3media 2008

Pullin, Tony: *Making Disciples – How Did Jesus Do It?*, CWR 2014

Sine, Tom: *The New Conspirators*, Paternoster 2009

Southey, Robert: *Letters from England*, first published in 1807, reprinted by Nabu Press 2013

Stark, Rodney: *The Rise of Christianity*, Princeton University Press 1996

Sweet, Leonard: *Nudge – Awakening Each Other to the God Who's Already There*, David C Cook 2010

Taylor, John V: *The Go-Between God – The Holy Spirit and the Christian Mission*, SCM Press 1972, reprinted 2010.

Taylor, Richard: *To Catch a Thief*, New Wine Publishing 2006

Trueblood, Elton: *The Company of the Committed*, Harper & Row 1961

Tunningley, Darrell: *Unreachable – One Man's Journey through Drugs, Violence, Armed Robbery and a Miraculous Encounter with God in Prison*, Sovereign World 2011

Tyndale, William: *The New Testament Translated by William Tyndale*, Cologne edition 1525 – see faithofgod.net/tynt/Prologue.htm.

Van Koevering, Helen: *Dancing their Dreams – The Lakeshore Nyanja Women of the Anglican Diocese of Niassa*, Kachere Series 2005

Walton, Roger: *Disciples Together – Discipleship, Formation and Small Groups*, SCM Press 2014

Walton, Roger: *The Reflective Disciple*, SCM Press 2012

West, Liz & Trevor Withers, *Walking Together – Making 21st Century Disciples*, Cell UK 2007

Wilkins, Michael: *Following the Master – A Biblical Theology of Discipleship*, Zondervan 1992

Willard, Dallas: *The Great Omission – Reclaiming Jesus' Essential Teachings on Discipleship*, Monarch 2006

Willard, Dallas: *Renovation of the Heart*, NavPress 2002

Willard, Dallas: *The Spirit of the Disciplines – Understanding how God Changes Lives*, Harper SanFrancisco 1991

Woolmer, John: *Encounters*, Monarch 2007

Wright, Christopher JH: *The Mission of God – Unlocking the Bible's Grand Narrative*, IVP 2006

Wright, Christopher JH: *The Mission of God's People – A Biblical Theology of the Church's Mission*, Zondervan 2010

Course materials

There are many published resources available to support those who wish to deepen their discipleship. The best are those which help people to become active apprentices of Jesus, learning together to do the works that he did, and in the process becoming more like him.

Anderson, Neil & Steve Goss: *Freedom in Christ – A 13 Week Course for Every Christian*, fficm.org

Bible Reading Fellowship: *Foundations21 – The New Way to Discipleship*, Foundations21.net

Cottrell, Stephen, et al: *Pilgrim – A Course for the Christian Journey*, CHP 2013-2015, pilgrimcourse.org.

Greene, Mark: *Life on the Frontline* and *Fruitfulness on the Frontine*, LICC 2012 & 2013, licc.org.uk

Gumbel, Nicky: *The Jesus Lifestyle Series 1-3*, Alpha Books 2007-2011, alpha.org

Morgan, Alison & Bill Goodman: *Season of Renewal – A Lent course*, ReSource 2007, resource-arm.net

Morgan, Alison & John Woolmer: *In His Name – A Training Course for Healing Prayer Teams*, ReSource 2008, resource-arm.net

Morgan, Roger: *Beautiful Lives – Sharing our Faith with Friends and Neighbours*, ReSource 2010, resource-arm.net

Morgan, Roger: *The God Who is There – A Discipleship Course for Small Groups*, ReSource 2011-12, resource-arm.net

Singlehurst, Laurence: *Discover – A New Discipleship Course Enabling You to Discover the Reality of Your Relationship with Jesus*, Cell UK 2013, celluk.org.uk.

Websites

Materials constantly come into and go out of print. But useful information about available resources can be found on the following websites:

- freshexpressions.org.uk/guide/discipleship/resources
- anglicanwitness.org/discipleship-courses
- calmonline.org.uk/resources/category/discipleship
- lichfield.anglican.org/growing-disciples
- chester.anglican.org/dev/docs/ministry/chester_discipleship _ resources_spring09.pdf
- oxford.anglican.org/wp-content/uploads/2013/01/ discipleship-resources.pdf
- goodbookreviews.org.uk

The CODEC Research Centre at Durham University has announced plans for the development of an online discipleship portal which will provide information about available discipleship resources.

- dur.ac.uk/codec/blog/?itemno=23791